Praise for *What They Didn't*

What They Didn't Teach Me on My PGCE i
where—a reminder of the joys (and lows)
profession.

Professor Dame Alison Peacock, DBE, DL, DLitt
Hon Fellow Queens' Cambridge, CEO of The Chartered College of Teaching,
Visiting Professor of the University of Hertfordshire,
Teach First trustee, author

Teaching is fundamentally a humane profession. Teachers tend to be attracted to it not only because they love learning but also because they love people and the relationships learning involves. This book captures the magic of this, as well as being full of practical (and often hilarious) anecdotes and advice. As someone who has spent most of her career working with new teachers, I really love the way it gives a sense of the journey as well as the inevitable ups and downs (and sometimes cul de sacs) this involves. It's also important to understand that it's not about knocking teacher training—it's about celebrating the wonders of all the things involved in being a teacher that could never be encapsulated in a course. Having said this, I thoroughly recommend it to teachers at every point in their career.

Professor Samantha Twiselton, PFHEA, FCCT, OBE,
Director of the Sheffield Institute of Education, Vice President of the Chartered College of Teaching, Chair of the DfE ITT Content Group

I was a proud teacher and school principal. From my days in Carysfort to this ministry, what I have learnt and wholeheartedly understand is that you can be clever, you can be brilliant, you can be knowledgeable, you can be creative, you can be a genius in your own lifetime. But if you don't use that genius and capacity to have a real impact on the learning of others, then you are not really teaching, you are just imparting facts. What is inspiring about this read is that we are keeping the passion-for-teaching light burning. It will motivate passionate teachers to be bright, shining beacons for their students.

Minister Mary Mitchell-O'Connor
Irish politician, Minister of State for Higher Education in Ireland

Rather than a critique of initial teacher education, this book stands as testament to the perpetual enriching of a teaching career, the constant learning, adaptation and improvisation required of really good teachers. Teaching, above all, is unpredictable. That is one of its joys and one of the reasons it creates such passion in those working in schools. And the stories within this book, stories of experience and learning and professional expansion and deep devotion to children, mark it out from the current crop of prescriptive and reductive texts that haunt staffrooms. It is a joy to read.

Professor Damien Page
Dean of the Carnegie School of Education, Leeds Beckett University

In this collection, Sarah Mullin has admirably demonstrated that to be a teacher is to be, first and foremost, an educator. To educate, according to its Latin origin, is to 'lead or draw out'—something she has clearly done in undertaking this text. While individual entries will no doubt have their own particular resonance for the reader, the real insights are ultimately in the collective. In bringing together the accounts of teachers 'in action', the power of narrative to help us make sense of our day-to-day interactions and the world of teaching is made vivid, and perhaps only in the way that a good story can.

Professor Dave Trotman,
Newman University, Birmingham

This book represents a wealth of heartfelt expertise that is given with generosity and an obvious love for teachers and teaching. Sarah has gathered a range of important and passionate voices that have created an indispensable volume that should be a constant companion for those embarking on what is the greatest profession, but also a reminder for those longer-serving teachers of why we do what we do day in day out. This book is one you'll take time to enjoy, and whilst you can dip in at any point and marvel at the insights, the journey through the book shows an unerring commitment to young people and championing the best teaching to achieve an inspiring education for everyone. A joy to read, and an important act of self-care for every teacher simply by opening this book and savouring every word.

Dr Steven Berryman
Director of Music, City of London School for Girls; Visiting Research Fellow, King's College London; Founding Fellow, Chartered College of Teaching

I have always felt that teaching is a permanent apprenticeship; I'm still learning new approaches having been in and out of the classroom since the late '70s. This engaging compendium is an invaluable resource for teachers at all stages of their career—whether establishing themselves in the first few years or looking for ways to keep that cutting-edge mid-career and beyond. It's a fact that the very best teachers, just like the very best in every profession, are always introducing incremental improvements to stay at the top of their game. The starting point is that the PGCE, and the multiplicity of other routes into teaching now, is positive and wholesome — but you can't learn everything as you qualify. It is a learning journey that extends way beyond the mentoring that teachers get in their first year. This book contains so much authentic, experience-based wisdom from authors whose passion for teaching shines through. So, when something happens or you are puzzled by a new situation, this is the book to turn to. I would keep a copy alongside me in the classroom and it would be well-thumbed!

Professor Colin Diamond,
CBE, University of Birmingham

If anyone thinks they know it all on their first day in this wonderful profession, they are wildly mistaken! *What They Didn't Teach Me on My PGCE* is a delightful collection of anecdotes and a reminder of the reality of a teacher continuing to develop their craft. We're all learning—every day truly is a school day!

Richard Gill, Chairperson of the Teaching School Council and
CEO of the Arthur Terry Learning Partnership

A lively collection of anecdotal vignettes and pearly words of wisdom, *What They Didn't Teach Me on My PGCE* is a joyful must-have for early-career educators that will have teachers chuckling and reflecting in equal measure.

Rachel Snape, Headteacher and National Leader of Education

I love this eclectic and authentic complication of voices in teaching. The authors mix humour with poignancy—from remembering not to sit in somebody else's seat in the staffroom to confessions of the most terrible times (and fabulous accounts of survival) to the recurring theme of the importance of relationships. A compulsive 'dip-in, dip out' book suitable for teachers and leaders at every stage in their careers!

Dr Emma Kell,
Author, Educational Consultant

Imagine yourself as a new student teacher or NQT, standing behind the lectern of a large lecture theatre in front of a full house of smiling and supportive education experts. Now imagine that they are all here to offer their wisdom, experience and research for you to ask any question you like about education. This is the situation Sarah has created in her new book *What They Didn't Teach Me on My PGCE.* This book is not only a unique collection of great advice and uplifting reminders of why we do what we do but also provides a personal introduction to some of the greatest educational voices out there. So, clear your throat, look that audience in the eye and ask that question you've been burning to find the answer to. This book will be your friend, your tutor, your mentor and your confidante and is full of support from all of us who've been there and are ready to welcome you into the teaching family.

Emma Turner, FCCT, CPD,
and Research Lead at Discovery School's Trust

What They Didn't Teach Me on My PGCE should be considered a handbook for new teachers. It is a wide collection of guides and narratives. It will inspire you to teach well, awaken your emotions and lift you up on tougher days. Sarah has collated these pearls of wisdom with care and passion. The contents reveal a 'who's who' of educators, from across age phases, disciplines and levels of experience. Each offers an insight into key aspects which affect your practice as a teacher, ranging from building relationships, improving your practice and dealing with challenges, to promoting wellbeing and reflecting on the funny times. As Sarah highlights, this book is not intended to replace the excellent initial teacher education which you are likely to receive during your training, but instead to complement it. These teachers' reflections will add depth to your knowledge and draw out important themes and learning points for new teachers to focus on, with the added bonus of some funny stories along the way. I will keep my copy close at hand as I enter the classroom, and cherish some of the lessons I have learnt from it. Allow yourself time to read and enjoy this book, and then return to it for guidance as the topics become familiar and you develop in the classroom.

Philip McCahill
Early Career Teacher Lead at Birmingham City University

What They Didn't Teach Me on My PGCE

*and other routes into teaching

Sarah Mullin

Word & Deed Publishing Incorporated
1860 Appleby Line, Suite #778
Burlington, Ontario, Canada, L7L 7H7

What They Didn't Teach Me on My PGCE

Copy editor: Steve Viau
Book design: Jim Bisakowski – www.bookdesign.ca

978-1-9994224-4-8
Word & Deed Publishing Incorporated
1860 Appleby Line, Suite #778
Burlington, Ontario, Canada, L7L 7H7
(Toll Free) 1-866-601-1213
Visit our website at
www.wordanddeedpublishing.com

Dedication

For my Granny—my best friend in Heaven. Granny, you taught me so many life skills that could never be learned in a classroom or lecture hall. You showed me the importance of being kind, generous and humble. You taught me how to be loving and giving. You simply made my world a better place, and there's not a day that goes by that I don't think about you.

For my parents Seán and Sadie who invested everything into giving me the best start in life and who continue to be my biggest supporters, along with my siblings James, Daniel, Helen and Thomas. Thank you for everything.

For my husband Ryan and for the most perfect children I could have ever hoped for—you bring absolute joy to my life. I am incredibly proud that you are growing up to be such thoughtful, loving and kind young people. Sean, Oisin and Susanna, this book is dedicated to you.

Thank you, Dr Darrin Griffiths for believing in the value of this project right from the very beginning. Thank you for giving me the opportunity to capture the narratives of hundreds of educators worldwide who are so passionate about making a difference in the world of education. Thank you for your continued support, guidance and positivity.

Thank you, Hannah Wilson, for your support, guidance and words of wisdom. I truly appreciate your unwavering support for this book.

For every single person who has supported me along this journey, and for every single contributor who has given the time to share their narratives, thank you. Without you, this book would not have been possible. Our pupils are truly blessed to have you as their teachers.

—Sarah Mullin

Contents

Chpt. 2. What They Didn't Teach Me About the Importance of Relationships – 23

Chpt. 3. What They Didn't Teach Me About Every Child Being Unique – 51

Chpt. 4. What They Didn't Teach Me About Growing as a Professional – 85

Chpt. 6. What They Didn't Teach Me About Pastoral Care – 177

Chpt. 7. What They Didn't Teach Me About the Challenging Times – 199

Chpt. 8. What They Didn't Teach Me About Collaboration – 221

Chpt. 9. What They Didn't Teach Me About Self-Evaluation and Self-Improvement – 243

Chpt. 10. What They Didn't Teach Me About the Funny Times – 263

Chpt. 11. What They Didn't Teach Me About Wellbeing – 283

Chpt. 12. What They Didn't Teach Me About Employment – 313

Chpt. 13. Parting Words of Wisdom – 357

Foreword

by Hannah Wilson, BA, SLE, NPQSL, NPQH, FCCT, FRSA Head of Secondary Teacher Training, University of Buckingham

Every adult has a story from their childhood that they can share about a favourite teacher, a much-loved lesson or a memorable moment like a trip or an event. *What They Didn't Teach Me on My PGCE* is an authentic, collective voice that captures the stories and advice of the profession. It is a compilation by teachers for teachers. Sarah has done a great job in collating a multiplicity of voices, capturing a cross-spectrum of experiences and perspectives.

The journey of a trainee teacher is an intense experience, and we learn as much about ourselves as we do about education—whichever route we take. I can still remember fondly the lectures, seminars, school placements and socials from my training year. I am still in touch with some of my fellow trainees, and it has been interesting to observe everyone else's journeys as educators alongside my own trajectory. As a teacher you will soon realise that a lot of your socialising will end up being with teachers, as you will share the same highs and lows, you will relate to one another's experiences and you will share the same holidays. Relationships as a teacher are key. I have kept cards, emails and messages from over the years that remind me about key moments and key people in my journey from trainee teacher to Headteacher to teacher trainer.

Our education system is ever changing, as are the routes to qualifying as a teacher. Schools constantly change to respond to societal changes; therefore, we as teachers need to constantly change how/what we teach too. Since I started my PGCE in September 2002, I have constantly evolved in my practice, but what I keep returning to is being authentic and being myself. Teaching can be such a physically demanding and emotionally draining vocation, and the pace of the profession—alongside the pressure schools are under—can become overwhelming at times. I wish I had had more candid input from peers when I was starting out. I wish someone had said to me 'good is good enough' when I spent hours on my lesson plans, lesson resources, displays and marking. As an avid tweeter for the last five years, the connections I have made and the conversations I have had have really helped to shape my educational philosophy and vision. Moreover, they have challenged me and supported me to find my right fit and fulfil my potential.

As a collection of stories about teaching and working in schools, *What They Didn't Teach Me on My PGCE* will encourage you to reflect on several important aspects of the profession: how we nurture hearts and minds in the children we teach. How we need to invest in our relationships with all stakeholders. How we need to remember that each child, each class, each school is unique and there is no 'one size fits all' approach to education. How we need to constantly reflect and evaluate our impact in the classroom. How teaching is more than just relaying knowledge, as we are there to shape the whole child. How learning difficulties are often teaching difficulties and we need to scrutinise our own teaching as much as we do the learning in our classrooms. How there will be highs and lows—teaching is an emotional rollercoaster and being resilient is key. How we are stronger together, and the more we connect/collaborate the less isolated we feel. How we will never be the finished article and we need to constantly learn and upskill ourselves. How we will laugh out loud most days. How we need to put our own oxygen masks on first, as we need to be well to teach well. And how hard it can be to find the right job, in the right school, at the right time.

The 13 chapters that Sarah has curated are crammed full of pearls of wisdom, hilarious anecdotes and sound advice from teachers at various points in their careers from contrasting contexts. The contributions capture the essence of the online community of educators who share their resources, offer their advice and give their support generously to enable other teachers to move from surviving to thriving.

Great teachers leave an imprint on our hearts and minds. Great teachers help us to make sense of the world, to have a sense of belonging and to become ourselves.

This book will reassure you that you are not alone, it will support you in plugging some of the gaps, and it will also make you realise that we will never be the finished article. So, join the conversation by dipping in and out of each chapter and each contribution, reflecting on your own practice as you find your own solutions. After all, you don't know what you don't know until you know it.

—Hannah Wilson
Head of Secondary Teacher Training at University of Buckingham
Former Executive Headteacher of two start-up schools in Oxfordshire
Co-founder of #WomenEd

Warm words of well wishes for the readers of *What They Didn't Teach Me on My PGCE*

As you take that step of faith, know you are supported as you make your way. You have chosen a precious career. Nurture it well.

Julia Skinner
Founder of 100 Word Challenge, Chair of a Trust, Chair of an SEMH Federation and Trustee for LinkAge

Teachers, I'm proud of you! Thank you for choosing to be an educator. It's not for everybody; you need to have the right skills, but you also need the right heart. Thank you for the passion you will bring to your work. Thank you for your commitment to making a difference for your children. You are creating a brighter future for your students, but also for all of us! You will do amazing things. Wishing you all the best!

Danny Steele
Educator, author, speaker @SteeleThoughts

To enjoy a happy, long and sustainable career in teaching, look after yourself first, before helping others, so that together you can make the biggest difference for the children.

Patrick Ottley-O'Connor
Executive Principal, Leadership Development Coach and Founding Director of Collaborative Leadership Ltd

You may be living in the present, but you're teaching the future. Yes, the curriculum is important, but so is shaping our nation. You not only teach, but inspire, encourage, support, nurture and grow. You're not just a teacher, you're an enabler: see each day as an opportunity to enable the future.

Nicola Brooks, FCCT
Reach South Teacher and lead for staff development and partnerships
Wiltshire Women into Leadership Champion

Teaching—quite simply—is a wonderful profession, which you hopefully already feel if you have got as far as completing your PGCE (or other route into teaching!). What you may not yet have experienced is that sense of wonder in those magical moments when you see your students in the flow of learning, overcoming obstacles and challenges, or just simply knocking themselves out, giving their absolute best. This magic still makes my heart sing after 23 years in schools. I'm sure it will make yours sing too!

Annemarie Williams

Executive Headteacher, National Leader of Education, WomenEd Regional Leader and winner of UK Literacy Association, School of the Year 2019

It's a joy to teach adults of the future; they will make you laugh and cry. They will exasperate and inspire you. When you're feeling down, there is nothing more nourishing than the special relationship between you and your pupils—and while teaching, your troubles will slip away.

Remember that you and your students learning together is the most important thing in your classroom, not a spreadsheet or the next data drop. Know your children well and value them equally.

Finally, don't burn out; good enough is fine. Teachers don't do perfect.

Jules Daulby

Literacy, Dyslexia, ADHD and Inclusion Specialist, podcaster, writer, National Leader #WomenEd

I tried my best not to be a teacher, but the inevitability of it all was apparent when I realised how much I loved working with young people—and realised the difference I could make. I'm sure it'll be the same for you. It won't always be a piece of cake, though. At times like these, by all means think of everything that you are supporting students to achieve, but what keeps me going are the subtler life-affirming moments you will enjoy almost every day; the stories, the jokes and the smiles. Children can bring a huge amount of joy—treasure those times and never forget them. Thanks for choosing teaching.

Tom Rogers

Assistant Headteacher, Teacher of History, TES columnist

The fact that you are reading this book means you are about to start the best job in the world! You may be feeling excited and nervous. That is completely natural. Everyone who has contributed to this book would have felt the same when they started. Rest assured that you are probably more prepared than you know. On behalf of governors, I would like to say thank you for what you will be doing for our children and wish you the best of luck.

Naureen Khalid

Trustee, Chair of Governors, co-founder @UKGovChat

Best of luck—and congratulations for finding one of the most inspiring, fascinating jobs on the planet. You'll be pushed to the very best version of yourself, and what a journey you will go on to get there. Remember that you have the power to show students all of the beauty of the world: they're just waiting for you to get started!

Kat Howard
Founder of Litdrive

Remember: teaching well is simple. Avoid unnecessary complications and you can relax and enjoy it.

Mark Enser
Head of Geography, Research Lead and SLE; TES columnist and author

Always remember, especially in any dark and possibly depressing moment, that what you do as a teacher is change lives. That is what you do daily. You are now part of an amazing profession. Go make a difference.

Chris Moyse
Head of staff development, Bridgewater and Taunton College Trust

I know that you are entering the best profession in the world because you want to make a difference to children's lives. My experience as an educator over many years has taught me that the primary job for school leaders is to create an environment in which all adults and children never stop learning. The greatest influence on the quality of children's learning experiences in schools is you, and the quality of teaching you provide. And the greatest influence on the quality of your teaching is the quality of your learning. So, my advice to you is to have fun and enjoy yourself. Never stop questioning, taking risks and making mistakes. Just like you want your children to do, reflect every day to continually improve. Never forget that you are all learning together. Believe in yourself and know that even though there will be ups and downs, it is the greatest job in the world and you will get there!

Dr Kulvarn Atwal, FCCT
Executive Head Teacher; Author of The Thinking School: Developing a Dynamic Learning Community

Congratulations for making the courageous decision to teach. It really is the best job in the world. Realise though that it comes with huge responsibility, as there is no other job which impacts positively on every aspect of our world's future. You have the power to give your pupils the gift of the joy of asking questions, taking risks, and making mistakes—in other words, the joy of learning. The children will make you cry, they'll stretch you and frustrate you, but they'll also bring you pride, joy and happiness. You'll laugh every day and they'll help keep you young—even if you feel old some of the time! Celebrate all the wins, big and small. Embrace the challenges too; set aside your anger or fear and see each tough moment as a gift, an opportunity to grow.

Alison Kriel, FCCT, FRSA,
Education leader, speaker, mentor, #WomenEd Strategic Lead

Before you can teach, you must be willing to learn. And as we learn, we grow into the people we want to become. Teaching has the potential to be transformative, and in choosing this as your vocation you are ultimately CHOOSING to learn and to grow into the educator you want to become. Listen with your heart, look inward before looking outward, share the space, be attentive, and be kind to yourself and to others. The best thing about this vocation is that it matters—it matters every day.

Dr Muna Abdi
Director of MA Education Consultancy CIC

Congratulations on choosing to join one of the most important and interesting professions in the world. It won't be easy, but nothing of value ever is. Some days will be good, others will be bad, but it will never be boring! There can be no greater honour than being trusted to teach the next generation.

Dr. Brendan O'Sullivan
National Chairperson, Irish Mathematics Teachers' Association

I feel privileged that I had a great career in teaching, fulfilling a range of roles across six schools in a thirty-year period. Whether you are in it for the long haul or trying teaching as part of a varied career portfolio, I wish you every success and happiness. I also very much hope that when you look back at the legacy you have left, you feel proud, energised and satisfied at all you have achieved, and at the difference you have made to the lives of the students you have taught and cared for, and the colleagues you have worked alongside. In my experience, there are far more good days than bad, and far more positive, joyful experiences than negative ones. It is hard work, and challenging at times, but never lose the conviction that you are carrying out a professional role which has purpose and impact. Enjoy it!

Dr Jill Berry
Leadership Consultant, Former Headteacher

Welcome to the profession. During your PGCE you will probably be given an abundance of information and pedagogy on how to be a good teacher. All of this will be vital information—take it and digest it the best you can and put it into practice. But there is a lot to teaching that cannot be taught: multitasking, patience, listening skills, how to pretend to be confident, and growing eyes in the back of your head to name a few. All of these intrinsic skills will come to you with time. Be kind to yourself, be patient with yourself, don't be afraid to ask for help from your mentor and other members of staff, follow through with anything you say you will do—and please get out of your classroom/department and spend time in other departments and in the staffroom. Good luck and I wish you a long and happy career.

Shonagh Reid
Assistant Principal for Behaviour

As the African proverb goes, it takes a village to raise a child. Remember that you are just one of the educators around the children in your class and draw on the resources, experience and skills of others. Your colleagues, your school leaders, governors, parents/carers and the rest of your 'village' can all play a powerful role. Working collaboratively with them will enable your learners to shine.

Karen Wespieser, FRSA,
Director of Operations at @DriverTrust, researcher, school governor

There is no job like teaching, on both a good day and a bad day. The children will see you through it all, and will become your pride and joy. As I begin my 26th year in the job, I have no regrets about the path I took. We are given people's most precious things five days a week to nurture and develop; it's hard to overstate what a real privilege this is. You will get out so much more than you put in. It is, quite simply, the best job in the world.

Kate Owbridge
Executive Headteacher, LLE, Consultant Head

As a teacher, you will be never be bored. There are huge highs and lows and (if you allow it) you will continue to learn every single day. You will shape lives, and even change them. At times, you will be the most important person in a pupil's life—and that's why this job is such a privilege. You will be the reason they achieve, but they will be your reason you love the job.

Sarah Watkins
Previous Head of School, teacher, writer

Teachers: be reflective but don't beat yourself up if something goes wrong—just take a breath and learn from it. Regardless of how long we've been at it, the teachers who have the biggest and most important impact are the ones who ask for help, try things out and take charge of their professional development. Do that and every child who walks into your classroom will be inspired and empowered by you. You've picked the best job in the world. Embrace it and enjoy it!

Shannen Doherty
Primary school teacher, Maths lead, Music lead, TES columnist

Your teaching training course is just the start of the journey. It gives you the beginning steps into a wonderful, rewarding, challenging career working in schools. The most important thing you can do is to be there for the learners in your class. Build relationships with them, enjoy their company, share their news, no matter how small, and show them you are listening. When you develop a strong relationship with the children, learning will soon follow. Go and watch Rita Pierson talking about every kid needing a champion and listen to her powerful words about the impact of the children having someone to look out for them. When it gets tough (usually around November when it's dark all of the time!), just remember why you are doing this.

Ian Addison
Year 2 teacher and Maths Leader at the Riders Federation of Schools

Introduction

I grew up in an Irish Catholic working-class family in South Birmingham. My parents truly believed in the transformative power of education. My father and mother instilled in my siblings and me a strong work ethic and a sense of ambition. Although we neither understood nor appreciated it at the time, our parents invested everything into giving us the tools we needed to fulfil our future ambitions, allowing us to overcome some of the barriers that might otherwise have stood in our way. Quoting Roald Dahl, my father would tell us, *'Make your dreams become reality or your reality will become dreams.'*

Those words still resonate with me to this day. My parents firmly believed that a good education would help us to become confident, articulate and well-rounded individuals with a strong academic background. They truly believed that with a good education, the world would be our oyster. Not every child is so fortunate to have had such a positive start in life.

I studied English with Linguistics at Queen's University Belfast before completing my Postgraduate Certificate in Education (PGCE). By becoming a teacher, I wanted to provide limitless opportunities for the next generation, helping to mitigate the impact of any barriers to learning that may arise for the children in my care.

Throughout my career, from English teacher to Head of English, from Assistant Head to Deputy Head, I have worked incredibly hard to ensure that all children are given the opportunity to maximise their learning potential. It is truly rewarding to have been able to make a difference to the lives of the children I have taught, increasing their life choices and instilling in them a sense of achievement, a sense of fulfilment, and a sense of enterprise, which I hope they will carry with them for the rest of their lives.

These achievements did not come easily; my passion, positivity and hard work have helped me to accomplish career success to date. I always remain confident, trusting in my Catholic faith that everything happens for a reason. Where there may be challenges, I try to present solutions. Rather than waiting for opportunities, I try to go beyond what is expected of me. Whatever barriers may stand in my path, I have a strong belief that hard work and a positive mindset will help me to achieve success. I truly believe that teaching is a vocation to which we are called, and my natural love for learning, my strong desire to drive social change and my unwavering commitment to helping others inspire me, making all that I do feel truly worthwhile.

In this book, I am delighted to be able to share with you a collection of narratives in a range of genres and styles from professionals at all stages of their careers. There are a wide range of perspectives from early career teachers to those who have been teaching for some time, from classroom teachers to senior leaders, from teacher educators and researchers, to inspectors, consultants and advisors. The accounts you will read are honest, heartfelt and written to offer you, the future generation of educators, an insight into our experiences. The views expressed in this book are each individual author's own and they may differ from the views, experiences or research of myself and others. We do not claim to be experts. We have simply united to offer you a book that we wished existed when we were starting our own journeys.

Each of the thirteen chapters you will read are broadly collected into themes, and you are invited to 'dip in and out' of each chapter. You will find recurring themes and patterns, paradoxes and contradictions throughout the narratives within this book. This is illustrative of the very nature of our profession: we are always learning, always growing as professionals and always finding what works for us in our own contexts. Some of the narratives you will read may act as signposts to further reading or research of your own. Some may enlighten you, some may amuse you and some you may disagree with! This eclectic collection provides a platform for authors to share with you their ideas, suggestions, reflections and tips. We hope you find this book to be informative, inspiring, empowering and uplifting.

As you begin your chosen route into the teaching profession, remember that this is just the beginning of your journey as an educator. I believe it is our duty as teachers to ensure that we provide a wealth of experiences which allow children to excel academically, grow spiritually and communicate confidently so that they may embrace every opportunity available in order to fulfil their dreams.

So, go into your teaching course and do well, but more importantly, go into the world and do good.

Aim high, dream big, and always, always believe in yourself.

—Sarah Mullin

Chapter 1

What They Didn't Teach Me About Opening Doors, Hearts and Minds

"Education is the most powerful weapon which you can use to change the world" – *Nelson Mandela*

As teachers, we have the opportunity to change lives. We are in the privileged position where we can equip learners with the knowledge, understanding and skills they need to survive and thrive as global citizens. In this chapter, authors reflect on their motivation for entering the teaching profession and consider the valuable role that teacher training programmes play in preparing teachers for their future careers in education.

#WhatTheyDidntTeachMeOnMyPGCE

Sarah Mullin

I have been coaching and mentoring teachers for over a decade. It is something I really enjoy, and I often find that I learn just as much from my mentee as I hope they learn from me. Back in 2017, I had just finished writing for another educational text, *The Leader Reader: Narratives of Experience,* when I had the idea to share my own career experiences with other trainee teachers, with the aim of inspiring and supporting the next generation of professionals.

Initially I thought about all of the things I had learned since my days as a PGCE student, which made me realise how many things that I wish I had known from the beginning—and this is how the title was born. I wish I would have known that the children would be just as interested in my daily outfits as in my lesson content. I wish I would have known that there would be days that my heart would break for a child and I would be limited in what I could do to help. I wish I would have known that I would spend more time with the children and my colleagues than my own family and friends. I wish I would have known how perceptive children can be and how they would pick up on the days when I was happy or sad. I wish I would have known how to deal with bumping into a parent in the middle of a supermarket or how I would be treated like a celebrity when pupils would see me outside of school. I wish I would have known that even though it has been fifteen years since I graduated with a PGCE, I would still be studying, still be learning, and still be growing as a professional. I wish I would have known that we get all those holidays for a reason. My PGCE year was fantastic—and so incredibly valuable—but there are just some things that teacher training cannot prepare you for; after all, no two days in the world of education are ever the same.

I firmly believe that the most valuable resources we have in education are each other's skills, knowledge and experiences. So with a book deal in place, an idea in mind, and the drive to put metaphorical pen to paper, I decided to launch a 'call for submissions' on social media, inviting others to share their informative, inspirational, humorous and even disastrous narratives for #WhatTheyDidntTeachMeOnMyPGCE. The response I received was incredible. That initial post was viewed, liked, shared and commented on over 83,000 times in the first twenty-four hours alone. It reached Europe, Australia, America, New Zealand, Canada and Africa. I had hundreds of professionals, some who have never written for the public domain before, keen to get involved. It was clear that we were all united in our mission: to inspire and support you, the future of education.

I had the most wonderful PGCE lecturers, and I truly enjoyed my training experience. This book is in no way intended to criticise your training programmes; after all, how would lecturers know to train us in how to deal with a pupil bringing a duck into school, or think to advise us not to leave a student on the roof during a science experiment? These are both real stories that happened to real teachers which you will read about in this book. How could your mentors possibly prepare you for projectile vomiting or little fingers getting stuck in test tube racks? Course tutors probably wouldn't consider the need to cover a session on managing children during a trip to the zoo, or a session on how to deal with the class erupting into hysterics due to the unfortunate misspelling of words on a white board. This book does not and cannot replace robust research. This book does not claim that one route into the teaching profession is preferred over any other. Whether you are studying for your PGCE, training through a School Direct programme, completing a Higher Education Institution programme, a distance-learning programme, a salaried ITT, training through Teach First, completing an undergraduate degree, or completing another route into teaching, this book is for you.

You will be training our sons and daughters, nieces and nephews. When we go to the doctor's surgery, it will be you who has taught our GPs, nurses, pharmacists and receptionists. When we answer the phone, it will be you who has taught our customer service representatives and engineers. When we go to a restaurant, it will be you who has taught our service staff, chefs and housekeeping team. You will be teaching our future police officers, sales managers, scientists and academics. Our transport staff, software developers, architects and recruiters will all have learned from you. It will be you who teaches the young people of tomorrow to be courteous and kind, tolerant and accepting; to be brave and thoughtful, critical and wise.

Being a teacher comes with a lot of responsibility but reaps so many rewards.

Welcome to our wonderful profession.

Making the Best of Your ITE Experience

Paul Hopkins

This narrative is for you if you are starting your teacher education either on a one-year course as a PGCE student in a HEI (Higher Education Institute), a Schools' Direct student attached to a University, a three-year B.Ed/BA student or another role. It might also be useful if you are in your first years of teaching and are looking back on your ITE time, hopefully with fondness.

The ITE period, especially if you are undertaking a one-year course, can be very intense; it is busy, crowded and even stressful. However, the role of the ITE course is not to produce the 'finished article'; it is to make sure you are ready for the post you will be taking up following your ITE period. This will mean you have satisfied the teachers' standards but still have lots to learn. The rest of this book will be filled with great anecdotes, tips and advice on these first years but I want to dwell on the ITE period. Remember this is your initial teacher education, the start of the exciting journey. You might think of the ITE period as getting you to the starting blocks of a long-distance race, or that your ITE is laying the foundations on which you will build your house.

Teaching is a mix of theory and practice. Lee Shulman (1986) talks about Content Knowledge (what you are teaching) and Pedagogic Knowledge (how you are teaching), and says that the teacher must have both of these (Pedagogic Content Knowledge or PCK). Pollard (2014) talks about the 'science of teaching', the 'craft of teaching' and the 'art of teaching' (Pollard, 2014, p. 302). The science is the underpinning ideas and theories about learning and about teaching, the craft is the day-to-day enactment of these things in the classroom, and the art is that 'je ne sais quoi' that you see in the experienced teacher, the 'responsive, creative and intuitive capabilities' (Pollard, 2014, p. 302). The ITE period is where you will develop the first two of these, and it is an opportunity to see the third in the teachers you encounter in the partnership schools. You will also develop this 'art' in yourself through experience. Also remember your ITE experience is the combination of time in the HEI and the time in schools. If you are on a one-year course then you will spend about 65% of your ITE time in your practice school(s). Use this time to develop both content and pedagogic knowledge to enhance what you learn in the sessions in the HEI. The time in the practice school(s) allows you to situate and embed the theory and knowledge you have learned in your sessions in the HEI. Aided by the expertise and experience of the classroom teachers, use this time to try things out, to experiment—remember this is the teaching 'practice'.

In your ITE year, you will have, or you will have had, the chance to explore a range of ideas and theories about teaching rooted in research and practice. Some of these will be long-established ideas and some new ideas. You will have a chance to reflect, critique, challenge and apply these ideas in your practice. All good practice is built, as Newton said, by 'standing on the shoulders of giants'. We tend to be cautious in HEIs and we want you to take the time to reflect on new ideas and theories and not 'rush in where angels fear to tread'. The skill of criticality, learnt during your ITE, will stand you in good stead when you encounter new ideas in your first years of teaching, allowing you to consider carefully how these apply to you in your classroom, with the children you teach, in the situation you are in. These will give you a chance to ask, 'what works for me?' When you are struggling with a new class the theory you studied in your HEI lectures and seminars may not seem immediately relevant, but critical exploration of these ideas will enrich and deepen your professional practice.

At the heart of most HEI courses is reflective practice. Jenny Moon (2008) describes it this way:

> Reflection is a form of mental processing that we use to fulfil a purpose or to achieve some anticipated outcome.

> It is applied to gain a better understanding of relatively complicated or unstructured ideas and is largely based on the reprocessing of knowledge, understanding and, possibly, emotions that we already process. (Moon, 2008, p. 8)

One of the great advantages you will have in your ITE year will be the time and space to share your ideas, thoughts, worries, experiences, highs and lows with your fellow travellers on the journey. The experienced tutors, most of whom will have extensive experience as teachers and/or mentors, will be your Sherpas—helping to carry the load and offering guidance. Use this time and space, and your fellow students, who will have been in a wide range of schools, all a little bit different, to help you reflect and situate your own journey. Once you are in the 'hurly burly' of a school, it is more difficult to do this.

When you do finish your ITE experience and begin a job, don't lose touch with the people you were in ITE with. Social media has now made it easy to maintain those support networks you developed and to make new ones. A personal learning network (PLN) is a very valuable asset to help you put things into perspective when you are feeling down. Twitter, for all its faults, can be a hugely supportive and instructive medium.

If you are currently teaching but are reflecting on the ITE period, you may want to take your own academic study further. If so, get back in touch with one of your tutors. They will be able to offer you support and guidance in your own academic journey. Who knows you might end up as one yourself!

Lastly, consider your ITE as a 'test' period. If you decide at some point during your ITE journey that this is not the path for you, then there is no shame and no failure in making this decision. Walking away takes as much courage as carrying on, C.S. Lewis put it this way:

> Progress means getting nearer to the place you want to be. And if you have taken a wrong turn, then to go forward does not get you any nearer. If you are on the wrong road, progress means doing an about-turn and walking back to

the right road; and in that case the man who turns back soonest is the most progressive man. (Lewis, 1952, p. 20)

References

Lewis, C. S. (1952). *Mere Christianity.* London: HarperCollins.

Moon, J. (2008). The reflective teacher. In P. Scales (Ed.) *Teaching in the lifelong learning sector.* Milton Keynes: Open University Press.

Pollard, A. (2018). *Reflective teaching* (4th ed.). London: Continuum Books.

Shulman, L. (1986). Those who understand: Knowledge growth in teaching. *Educational Researcher, 15*(2), 4–14.

Paul Hopkins is a lecturer and researcher at the University of Hull working on teacher education, research and general education programmes. He has previously worked in primary and secondary schools as a teacher, senior leader and governor, as well as an LA advisor and consultant. He writes and researches internationally in primary and secondary education with a focus on technology-enhanced learning.

What They Didn't Teach Me About

Minding the Gap: How to Navigate the Space Between School and University Worlds as a Beginning Teacher

Jo McShane

Looking back on the experiences shared by the hundreds of trainee teachers and NQTs I've had the privilege to work with, one of the biggest hurdles to jump is almost invisible. Hidden behind the boulders of behaviour and ascents of assessment lurks a far swampier terrain; that space between the home base of the university or ITT provider and the placement school. I hope this brief reflection helps you to make a smooth transition between the two educational worlds that will mould you.

University and provider-based sessions create a double-edged sword. On the plus side, you get to meet your cohort, have access to Starbucks, enjoy a gentle, philosophical induction to the purpose of education and find yourself steered by pastoral, phase and subject tutors. If you find yourself wandering around faculty with your map upside down, someone is always there to steer you gently towards a warm and cheery session on 'Metacognition and Self-Regulation'. Budding fellow teachers admire your new pencil case and lend you a hand when you stare dumbfounded at that QTS portfolio thing. The negative side can be summed up in the words of Kirsty, a SCITT trainee I worked with a few years back: 'I love training sessions, but they're like driving lessons. All you want to do is pass your test and hit the road'. After the sheen of your fancy paperclips and matching treasury tags wears off, the home base of the provider can feel a bit constraining, surreal and kind of irrelevant. Year after year, I've watched trainees mumble a weak bye-bye through barely concealed tears as they head off to live out their pedagogical dreams. And each year I've whispered knowingly in their wake… 'You'll miss us, you know'.

It's not that the provider home-base is irrelevant while school is real; rather they complement each other in ways you cannot possibly grasp until you've made that leap from workshop to classroom. You'll spend at least 120 days learning in school, and my advice is to enjoy the moment in that 'other' third of the course you spend in training sessions. Practicing and time-served teachers often rush to provide sessions at the university because of the importance of reflecting on practice in a context that affords you the luxury of space and time to learn as a community of professionals. When you look around school, it will become clear that time is the most valuable resource; the mystical elixir that can turn a horrific week into a success, or a bad lesson into a good one (especially on a chilly, grey Friday afternoon in November). Your school colleagues may secretly envy your un-pawed copy of *Rise and Rosenshine* (made up title, though I might write it now I've noted its excellent potential), and, with CPD budgets being restricted, your access to current thinking about research-informed practice that works. Remember that your placement school and ITT provider share the same, broad professional aims embodied by education: high expectations, meaningful learning and development and the maximisation of personal potential. You are the embodiment of the bridge between these complimenting spheres, so thread them together to build the strongest possible practice. It is important to note that reflection is key to drawing the benefits from your theoretical and practical learning experiences. Though formal reflection on lesson plans and assignments will no doubt be required during your PGCE, personal reflection plays a huge part in making sense of the different ways you can understand your changing professional identity. Take some time to recall why your tutor made space in that behaviour session about Maslow's Hierarchy of Needs when you review the challenges you've experienced settling your class during morning registration. Recognise that when your mentor appears to be curious about the potential of Rosenshine's Principles in the classroom, they are genuinely interested in what your cutting-edge learning can bring to the department. Remember that the innovative blending of theory with practice that you encapsulate is why so many teachers reach out to embrace trainee teachers.

Your PGCE, and your subsequent journey into the wild and beautiful seas of education, are like a crazy, beautiful tapestry. If I could give you just one piece of advice, it would be to stand back and recognise how the myriad of facts, failures, wins, light-bulbs, reflections, face-palms, assignments, shining feedback notes, teary phone calls to your fellow travellers and hastily scribbled journal annotations stitch together to create the complex and rich fabric of knowledge that will inspire a generation of learners. Enjoy!

I'd like to leave you with some practical tips:

- **Expect the unexpected.** There will come a point at which you do miss the home base of your ITT provider. This can sneak up on you, so anticipation is key. Consciously acknowledge how distinctive the learning experiences of school and university feel, and how one may naturally be more anxiety provoking than the other.
- **Maintain contact.** This includes a wide range of people, ranging from your tutor, central services at the university/provider and your peers. Being part of strong learning communities is incredibly valuable and supportive during the times when you want to share your wins or take solace.
- **Avoid the group of fear.** Sometimes certain groups and collectives on social media platforms manage to create a gulf between the value of school and provider-based learning. Forge your own path: avoid being dragged into moaning and seek out your own truths.
- **Find your marigolds.** Find the people who help you to flourish and stick with them; for example, a wise, Deputy Headteacher called Jane Rayson has inspired countless beginning teachers by expertly relating a blog post from Jennifer Gonzales to their professional growth. She found someone to help her flourish and

successfully passed that on to others. Work to do the same—you'll be glad you did.

Jo McShane is a senior lecturer in education at the University of Sunderland, working across Primary and Secondary Programmes. She has worked as an ITT lead in several university and SCITT settings and has many years of experience as a Secondary RE Teacher, Senior Leader and International Consultant.

Finding Your 'Why'

Sarah Mullin

> *'Watch with glittering eyes the whole world around you because the greatest secrets are always hidden in the most unlikely places. Those who don't believe in magic will never find it.' —Roald Dahl*

Nobody ever said the job of a teacher was easy. Many of us feel that teaching is a vocation, that we have been called to play a part in giving children the very best start in life. The role of the teacher is incredibly diverse. We are the child's parent figure during the day, providing stability, consistency, routines and love. We are the child's support, helping them to build happy memories as they grow and learn. We are the child's coach, encouraging them and cheering them on when times are tough. Our job is to equip our pupils with the skills they need to be healthy, caring, responsible global citizens.

It is always important to remember what it is that drives you in your career. Why is it that you have chosen to be a teacher? Whether you are studying to be a teacher, working as a newly qualified teacher, or have been teaching for some time, it is important to periodically reflect on what it was that motivated you to enter our wonderful profession and consider what your career goals may be. In short, dig deep inside and think: What is your 'why?'

> *'There's no greater gift than to honour your life's calling. It's why you were born. And how you become most truly alive.' —Oprah Winfrey*

What They Didn't Teach Me About
Changing Lives

Mary Mitchell-O'Connor

The summer of 1977. Fleetwood Mac's *Rumours* was the soundtrack to our lives. The nation was gripped by discomania as we all swooned over a young John Travolta in *Saturday Night Fever*—and Elvis died while eating a burger sitting on the toilet!

I, however, was oblivious to all of that. Successful Leaving Certificate in hand, I had just been accepted into Carysfort Teacher Training College to study a Batchelor of Education from NUI. The smell of freedom was intoxicating. One of my favourite quotes was from W.B. Yeats: 'Education is not the filling of a pail but the lighting of a fire.'

Roll on four decades. I certainly have a perspective on how my time in Carysfort shaped me as I progressed through my career. Education, and the importance of it, is imbued in every cell in my DNA. Life changes, it alternates, throws us curve balls, challenges us, surprises us and sometimes leaves us floored and confused. From my standpoint, however, the impact of learning remains constant. It paints a portrait of possibilities.

Education really does matter and it changes lives. Education starts as soon as a newborn is handed to its mother, the first caregiver, and continues throughout the lifespan. We are always learning. As a society we guide and structure learning through preschool, primary, secondary and tertiary education on into adult education and beyond. It is what sets us apart and enriches our experience. It is delivered by the battalions of committed and creative teachers, tutors, lecturers and professors who nurture our students in the country's educational institutions.

I was a proud teacher and school principal. From my days in Carysfort to this ministry, what I have learnt—and wholeheartedly understand—is that you can be clever, you can be brilliant, you can be knowledgeable, you can be creative, you can be a genius in your own lifetime. But if you don't use that genius and capacity to have a real impact on the learning of others, then you are not really teaching, you are just imparting facts.

Mary Mitchell-O'Connor is an Irish politician and Minister of State for Higher Education in Ireland.

Why We Wanted to Become Teachers

'I decided to become a teacher in my final year of university. I went to a career talk about educational inequality which struck a chord with my own background. I was also beginning to get into politics at the time and I realised that so many societal issues could be remedied by better education for all.' —*Alex Jose, English teacher and Assistant Head of Sixth Form*

'I wanted to become a teacher because I wanted to give back. I was lucky because I had so many supportive teachers who said from day one I should go into teaching as I would be good at it. I wouldn't be where I am now without them. In all my placements with all my groups, the students have been the best bit. I can't wait to have my own classes as an NQT!'—*James Roden, Secondary English NQT*

'A lot of teachers were inspired by someone at school to teach. For me it was that I really didn't enjoy my experience. I felt like surely there were more exciting ways to learn. I became a teacher to help children love learning.' —*Cate Knight, qualified teacher and private tutor*

From a young age, I always struggled at school; I was always that child who didn't understand the work and needed that little bit of extra support. Since growing up, I have discovered my love and passion to help other people with their education, from helping my disabled brother with his maths homework, to running GCSE revision classes during my GCSEs, to setting up my own educational resource business. This is how I knew I wanted to be a teacher, to help inspire the next generation, making positive change, even if it's only in small amounts. Remember #InclusionMatters! —*Thomas Saunders, studying BA (Hons) in Special Educational Needs, Disabilities and Inclusion*

I chose to be a teacher because I wanted to make a difference. I wanted to inspire children, from all backgrounds, to achieve greatness. My advice to any aspiring, training and early career teachers is to enjoy it. You often get lost in the pressure of the role, to the point that you forget all of the amazing things about it. Have a laugh with your children, get to know them and build that relationship. You are working with the most incredible little people; let them know how important they are. *—Zack Mitchell, Newly Qualified Teacher*

I wanted to become a teacher because of where I come from. I'm from a deprived inner-city area in Birmingham; I have watched friends go down the wrong path first-hand. I want children in my community to succeed and I want to contribute towards narrowing the gap. *—Abed Ahmed, Maths teacher with a stammer, TES Teacher of the Year 2019, #Brum30under30*

The reason why I chose to become a teacher is linear. I was inspired by my teachers who helped me find the subject that spoke to me about understanding my place in the world. More than that, they believed in me and encouraged me to pursue opportunities that I had never thought were open to me. I decided to teach so that I could have the chance to help change the lives of children for the better. *—Dominic Weir, NQT*

Our Proudest Teacher Moments

'When the parents of a student in the same class greeted me at a parents' evening with "Oh you're the one she keeps talking about; she loves your lessons!" This was at a point when I could not ever conceive that I would be that teacher for someone. Also, when greeting a Year 10 pupil at the door and she responds with "How come you're always so happy and smiling miss?" And my honest response was "because I love teaching you!"' *—Melissa Wells, English NQT*

'Watching my Year 8 pupils present the news after a successful BBC School Report, including one child who had been mute until the age of twelve. Also, taking a group of students, including those labelled 'troublemakers', to complete controlled-assessment surveys and seeing them tuck in their shirts, straighten their ties, and polish their shoes as they were so excited about being trusted to talk to 'real people' in public.' *—Jo Coles, Assistant Head, Teaching and Learning*

'In 2015 I received a communication from a former student. I had to drag him through his GCSE English and he had achieved a grade of C. It was hard work for all involved! He thanked me for not giving up on him and told me that he was at university. I cried when I read that message.' *—Laura Larkin, English Teacher*

Chapter 2

What They Didn't Teach Me About the Importance of Relationships

> I have come to the frightening conclusion that I am the decisive element. It is my personal approach that creates the climate. It is my daily mood that makes the weather. I possess tremendous power to make life miserable or joyous. I can be a tool of torture or an instrument of inspiration. I can humiliate or humour, hurt or heal. In all situations, it is my response that decides whether a crisis is escalated or de-escalated, and a person is humanized or de-humanized. If we treat people as they are, we make them worse. If we treat people as they ought to be, we help them become what they are capable of becoming.
>
> —*Haim G. Ginott,*

It is said that the triangle is the strongest shape found in nature because the force is distributed evenly between each of the three sides. I firmly believe that to ensure the best academic and pastoral outcomes for every child, the school, the child and parents/carers must share in the child's learning journey, forming a united triangle of support, positivity and encouragement. By working collaboratively, we can support one another, becoming a united force of solidarity to maximise the learning potential of each child entrusted into our care.

In this chapter, you will read narratives from professionals who discuss the value in establishing and maintaining positive working relationships with pupils, parents and colleagues.

What They Didn't Teach Me About
the Lasting Effects of Kindness

Dr Brendan O'Sullivan

When I began teaching, one of the big tips was never to smile before Christmas. The idea being that the new teacher would establish firm discipline and convey high expectations using an austere, authoritative air. Of course, some took this to an extreme and lost the opportunity to establish relationships with the children that they taught. The learning environment requires firm boundaries, established through fair and just sanctions. However, in my view, it can never be at the cost of kindness.

Never underestimate the power of a smile: you can exude kindness simply by engaging in the act of smiling. It makes everyone feel more comfortable and it ultimately leads to students finding you more approachable. Greeting them as they enter the room, showing an interest in their lives and saying goodbye are all simple acts of kindness. I often think that our students do not care about what we have to teach them until they are assured that we care about them as people. True engagement with students leads to deeper relationships, which fosters greater learning in the classroom. Another way that kindness can be conveyed is through patience, one of the most powerful virtues that a teacher can possess. Some learners need more time than others to grasp concepts. They need to be encouraged to try, try and try again. Rather than dwelling on failures, the student is afforded the opportunity to develop without feeling rushed or under pressure.

Having taught for over twenty years now, I sometimes have the good fortune to meet past pupils. I must confess that initially they often remember more of me than I do of them. However, after a few minutes of conversation, they start to recount anecdotes that spark my memory, and the passage of time melts away. I remember one particular encounter where a woman in her mid-twenties informed me that she 'always loved learning' in my class. I asked her what great pedagogical technique made the difference for her. She answered 'you were so kind and that's what I needed'. I doubt that our work on equations or mathematical expressions had much impact on her life but it brought home to me the lasting effects of kindness. Aesop tells us that 'the level of our success is limited only by our imagination and no act of kindness, however small, is ever wasted.' My meeting with this adult, whom I had only ever known as a teenager, made me reflect on the impact that kindness can have. If I can give you two words to guide you on a hopefully long journey in teaching, they are these: 'be kind'.

Dr Brendan O'Sullivan is the National Chairperson of the Irish Mathematic Teachers' Association.

What They Didn't Teach Me About
Safeguarding

Philip McCahill

No doubt during your training you will have heard a lot about safeguarding pupils: keeping children safe from harm and maltreatment; promoting their wellbeing and best interests. Most importantly, you will know that safeguarding is everyone's responsibility, and have received training about how to recognise and report concerns. Safeguarding pupils is a vital part of our role as teachers, and underpins everything we do in school. In my experience, it is also a source of uncertainty and confusion for many new teachers, so I will break down the different elements of safeguarding you need to familiarise yourself with before you enter the classroom.

1. Know the difference between safeguarding and child protection. Safeguarding focuses on prevention and keeping all children safe, whilst child protection describes activity undertaken to protect specific children at risk of harm.
2. Keeping Children Safe in Education is the statutory guidance from the DfE, which you must read. It includes your responsibilities as a teacher, as well as the different types of harm, abuse and neglect, how to recognise them and how to make referrals for support. You should also be aware of your legal responsibilities; for example, if you become aware of an incident of female genital mutilation, you have a legal duty to report it directly to the police. You must ensure that you are conversant with Part One and Annex A of the most current version, which you should access via the DfE website.

3. Make sure you're familiar with your setting's child protection procedures, including who your Designated Safeguarding Lead (DSL) is, your local Early Help process and how to deal with concerns and disclosures. The most effective way to ensure you are sufficiently aware of these is to know your school's Safeguarding and Child Protection policies and meet with your DSL to complete a safeguarding induction.
4. Safeguarding encompasses many aspects of school life and pupils' wider experiences that you should consider: a safe and secure school environment, their home lives, their online behaviour and their relationships with others. You should be mindful of all of these, as well as understanding which of these has a particular prevalence in the lives of individual children and in your wider context. As part of this, it is essential that you understand the local safeguarding priorities relevant to your particular school, and the implications these have to your daily practice.
5. As a teacher, you have an opportunity to teach children to keep themselves safe. Through a programme of PSHE and RSE lessons, children can be taught at an age-appropriate level about how to recognise risks, how to seek help and how to keep themselves safe from harm. Consider how you might teach pupils in your class about these issues in the most effective and appropriate way, and explore your school's PSHE curriculum provision to find out how they aim to teach pupils about safeguarding issues.

Underpinning safeguarding is the positive, professional relationships you have with your pupils and key colleagues. Through these, you will gain insight into pupils' lives and recognise those who are vulnerable or may be at risk. If you have a concern about a child's welfare, your identification and response to it could help to keep your pupils safe from harm.

Philip McCahill is a newly qualified primary teacher in the West Midlands, and a safeguarding governor at a small primary school in South Birmingham. Additionally, Philip is a member of the Chartered College of Teaching and leads the Early Career Network based at Birmingham City University to offer support to new and student teachers across the region.

What They Didn't Teach Me About
the Complex Relationship Between Teacher and Student

Neil Gilbride

What they didn't teach me on my PGCE was how deeply complex the relationship between teacher and student is. Relationships are the dynamic between people, a tricky web of thoughts, feelings and actions. And within this web lie both warnings and glorious opportunities to do some good.

I'll begin with the caveat that what I am about to tell you isn't something you can necessarily learn by being told. I have come to believe that if anyone had told me these observations prior to starting my training, I wouldn't have paid much attention. So, what can I hope to achieve in telling you? Some of you may absorb these observations like sponges, and some of you may revisit the seed I'm planting with fully fledged thoughts of your own. My hope is that these observations paint a picture of how tricky yet remarkably rewarding it can be to manage the dynamic between yourself and your students.

Observation 1: This observation came from a Year 9 class. They had previously gone through five teachers in two years. When I arrived as a preppy, bow-tie-wearing, Harry Potter-esque Teach Firster, I was confused why they treated me with such disdain. I really cared and tried so hard, why was I getting a rough time?

It wasn't until the fourth lesson, when a student muttered 'He'll be gone soon, just like the others, why should I do what he says?', that the penny dropped. There was absolutely no reason why those students should have trusted me—their experience had told them to do otherwise. I needed to build their trust, something that takes time.

What I learnt from this is that trust is different to obedience or respect. Trust is held far deeper and goes beyond you and your role, and it can operate both on an individual level and on a collective level. It takes time to build and one mistake to ruin. No matter how committed you are to your job, you need to take the time to build it. Especially with students who, whether struggling at home or at school, have a justified reason to second-guess you and your motives.

Observation 2: The impact you can have on individual students is far beyond what is immediately observable. This observation came from a student that I'll call Sarah. In lessons, Sarah interacted with disinterest—she wasn't disruptive... but she wasn't waxing lyrical about my lessons or me either!

However, every week (about 15 minutes before the end of lunch) she would come and sit in my room whilst I prepared for our lesson. I'd say hello, but she would mainly sit there and draw. Sometimes we would chat, but it was polite conversation. Any time I asked if there was something wrong, she wouldn't engage beyond 'fine'. So, I mainly put her coming to my room early as just having somewhere to sit where she could draw, and that was that.

Until her final day. On my desk, there was a card. In the card, Sarah explained how my classroom was 'the only safe space which she knew in the school', that I was an inspiration to her and she was grateful for my help. All I did was let her in my classroom early and ask how she was—no major intervention, no dramatic recovery of her academic grades. That was it.

What I learnt from this was the extent to which we have impact on our students is beyond our field of view. We don't just impact them in the explicit plans and strategies we put in place, we impact them by who we are and by the smallest acts of kindness. It's almost unfathomable. In a sea of action and demand, we can forget that just being our kind and truest selves can impact individuals beyond measure.

Observation 3: The difference you will make continues beyond your time with them. This observation was far more recent, primarily because it requires the passage of time. You will realise that you made a difference because of things such as the random email you receive after seven or so years saying, 'I'm training as a teacher because you inspired me'. Or, 'I wouldn't be doing a Masters without you.' Or when you see ex-students working hard in a shop and they come from round the counter to say hi (and even, 'Mate I was so horrid to you, please forgive me!'). These experiences showed me that the impact you have on the life chances of the young people you serve can neither be predicted nor measured. The thoughts and ideas you give them can stay with them way beyond the end of your teaching relationship.

What do I hope you can see within these observations? I hope you realise that there are factors operating beyond your control. Be patient. Listen and be kind to yourself. Slow the world down a bit and you might begin to see why students aren't responding. I hope you will realise that our small actions and ways of being are powerful beyond measure. It's not all about interventions and our intentional actions; how we conduct ourselves and look after our students can—literally—change their lives.

What they didn't teach me on my PGCE wasn't, indeed, teachable. But I hope that these observations might focus your attention on the dynamic between you and your students and give you the belief that you can change the world of the young people you serve.

Neil Gilbride is a lecturer in education at the University of Gloucestershire. He has a multidisciplinary background stretching over twelve years, which he uses to research new ways of exploring school leadership and organizational life. Neil is an alumnus of Teach First 2011.

What They Didn't Teach Me About
Mutual Respect

Fiona Ruck

My PGCE interview was nothing short of horrendous. Graduating with a BA in Human Geography, my subject knowledge of physical processes was put to the test and, in my mind, I had failed miserably. I remember how desperately I longed for the place on the course, and how I cried for hours as I walked out following my inability to correctly answer questions on my 'specialist subject'. I wanted the ground to open up and swallow me whole. Where would I go from here? What would I do now? My career was over before it had even started.

At the time I was oblivious, but now, ten years into my teaching career (yes, they gave me that place!), I see that interview as one of my most valuable lessons, a pivotal moment to shape my future as a teacher. Indeed, teaching is very much about being an expert in your subject. It is imperative that you constantly develop and broaden your depth of knowledge and understanding as time progresses; remember, your subject area moves forward too. But equally, we are teachers of people who need your respect, your encouragement, your inspiration, and your motivation. They need someone to nurture their growth, to instil in them a love of learning and to take them on a journey of personal endeavour and achievement. They need someone to believe in them so that they can believe in themselves. This is the exact same belief that my PGCE tutors had in me. What they saw in me that day was not my impeccable ability to explain in detail the formation of arêtes, but my passion for teaching; my determination to become a teacher of children and not simply a teacher of Geography. This, for me, is the most significant aspect of teaching.

My first teaching post was at the school where I completed my first PGCE placement (and coincidentally, the school that took me on a fieldtrip to Iceland where I learned exactly how those dreaded arêtes are formed!). Ten years later, I am still at my first school. It is a real passion of mine to ensure that all of my pupils enjoy our lessons, whatever their ability, and that all of them feel safe and encouraged throughout our time together. I remember vividly being told on my PGCE not to smile at the children before Christmas. I have quickly learned, however, that a smile as they walk through your classroom door can shape your relationship with your pupils. And these relationships are key to learning and progress.

I am all for being firm, setting boundaries, and being in control of what happens in my lessons—and I learned some great strategies for this on my PGCE. But I have since learned that these must promote mutual respect. I have rules, but more importantly what we have are high expectations of each other. I am not a dictator in my classroom. I am a fellow human, just an older and supposedly wiser version with the ability to stretch and challenge my pupils to scaffold their learning and help them to achieve their full potential. Model the behaviour that you expect from them. Make it obvious that you follow the same expectations as them. One of my personal favourites is when I am in task transition, and using wait time (another really fabulous strategy in itself) to gain the attention of the whole class. I will state for example, 'I will not talk over you, as I wouldn't expect you to talk over me'. Show them that you respect them; show them that you are there to work with them and not against them. This can also be a strategy to use with other members of staff. They didn't teach me on my PGCE how to deal with colleagues, but that's a whole other chapter!

Modelling behaviour does not just mean not pole-vaulting over those imaginary lines where behaviour becomes a concern. We can model our emotional behaviour too, share our experiences, show the importance of empathy. I will always remember my Geography teacher at school used to tell us about the farm she lived on (we lived in an inner suburb of Birmingham) and we hung on her every word. Turns out it was a load of rubbish! But she had us all engaged. She built a relationship with us where she shared a part of herself (albeit a fake one) and we respected her for it. Share your experiences with your pupils (real or imagined). I teach Year 8 about migration. I encourage them to share their family migration stories, but I always start with mine. How my ancestors had left Italy in search of the American Dream, and how if the ship hadn't broken down and docked in Cardiff, I wouldn't be there with them. Allow them to see that you have experiences and emotions in the same way that they do. They will respect you for it.

There will of course be many situations where this mutual respect is put to the test. There will be times where behaviour is a concern and we struggle to deal with emotions in a rational manner—and I'm not just talking about the children! When I first qualified, I remember a particularly challenging Year 9 class, with some particularly trying pupils. I remember having removed a young man from my room to discuss his behaviour and have a restorative conversation, when another member of staff walked up and exploded at this young man. As a newly qualified teacher, I was petrified and the pupil in question certainly had no choice but to listen and agree. At the time, I'll admit I was a little bit in awe of the respect he seemed to gain and the fear that the students had of him. They dared not misbehave. But in retrospect, that is not the kind of teacher I want to be. I have worked hard to develop discipline techniques that do not involve reacting aggressively or hot headedly.

It may sound obvious, but when we build these relationships based on respect, and we teach our pupils to take ownership of their behaviour and emotions, we need to remember that we are the adults. We are the ones they look to for a model of how to cope with the anger, the frustration, the utter despair when they think the whole world is against them. Choose your words carefully. Use phrases such as 'I've noticed that…' which tend to be more positive and elicit a constructive response. Try to remain calm. I'm not saying you will never lose your cool or you'll never want to scream at the top of your voice. But on your PGCE when you are taught these discipline strategies, what you sometimes fail to understand immediately is that, for some pupils, you will be their only adult role model, the only person they can rely on to support them and encourage them and forgive them when they make poor decisions or struggle to deal with their own emotions. Remind them that we all make mistakes and have to learn from them. Only then will you maintain those all-important relationships based on mutual respect and high expectations.

Fiona Ruck, BA (Hons), PGCE, MEd, is second in Geography at Archbishop Ilsley Catholic School in Birmingham. She is passionate about engaging and enabling students through teaching and learning strategies as well as developing positive relationships through effective behaviour management.

What They Didn't Teach Me About
Pupil Feedback

Nina Rogers

As a trainee secondary teacher with no real prior classroom experience—or even general experience with teenagers—the thought of gaining teenagers' respect was a daunting prospect! I constantly thought about ways to connect with them, but definitely did not want to be *that* cringe-worthy teacher who tried to be cool.

Over the lessons I had with a group of Year 9 pupils, I found some just openly chatted to me about their day, and I would follow this up with them if they arrived early to my class. It was a nice, simple way of showing I was interested in them and fostered a positive working relationship. I really enjoyed hearing snippets of their lives too.

The best bit though came a few lessons later when I had made a picture quiz on a biology topic for whole-class engagement. One of my pupils said they really enjoyed what I had done and asked if I could make another one sometime. I made sure to incorporate another picture quiz a few lessons later as a way of teaching them about a concept and I informed the pupil beforehand that I had considered their feedback. The pupil smiled at me when they realised I had devised another quiz for them. It was by far one of the best lessons I have taught, and I found the pupils worked well for me when they knew that I cared about them and their contributions.

Nina Rogers, BSc (Hons), is a trainee secondary teacher in Birmingham, UK. Nina is dedicated to providing pupils from all walks of life with opportunities to achieve success and build self-confidence.

What They Didn't Teach Me About
the Power of Listening

Lucy Whittington

When I first began my teaching career as an NQT in a large primary school in inner-city London, it was exactly what I had hoped for: diverse, challenging and exciting. What I wasn't prepared for, however, was the number of angry outbursts I would experience from some of the children in my class, and I wondered what on earth I was doing wrong. My lessons were engaging and well planned, pupils were making good progress, I regularly received good observation feedback, and when a pupil became disruptive, I would follow the behaviour policy to the letter; even so, outbursts of anger still happened again and again.

Then, one autumn morning, I decided to change my approach. When the first incident occurred, I took the opportunity to speak to the pupil one to one. I made a conscious effort to listen properly to what the child was saying to me, and to make eye contact with the child in a calm and understanding manner. It was during this conversation that I realised it's so easy to be preoccupied as a teacher. You can be speaking to a pupil whilst also thinking in your head what you need to do during break-time, or be reminding yourself to chase an email up, and the pupil knows they're not receiving your full attention. Therefore, they don't *truly* speak to you because they know you're not completely listening.

It can be easy to get caught up in the academic side of teaching, especially with the focus schools may place on marking, assessments, league tables, and Ofsted visits. But with mental health issues in adults on the rise, it's important to remember that these issues often develop from a young age. It's our job as teachers to encourage positive wellbeing and mental health in pupils, and one way of doing this is giving pupils the opportunity to talk whilst you take the role of an active listener. Active listening is where you put down your pen, go down to the pupils' level, make eye contact and turn off any thoughts preoccupying you. This strategy will build trust and respect and will help you to support the pupil with any issues they may be experiencing. Don't dismiss an issue as not being important; to that child it could be their biggest cause of anxiety, which could then manifest itself in aggression towards a 'safe' person—which could be you. There's always a reason for a child 'lashing out', and if they're doing it towards you it's because they want you to listen. They know you can be trusted and that you won't lash out at them, and most importantly they know you can help.

The power of listening in an age where more and more people don't have conversations in person but rather over the phone or on social media is stronger than ever. By listening, you make that child feel important, cared for and understood, and this can change their mindset in the classroom. It certainly made a marked difference in mine: the frequency of the outbursts reduced, and the pupils knew I was there to listen and help.

I then improved mental wellbeing in my class further by implementing opportunities for talking and active listening throughout the school day, not just with the adults in the room but with each other. I used other adults in the room to help me model this and provide pupils with a framework for their own conversations. Pupils gained respect for one another, shared ideas on how to problem solve, and had a greater understanding of their emotions and how to deal with these more effectively.

Think carefully and answer this question: when was the last time you saw an adult not looking at their phone? When was the last time you looked at your phone? When was the last time you had to ask someone to repeat what they had said because you were preoccupied? It's easy to be preoccupied with technology or work life but often that's all our children see. In this technology-filled age, it is vital that we use the power of listening to help our pupils and staff understand that their thoughts and opinions are valued so that we can promote positive mental wellbeing.

Lucy Whittington, BA (Hons), PGCE, NPQML, is a former middle Leader at ARK Franklin Primary Academy, London. Lucy is passionate about raising standards through mentoring and coaching peers, being a reflective practitioner and raising awareness in the importance of child mental health through 'knowing every child'.

What They Didn't Teach Me About
Building Trust with Parents

Michael Power

For a teacher, the relationship between home and school can be crucial in both getting the most out of your students and dealing with issues whenever they occur. Unfortunately, as someone new to the classroom, little can prepare you for facing a disgruntled parent, or the parent who feels that you should be doing more to support their child.

As an NQT, I would willingly call home to parents and explain when their child had been up to mischief. One day I called home to explain that a child had been throwing food around the playground and would need to complete a detention. What followed was a barrage of questions, then the parents proclaiming that the child said he was nowhere near the incident, and then an outraged finish asking, 'Are you calling my child a liar?' I had witnessed this incident with my own eyes, so I responded, 'I am simply saying I saw it myself.' The parent asked again if I was calling their child a liar. This time, I responded, 'I guess I am then yes...' The phone went dead. Without any guidance on how to work with parents, I had created a scenario where the trust between parent and school was at an all-time low. Now with more experience working with parents, I am able to see that this situation should have been dealt with in a different manner.

You are tasked with looking after the parents' most precious possession, their child. They will act to defend their child no matter what because that is their job. This is always a useful starting point when looking at your interactions with parents. What parents sometimes forget in times of disagreement is that, as the teacher, you also want what is best for this child.

Quite often, the parents you deal with will be in an anxious or angry state. Make it clear that you are expecting the outcome to be positive for everybody involved. Give the parents clear and easy-to-understand information, particularly if you are talking about levels of progress or steps within your behaviour system. Parents often left school some years ago and things may have changed significantly, which can lead to confusion, which serves nobody well.

If you promise to complete any follow-up in your contact with a parent, make sure you do it. Nothing can damage the relationship between home and school more than a broken promise.

And most importantly—don't call their child a liar!

Michael Power is a Head of Year and teacher of History in a Greater Manchester secondary academy which recently joined a multi-academy trust. Michael holds an MA in Educational Practice where he focussed on tackling educational disadvantage and the role of interventions.

What They Didn't Teach Me About
Working With Your SENCO

Abigail Hawkins

In your training year, you met children with dyslexia, autism, and who spoke English as an additional language… so SEN and EAL are covered, right? Your new class as an NQT has a couple of those too, so you can do the same thing, right? Nope!

Whatever you think you learned about meeting the needs of individuals in your class, prepare to be re-educated. Even after 23 years as a SENCO, there will always be a child who doesn't quite fit my understanding and knowledge of a particular need, or an unusual diagnosis that appears in my register. I have to research and learn new things all the time. As an NQT, you are not expected to know it all. Just because you taught a child with Fragile X last year doesn't mean you know how to teach the one in your class this year—although you have a head start on anyone who has never taught a child with this syndrome.

First, gather as much information as you can about the children, remembering that they are not SEN students primarily. You will want to know what their strengths are so that you can play to them, and where they struggle the most so that you can scaffold work so they achieve. If you have the chance to observe the children in their previous class, take the opportunity. You'll see what they're able to do, and what they struggle with. It will also help you when you face the inevitable 'lost all skills over the summer' syndrome—as teachers we know that yes, there might be a small dip, but they don't completely lose the ability to open a book and write a title! Talk to their teachers and teaching assistants and make sure you see them at break time too—you'd be surprised how some difficulties vanish when the pressure of the classroom is removed.

If your school offers a summer parents' evening, see if you can attend and meet the parents of some of those children. They will give you insight into their child's home life, and you will able to see the child in a slightly different context too. Look for little clues, and file them away for the coming school year. Does Mum tell them to fasten their shoelaces or do it for them? How does this match with what you've seen in the classroom already? Make friends with the SENCO; we're not that scary (I promise), just incredibly busy! But, we'd rather talk to you early on and teach you what you need to be successful with students than try to help a student after conflict or issues have begun. I've seen many primary students become 'school refusers' because their teacher didn't ask for help early enough, and just muddled through without meeting the child's needs. Ask to see any plans or records about children in your classes, and ask how you will be kept informed of any updates to that information. It can be useful to find out if children in your classes are involved in any interventions or provisions and when these will be happening. Correspondingly, it's important that you manage their absence from your classes carefully.

When planning your lessons, aim high and then provide lots of scaffolding, support and guidance. Key words or vocabulary mats help everyone. You can have different versions for different levels in your class, and even leave space on them for EAL pupils to add words in their own language. Don't underestimate the power of a picture; it really can convey a thousand words, most of which your SEN pupil might not be able to read independently. Sentence starters are useful at every level too, from the simple through to the complex, using connectives and conjunctions. Don't make assumptions that every child with dyslexia will want yellow paper and every child with autism likes to spin wheels—you will come unstuck very quickly. Rather than looking at any diagnostic label, the child is an individual with their own profile of strengths and difficulties.

Finally, ask questions. Twitter, Facebook groups and staff in the school can all be great resources. The NQT year is the start of your career, and there is a massive learning curve. Answers to questions provide the handrail that stops you from falling off the trajectory!

Abigail Hawkins has been a SENCO for nearly 25 years. She is also the co-ordinator for Pupil Premium, English as an Additional Language, Looked After Children, Family Learning, Assessment, Designated Safeguarding Lead, and NQT Mentor. See www.sendcosolutions.co.uk for more information.

What They Didn't Teach Me About
Emotional Engagement

Dr Gillian Judson

We don't talk much about feelings in education. There are many reasons for that, but I think one of the most important is that many people don't see what feelings have to do with 'serious' learning—that is, the *serious* learning of the 5-year-old making sense of colour, the 12-year-old exploring trigonometry, the 17-year-old studying literature, or the 37-year-old advancing quantum physics. But here's the problem: when we ignore the role of emotion in learning, we neglect one of the most powerful ways human beings make meaning of their experiences.

No one told me in my teacher training that I needed to evoke my students' emotions if I wanted my teaching to be meaningful and memorable. However, research shows that this is exactly the case. Mary Helen Immordino-Yang's (2016) research in affective neuroscience disproves old beliefs that emotions interfere with our ability to think and reason. It simply is not true. In fact, the reverse is true. She notes, 'It is literally neurobiologically impossible to build memories, engage complex thoughts, or make meaningful decisions without emotion.'

She asserts that emotional engagement is crucial in all subject areas and for all ages of students. The educational implications are huge: educators need to leverage emotions in *all* learning contexts if they want to maximie learning.

References

Immordino-Yang, M. (2016). *Emotions, learning, and the brain* (1st ed.). New York: W. W. Norton.

Dr Gillian Judson is member of the Faculty of Education and Executive Director of the Centre for Imagination in Research, Culture and Education at Simon Fraser University in Vancouver, B.C., Canada. She's interested in the role of imagination in all learning contexts, imaginative and ecological teaching practices, educational programme design, educational change, educational leadership and imaginative online learning. Her recent books include Imagination and the Engaged Learner: Cognitive Tools for the Classroom *(2016), and* A Walking Curriculum *(2018).*

What They Didn't Teach Me About
Behaviour Management

Steve Russell

Looking back on my PGCE, as much as I got from it, when it comes to 'behaviour management', it was very minimal. So, faced with my first class, I fell back on the conventional 'what are going to be our classroom rules?' discussion. I say discussion, but it was more a case of us going through the motions of setting the rules that, as Year 4 students, they knew to trot out. So, rules were 'agreed' on, but with very little true buy-in.

Fast-forward over 10 years later—I came across a different way of establishing a classroom agreement using a process called contracting. It might not seem very different to what I've just described, but its power and effectiveness lies in the subtle differences in how the discussion is carried out. It's a co-creative process, where the teacher is still in charge, but where the pupils' views and engagement are actively sought.

Top Tips for Setting Classroom Rules

- **Start with the big picture:** By this I mean ask what the pupils think the head expects of the adults, and vice versa. Then the expectations the head has of the pupils. When they say 'to learn' or 'to behave,' tease this out into specifics 'so when Mrs Jones comes into our classroom and sees you behaving, what will she see?' For older pupils especially, starting with the big picture can help to depersonalise some of the potential conflict: 'I know you don't like maths, but if I don't teach you maths, I'm going to end up having a very tricky conversation with the head.'

- **The miracle question:** The agreement between yourselves and the pupils—the following, or a variation thereof, can be very useful: '*Imagine that when you come into the class tomorrow, the magic has happened. You don't know how or by whom, but this is the best classroom it could be for you. Describe what you see and hear?—pupils, yourself, adults.*' The discussion focuses upon what needs to happen for it to be the best classroom you can collectively create.
- **Two killer questions:** '*What could I do to help you get the best out of your learning?*' and '*What could I do, quite accidentally, that could get in the way of your learning?*' If you can hold yourself to hear their responses, you will be rewarded with rich information to help you in your planning.
- **The five 'R's:** Frame the subsequent conversation around these five 'R's: Rights and Responsibilities (e.g., everyone has the right to learn/teach; to be treated with respect; to be and feel safe'); Routines (e.g., entering and leaving the room; getting equipment; asking for help); Rules (note these come after the other 3 'R's); and, Relationships, which is the bedrock for a happy, stimulating classroom.

Steve Russell is passionate about behaviour, wellbeing and leadership. Having worked as a class teacher, behaviour support teacher, and a senior school improvement consultant, he is now an interdependent consultant, coach and trainer and the owner of Beyond Behaviour.

What They Didn't Teach Me About
My Work Family

Laura Reader

I was never taught the value I would come to place on my work family. I wish I had known how things would change in the blink of an eye, how the fragility of life would reveal itself to me at such a young age. My advice to student teachers and NQTs is to take a chance, invest in the right school and accept the love you are given.

I recently left the school where I trained, was an NQT and received several promotions. I left, on happy terms, to become a Vice Principal in a local SEMH through-school (literally, a total 'ticks every box' kind of dream opportunity). Having spent eleven years in the same place, I was part of the furniture. Come the big day of my leaving speech to the staff, I didn't know where to start.

Starting life as an Economics graduate with a PGCE in French, I was quickly shoehorned into a growing English department, which had been struggling to recruit. There, I met the woman who would become one of my lifelong friends, Jo, my Head of Department, and, in later years, the women who would become friends for life. All I had ever wanted was to teach, and I thrived in a busy, challenging school facing huge deprivation and full of bubbly, warm, 'salt of the earth' children. Life was good.

My NQT year flew by, although not without event. By the end of the year, I was pregnant, and my mum was dying, facing her final struggle with breast cancer. The end came very quickly and SLT forced me to leave work early for the summer to be with her... something I will never forget, and for which I will be forever thankful. By the first week of the holidays, she had gone. I began to learn that family came first, that the job would always be there.

In a time of heartbreak, I gave birth to my little girl. Rather than let the turn of events hold me back—my team pushed for me to come back fighting—I secured the role of Second in English whilst off on maternity leave. I learnt my children would be my motive, and motherhood my energy.

My second pregnancy followed, and again, aged just 24, vulnerable and without my mum, my work family stepped in. At 29 weeks, when I was told to be off my feet due to risk of immediate haemorrhage and stillbirth, they swooped in and gave me desk duties, an office, and most importantly, the tea, cakes and love I needed. I learnt the job could, and would, wait.

Time went on, and I forged friendships for life with the women around me. We grew up together. We loved, we lost, we saw horrendous things; but ultimately, we were there, day in, day out, with a hug and the understanding needed to make each other's darkest times a little more bearable.

My career went from strength to strength as I became Head of Department, an associate to the leadership team, and later a fully-fledged Assistant Principal. I didn't always get it right, but I tried to show my teams the love and support I had been lucky enough to experience myself. Leaving was the hardest decision I ever had to make; I wasn't just leaving a school, but a family, my security. Standing before the whole staff and thanking them for their love and support was one of the most humbling experiences of my life. For NQTs out there… find that place. The one that feels like home, where your team has your back, and where you can grow up, make mistakes, and eventually pass on the support yourself.

Laura Reader is the Vice Principal at Springwell Leeds South. As an SLE and former PIXL Associate, Laura has supported senior- and middle-leadership teams across the country in school improvement. Now, leading within an SEMH setting, she believes every child is capable of great things, and in giving teachers the skills to release this potential through excellent teaching and learning.

What They Didn't Teach Me About
Department Dynamics

Lorna Allwright

'Why are you sat in my seat?'

In a school, you may expect these words to be said by children to other children, not by one staff member to another. Yet I found myself in this situation recently—just one of the many examples I could draw upon to discuss the issue of department dynamics. The working relationships one builds up with colleagues can make or break the experience of working in a school. However, they are incredibly hard to perceive or predict during the application and interview process of joining a new school. Regardless of how good the dynamics may be of your own department, the following are two suggestions for how to build a positive working environment:

- **Get to know people outside of your department.** Whether they are also trainees, NQTs or someone entirely different, having someone to talk to, get advice from and eat lunch with outside of the department is incredibly positive. If relationships with your department are strained, this can be a lifeline. Just make sure you don't spend the whole time moaning about the team, as gossip travels fast in a school!
- **Intentionally seek out a mentor** (either within or outside of your department) who you can speak to in confidence. It can be very daunting for inexperienced teachers to approach a Line Manager with negative issues. A mentor can act as a sounding board, allowing you to voice ideas and concerns in a safe environment, without rocking the boat within a tense department.

Lorna Allwright is an English Teacher at Wyvern St Edmund's in Salisbury, UK. She is convinced of the transformative power of reading and literature and aims to instil the same passion in each of her pupils.

Chapter 3

What They Didn't Teach Me About Every Child Being Unique

A child is like a butterfly in the wind
Some can fly higher than others
But each one flies the best it can.
Why compare one against the other?
Each one is different.
Each one is special.
Each one is beautiful

—*Anonymous*

For a teacher, your greatest privilege is being responsible for the children entrusted into your care. Within your class, each child is an individual with their own unique social, emotional, intellectual and physical qualities. That is what makes each child special. In this chapter, authors explore some of the individual needs that teachers are advised to consider in their planning, preparation, teaching and relationship-building.

What They Didn't Teach Me About
Working with Hungry Children

Helen Abbott

We might be familiar with Maslow's hierarchy of needs, but I never understood just how important it is for children to be fed properly. During my first few months at a boy's behaviour school (Last Chance Saloon as I fondly nicknamed it), I came to realise the impact that a lack of—or even a potential lack of—food can have on the teenagers I was working with. The boys received breakfast, snacks at break and a full two-course lunch every day, and, while it happened occasionally, it was very rare for behavioural issues to present themselves during these eating times. How can we expect anyone to function appropriately when they are hungry? How can we expect them to make the right choices when they haven't eaten a decent meal for a few days? I once caught a lad sneaking out of the kitchen with a full block of cheese up his sleeve, a chunk having been bitten off; there's no way that student was able to learn properly during our lesson time. Food is something I'm very aware of now, and at our school (now an alternative provision academy), all pupils receive a free lunch and breakfast. How can we expect anything from children if their basic needs aren't being met? If you are faced with a challenging child, it's certainly something to think about.

Helen Abbott, NPQML, is Head of foundation curriculum at an alternative provision academy in the North West. She is an art specialist, fervently believing in the therapeutic benefits of the subject. Helen is currently working on her NPQSL, completing a whole school project on Mental Health and Wellbeing.

What They Didn't Teach Me About
Looked-After Children

Bretta Townend-Jowitt

Do you know if you have an adopted, looked-after child or a child with a Special Guardianship Order in your class? Training and information in ITT is certainly not as informative in this area as it ought to be, and there are many teachers who do not have adequate knowledge and awareness of adopted, looked-after and children with special guardianship orders.

Looked-after children (LAC) are those who are in the care of a local authority. Previously looked-after children (PLAC) are those who immediately after being in care became subject to an adoption order, child arrangement order or special guardianship order. A Special Guardianship Order (SGO) is an order appointing one or more individuals to be a child's 'special guardian'.

Adopted (PLAC) and looked-after (LAC) children are one of the most vulnerable groups. Research demonstrates they experience higher rates of social, emotional and mental health needs than any other group. Academic achievement can also be severely impacted. Fewer PLAC and LAC pupils achieve age-related expectations compared with non-adopted/looked-after pupils and are much more likely to be permanently excluded from school.

The DfE collects information on looked-after children at both national and local authority levels each financial year, producing statistical release and methodology documents:

72% of those adopted in 2013–14 entered care due to abuse or neglect. Their needs do not change overnight and they do not stop being vulnerable just because they are in a loving home. Their experiences in early life can have a lasting impact which can affect the child many years after adoption. We therefore believe that teachers and schools have a vital role to play in helping these children emotionally, socially and educationally by providing specific support, to raise their attainment and address their wider needs. (DfE, 2014)

For many PLAC and LAC children, SEMH is both their primary need and main barrier to learning. Other SEN needs are also more prevalent, including: speech, language and communication needs; attention/concentration difficulties; developmental delay; and foetal alcohol spectrum disorder.

Adopted and LAC children often experience a number of moves of home (sometimes even unplanned and without their siblings), which disrupts their life in context of their place in a family. And remember that LAC children already faced additional challenges and experienced difficult issues that needed intervention by professionals prior to becoming looked-after. Also, some placements may be temporary, and secure attachments and relationships cannot be formed until they are in a more secure/permanent placement. Placement moves also affect schooling and learning; all changes of school are difficult, but for a PLAC/LAC child they are coping with a new family placement as well as a new school placement. It is vital that we are accepting of pupils who are looked-after or adopted.

As teachers, there are a number of ways that we can support pupils:

- Use the term 'birth' parents rather than 'real' parents to avoid implying that adoptive parents are not 'real'.
- Check your curriculum and think about areas which may cause difficulty; for example, things such as family trees, mothers'/fathers' days, or baby photos.

- Communicate with carers and foster parents. Remember that a parent of an older adopted child may not have come into contact with schools before as a parent—they are suddenly dealing with instant parenthood, maybe of more than one child.

Note that adopted children want to be treated the same as everyone else, so the awareness and support needs to be ongoing, but in the background.

Reference

Elias, L. 2014. PAC-UK. [Online]. [26 November 2019]. Available from: https://www.pac-uk.org/department-education-response-main-queries-adopted-children-pupil-premium/w

Bretta Townend-Jowitt is the headteacher of Kingham Primary School, Oxfordshire. She is a member of The Advisory Board for Teacher Toolkit and Learner Engagement Board, Oxfordshire County Council. Bretta is passionate about staff well-being (holding a Gold Award from Teach Well Alliance) and coaching by being a coach for Women Leaders in Education.

What They Didn't Teach Me About
Working with Children with SEMH Difficulties

Jill Turner

Before starting my PGCE, I worked for seven years in a school for children with profound and multiple learning difficulties. I thought I knew all about working with children with SEN—how wrong I was.

As a teacher, the progress of all children in your class is your responsibility (Code of Practice [DfE, 2015] section 6:521). This includes the time you aren't directly teaching them; for example, if they go to an alternative provision for a short time you are still responsible. If they have an intervention with a TA every afternoon, you are still responsible. It is quite a sobering thought and means that you need to ensure that you know what is happening. If you don't know—ask!

One of the things that you have minimal to zero influence over is what happens at home for these children. Many of the children on the SEN register may be there for social, emotional and mental health (SEMH) reasons; to the uninitiated they may just look like 'naughty children', but these children have a myriad of difficulties. There may be an undiagnosed medical condition such as autism or ADHD, or there may be other mitigating circumstances; this doesn't mean that their difficulties aren't real or that they don't need to be on the SEN register, but it definitely does mean that you need to be trying to do something to help.

For many children with SEMH difficulties (and even for some without), school is their safe place, their sanctuary; they hate holidays. School is predictable, the day is structured, rules remain consistent and adults are generally kind. They hate the holidays and challenging behaviours can increase in the week before a break. This certainly came as a shock to me; I had always presumed that all children would look forward to holidays in the way I had as a child.

As a teacher who has children with SEMH difficulties, what can you do to help? You aren't (or are unlikely to be) a paediatrician, a mental health worker or an educational psychologist—but you need to have a lot of those skills! There are many simple things that you can put in place as part of your graduated response that will help the children. A few easy to implement, cheap strategies include:

- regular down-times in a quiet area
- time-out cards or alternative places for children to eat lunch, away from the busy dining hall
- allow a teddy to sit on the window sill to 'watch' the child
- alternative routes into and out of school to avoid noisy playgrounds
- social stories

Remember all behaviour is communication, and as a class teacher it is your responsibility to try to work out what these children are trying to tell us. At the time they may feel like the most difficult and irritating children but, believe me, if you get it right, 20 years on, these are the children you will look back on with the fondest memories. As Russell Barkley said, 'The children who need love the most will always ask for it in the most unloving ways'.

References

DfE. (2015). Special educational needs and disability code of practice: 0 to 25 years. DfE-00205-2013. London: Department for Education.

Jill Turner has been a primary school teacher since 2000, following several years as a TA in a school for children with profound and multiple learning difficulties (PMLD). She became a SENCO in 2013 and an SLE (Specialist Leader of Education) for mainstream primary SEN in 2019. Since 2013, Jill has been working in a school in an area of high deprivation where she has worked on a variety of strategies to help to improve the outcomes for children with SEN, particularly Social, Emotional and Mental Health (SEMH) and Speech, Communication and Language Needs (SCLN).

What They Didn't Teach Me About
School Refusal

James McBride

School refusal has been evidenced to disrupt the emotional and social development of young people and is predictive of problems through to adulthood (Melvin et al., 2017). In a ten-year follow-up in a study of 168 school refusers, 30% received treatment for psychiatric disorders, 14% had seen a psychiatrist and 5% had been admitted for psychiatric treatment (Prabhuswamy, 2018). School refusal impacts families across all socio-economic groups, occurring within affluent and less privileged families, and is equally prevalent amongst boys and girls (Garfi, 2018). It is relatively common, impacting between 1 and 5% of school-aged children (Prabhuswamy, 2018). School refusers often express a desire to go to school, but that they can't due to genuine distress, which causes them to become tearful, defiant or angry (Garfi, 2018). Other known symptoms include excessive fearfulness, misery and complaints of feeling ill without obvious cause when faced with going to school (Prabhuswamy, 2018).

As school refusal can have many causes, parents, students, mental health professionals, paediatricians and educators are key stakeholders (Prabhuswamy, 2018). Evidence shows that parents often lack the skills required to respond effectively when their child faces severe emotional and cognitive stress (Garfi, 2018). Young people who refuse to go to school may be oppositional and aggressive towards those who try to enforce school attendance (Melvin et al., 2017). Parents often have very high individual stress, leading to burnout and family conflict (Prabhuswamy, 2018). Burnout can result in parents presenting as being unmotivated, sceptical or resistant (Garfi, 2018). Family conflict is one of the major stressors associated with the onset of school refusal in adolescence, and parents may lack confidence in their ability to manage this issue (Heyne, Sauter, Van Widenfelt, Vermeiren, & Westenberg, 2011). By giving in to their child's pleas or tantrums, parents reinforce their fear and teach them that they can avoid school through these behaviours (Garfi, 2018). Families need as much support as children to remain strong in the face of adversity (Garfi, 2018).

Up to 80% of school refusers meet criteria for an anxiety disorder, showing symptoms of persistent and excessive worry and vigilance in preparation for an anticipated danger, which impacts on rational thinking and action and can lead individuals becoming avoidant (Garfi, 2018). It is important to consider the presence of separation anxiety, generalised anxiety or a depressive disorder as an added criterion (Prabhuswamy, 2018). Diagnoses and the circumstances known to trigger symptoms should be targeted with treatment tailored to the individual (Mcshane, Walter, & Rey, 2001). Early recognition and appropriate intervention can prevent the medium to long-term psychosocial consequences for young people and the associated economic burden to society, the cost of which is unknown (Prabhuswamy, 2018).

Cognitive behaviour therapy (CBT) is the most commonly evaluated treatment for school refusal, showing efficacy for improving attendance and reducing emotional symptoms, with research showing that after intervention, approximately two-thirds of participants were free of the disorder at follow-up (Heyne et al., 2011). Interventions involve psycho-education, relaxation training, graded exposure and social skills training (Melvin et al., 2017). Other interventions focus on family communication and problem-solving skills and working on the inter-relationship between thoughts and feelings (Prabhuswamy, 2018). This can be very useful for severe cases of school refusal, as relaxation training provides coping skills that can be used by young people when approaching school grounds, social skills training to improve interaction with peers and anxiety-provoking thoughts can be reduced through cognitive therapy (Heyne et al., 2002). If young people display high levels of depression, psychopharmacology is an important consideration to reduce symptoms (Heyne et al., 2002).

The involvement of medical professionals in the initial stages of intervention is necessary, as unexplained somatic symptoms must be assessed to rule out medical reasons for symptoms (Prabhuswamy 2018). In a study of 63 school refusing adolescents with anxiety and depressive disorders, 54% of adolescents receiving treatment of CBT and antidepressant medication achieved 75% school attendance compared with 17% of those in the placebo group (Melvin et al., 2017).

Teachers can influence the environment that the young person will return to once the reason for the school refusal is understood. Garfi (2018) states that returning to school may be stressful, but the stress will be short lived if help is provided to academic results, bullying concerns are addressed and friendship issues or issues with teachers are resolved. Collaboration between the school and the family is needed to explain the rationale for the skills being taught and checking the child's understanding, facilitate collaborative problem-solving discussions, rehearse and model the skills being taught and providing positive feedback (Prabhuswamy, 2018). Complex issues may exist, and should be rectified where possible before the child returns to school so that stress experienced by the young person is short-lived (Garfi, 2018).

When planning for a return to school, teachers should ensure that the young person is aware of their timetable, an adult leader is in place at home, safety strategies are implemented at the school and practice runs are conducted to reduce anxiety by exposing the young person to the environment (Prabhuswamy, 2018).

References

Garfi, J. (2018). *Overcoming school refusal: A practical guide for teachers, counsellors, caseworkers and parents.* Bowen Hills: Australian Academic Press.

Heyne, D., King, N. J., Tongue, B. J., Rollings, S., Young, D., Pritchard, M., & Ollendick, T. H. (2002). Evaluation of child therapy and caregiver training in the treatment of school refusal. *Journal of the American Academy of Child & Adolescent Psychiatry, 41*(6), 687–695. doi:10.1097/00004583-200206000-00008

Heyne, D., Sauter, F. M., Van Widenfelt, B. M., Vermeiren, R., & Westenberg, P. M. (2011). School refusal and anxiety in adolescence: Non-randomized trial of a developmentally sensitive cognitive behavioral therapy. *Journal of Anxiety Disorders, 25*(7), 870–878. doi:10.1016/j.janxdis.2011.04.006

Mcshane, G., Walter, G., & Rey, J. M. (2001). Characteristics of adolescents with school refusal. *Australian & New Zealand Journal of Psychiatry, 35*(6). doi:10.1046/j.1440-1614.2001.00955.x

Melvin, G. A., Dudley, A. L., Gordon, M. S., Klimkeit, E., Gullone, E., Taffe, J., & Tonge, B. J. (2017). Augmenting cognitive behavior therapy for school refusal with fluoxetine: A randomized controlled trial. *Child Psychiatry and Human Development, 48*(3), 485–497. doi:10.1007/s10578-016-0675-y

Prabhuswamy, M. (2018). To go or not to go: School refusal and its clinical correlates. *Journal of Paediatrics and Child Health, 54*(10), 1117–1120. doi:10.1111/jpc.14198

James McBride is a social worker in Australia where he works with families to avoid child protection intervention and helps young people to transition from living in care to living independently. James is passionate about working alongside his clients to assess their needs, strengths and dreams and takes a strengths-based approach to empower clients to set goals and act to make their dreams a reality.

What They Didn't Teach Me About
Attachment

Bretta Townend-Jowitt

Attachment is probably one of those phrases you have or will hear about in schools, but it is likely no one has truly explained what it is or the impact for the pupils in your care.

Bowlby (1988) described attachment as a 'lasting psychological connectedness between human beings'. This means that children need to develop a secure attachment to their main caregiver early in their lives to ensure emotional well-being, self-regulation, the ability to develop relationships and capacity to learn. Children who live through a disruptive childhood, may face attachment difficulties. Factors which may present a risk include the following: poverty and homelessness; exposure to drug and alcohol abuse; exposure to abuse; parents with mental health difficulties; and, family breakdown or conflict. Understanding these disruptions and the vulnerable groups (adopted and looked-after pupils; pupils with SEND; refugees and those traumatised by conflict or loss) enables us to plan support more effectively.

There are 4 identified attachment types:

- **Secure attachment** comes from experienced and sensitive care givers, and as such, children with secure attachment trust teachers to meet their needs and are able to form relationships with others. Securely attached children are more likely to be better at problem-solving, be more co-operative with others and more self-aware.
- Children with **avoidant attachment** have experienced insensitive or rejecting caregiving; they subconsciously believe their needs

probably won't be met, and as such, appear independent and self-reliant, avoiding close relationships and rarely seeking help from others. In the classroom, they focus primarily on the task rather than asking for help, as they find trusting a teacher difficult.

- **Ambivalent attached** children may have experienced inconsistent or unresponsive caregiving, so cannot rely on their needs being met. As such, they are easily frustrated and can present as both clingy and rejecting as they seek comfort but are often unable to be comforted. They sometimes present as attention-needing and hyperactive. These pupils want the attention of the teacher and this can become a pre-occupation, meaning the task is overlooked and insist on adult support before they engage in the task.
- **Disorganised attachment** comes from caregivers who are neglectful, abusive or chaotic. The child often has no attaching behaviours and is confused or apprehensive. They are highly vigilant yet easily distracted and may also present unpredictable behaviours. For these pupils both the task and the adult can be a challenge; they mistrust adults and are unable to complete tasks if they feel there can be any chance of failure. They often feel helpless and this leads to the teacher, task or others being the target of their anger or frustration.

Schools can offer a 'safe haven' for pupils, and our understanding of attachment theory in turn helps us to understand the issues and problems we are dealing with so that we are able to focus our practice on the individual child's needs. Teachers and teaching assistants can therefore provide important attachments for children which will help them succeed in school.

So why does attachment matter? Quite simply, most children are successful in school and enjoy their lives, but some children can struggle from an early age. This means they could be disruptive, unfocussed, withdrawn, distracted, controlling, destructive and lacking in self-esteem and confidence. This in turn means they often underachieve in school and are classed as pupils with behavioural difficulties and are at risk of exclusion.

References

Bowlby, J. (1988). A secure base: Parent–child attachment and healthy human development. New York: Basic Books.

Bretta Townend-Jowitt is the headteacher of Kingham Primary School, Oxfordshire. She is a member of The Advisory Board for Teacher Toolkit and Learner Engagement Board, Oxfordshire County Council, an Advocate for The Chartered College and the Maternity Teacher Paternity Teacher Project. Bretta is passionate about staff well-being (holding a Gold Award from Teach Well Alliance) and coaching by being a coach for Women Leading in Education.

What They Didn't Teach Me About
English as an Additional Language (EAL)

Joe Denny

As a passionate linguist, I was enthusiastic about an entire day of training dedicated to supporting learners with English as an additional language. The host school was a two-form entry primary school with 100% EAL pupils. Could there be a better place to learn the ins and outs of such an important element of classroom practice? By 9:15 am, I concluded that yes, yes there could. The opening statement of the day set the tone for the most confusing course I have attended to date: 'we don't really have to do anything for EAL because everyone here is EAL'.

Even as a person with little knowledge of the school context, I felt the trainer's outlook did not map to successful English language learning. How could the school feel their non-action was something worth celebrating? The following day when I met my class on my first placement, there were 17 EAL pupils with 8 different first languages, I began to wish I'd learned something about how to teach them properly. So, allow me to share a few tips about teaching EAL learners I wish I had known before I began teaching groups of bewildered pupils.

- Osmosis is not a strategy you should rely on as a teacher. If you want EAL pupils to learn something, you have to teach them. If you want EAL pupils to do something, you simply must show them how to do it. I know how obvious this may sound, but it is worth remembering when you are in the classroom.
- Teaching academic language involves two key elements: teach the meanings of key language, including the definitions of key words and model using key language. Allow pupils to demonstrate their

understanding of the key language using four communication skills: speaking, listening, reading and writing. Give pupils clear, constructive feedback and allow them to practice repeatedly. It requires hard work, determination and resilience to get this right, but it is 100% worth it.

- When differentiating, remember that EAL is not a special educational need or disability. EAL learners can also have SEND, but it is important that you do not confuse the two.
- To differentiate effectively, it is important to scaffold pupils' use of English so that they develop their understanding of academic language. When you get it right, they can achieve the same lesson objective as their peers. Never differentiate by giving EAL pupils an alternative task to their peers with a lower level of cognitive challenge. It may be that pupils can complete their task independently and confidently, but be clear that this does nothing for their language development.
- Finally, the most wonderful thing about teaching is the opportunity to reflect and improve. Be grateful for every cringe-worthy moment you produce or witness, as those moments will teach you more than your successes ever will. Actively look for positivity, even in the unlikeliest of places, and you will be well-equipped to survive the more difficult points along your PGCE journey.

Joe Denny is an EAL lead teacher at a large primary school in Oldham, Greater Manchester. Joe is passionate about enhancing pupils' academic language skills and empowering teachers and support staff to help pupils achieve their goals.

What They Didn't Teach Me About
Dyslexia

Lorraine Loveland-Armour

It is so easy for students with dyslexia to blend into the background in schools. There are so many misconceptions, including understanding what dyslexia is and how it can be observed and differentiated from garden variety poor readers. Too often, especially as new teachers, we are caught up in what we can observe, especially through assessments. Dyslexia becomes something associated with reading, writing and/or spelling, and the time to understand the underpinning cognitive skills associated with consistency in these academic areas, including working memory (see Sue Gathercole's work), processing speed and phonological awareness, is lost.

When I started teaching high school English (25 years ago), my misconceptions about dyslexia were rooted in assumptions informed by poor literacy being core to dyslexia. I was suddenly responsible for over 150 students. I had a class of 36 Year 11s, and 20 of these students were identified with dyslexia. Whilst their literacy skills were often erratic, what became clear very quickly is that that the majority of these young people had strong verbal and reasoning skills, but these abilities weren't always reflected in their written work. They also believed they were 'stupid' and incapable of meeting any of the learning outcomes I set. What was most alarming to me was that they spoke in a collective pronoun: 'we can't do it!'; 'you expect too much from us!'; 'we're never going to go to university!'

Being a new teacher, I took my attendance register to our educational psychologist—we were lucky enough to have one onsite back when I began—and I asked to see the individual education plans (IEPs) for the students with dyslexia. They had a system of using an asterisk and a letter code to indicate the type of additional needs that students had been identified with. Reading these reports raised so many questions about what had happened in these students' educational journeys, and made me realise that clearly the structure of our educational system had failed them.

Over my years teaching I learned how important it is—especially when you are bogged down in data, marking and feeling overwhelmed—to remember, and focus on, students with dyslexia. These students:

- may be tremendous spellers, especially when spelling words in isolation;
- are often very keen readers, especially when they can select the texts;
- are likely to remember you if you take time to know them, but equally if you dismiss their capabilities;
- may write well, but in unstructured or in non-sequential ways—teaching writing processes, beginning with a range of planning strategies and writing prompts can be liberating;
- require a bit more time, not because they are slow learners, but because they are reasoning through possibilities in often interesting and creative ways—it is worth the wait!

Finally, students with dyslexia may blend in with classmates performing at all ability levels—be sure you know how to really see their abilities amongst their difficulties. These may provide illuminations to support you to recognise dyslexia, and perhaps you can be the teacher who shifts the learning journeys students with dyslexia embark upon!

Lorraine Loveland-Armour is the Team Leader of Dyslexia Support Services at Newman University. She started her career in education as a teaching assistant and went on to train as a high school English teacher, teaching in both California and Washington states; she then specialised in dyslexia at Antioch University, Seattle where she gained her MA, Ed. Lorraine is in her final year of her EdD and her research interests particularly focus on dyslexia and adults, university education, lived experiences and phenomenology.

What They Didn't Teach Me About
Teaching 'Lower Ability' Labelled Students

Laura Larkin

When some people look at my timetable, full of 'bottom set' groups, they exclaim 'What have you done to deserve that?!' It's at this point I take great pleasure in telling them that it's a timetable I asked for. I still get frustrated by this attitude because my students aren't any less deserving of a good teacher than anyone else—why shouldn't they get someone in front of them who wants to teach them?

Way back at the start of my career, I saw lower-ability classes as students to be won over; to engage them meant getting the pencil crayons out at every opportunity (but not felt tips, they only came out on special occasions and with classes I could completely trust!), and I had my worksheets differentiated at least three ways with each version on different coloured paper.

Now I realise that what these classes need is the very highest of expectations. The first thing I tell my classes each September, and I reiterate it throughout the year, is that I don't care what number is assigned to our class, we are going to work hard and to the very best of our ability. I make sure that they agree with my aims: I want the best for them all; I'm going to make sure they work hard, with no excuses; and, I will keep pushing them even if they think they're done. They all agree to these aims, and I hold them to that agreement.

My students are challenged from the moment they step foot in the classroom. Every student I teach is treated the same. They are expected to follow the rules of my classroom. They are expected to use the best vocabulary they have—and if they haven't got the best vocabulary, I give it to them! They are expected to read aloud, even if it is just one sentence. They are expected to write in full sentences. They are expected to contribute in some form to our discussions. And they rise to it. Every time.

It can be hard sometimes when the message of high expectations for every student isn't shared across the whole school, and you do have to constantly remind students that you expect the best; that's ok though—that's how you build a relationship with students. I strongly believe that when you share the high expectations with students consistently, they start to believe it themselves, and that in turn develops them into students with higher levels of motivation and better behaviour. Chocolate and pencil crayons aren't the secret to engaging lower-ability students; it's your belief in them that is the key.

To summarise my advice, believe that your students can achieve the very best outcomes, and teach them how to achieve them. Don't fall into the trap of thinking that having a 'lower ability' student means they can't do something; they can and will with your help.

Laura Larkin has been an English teacher for almost 15 years, and, in that time, she has been KS3 lead, KS4 lead, second in department, and she is currently a Lead Practitioner at Cockshut Hill School in Birmingham. This job enables Laura to focus on developing Teaching and Learning strategies that will support the students in her school.

What They Didn't Teach Me About
Reflective Practice

Michelle Stephenson

When I signed up to be a teacher, I wish they had told me that I would also be a nurse, a doctor and a social worker. We are all of those things.

It is our responsibility to spot signs of abuse, to talk to children about emotional issues, to deal with bereavement and trauma, to help pupils get appropriate help when they take drugs, can't manage a day in school, or a day without alcohol, or are fighting the urge to cut or burn themselves. Nobody talked about that in our PGCE.

Camran doesn't like male teachers standing beside him to check his work; he has had too many aggressive men towering over him. Olivia is freaked out by teachers who call her 'Princess' or 'Sweet Pea'. Jack reacted violently when his maths teacher said, 'Good work, son'. Teachers think they are being friendly and non-threatening, but children can see them as crossing boundaries.

Many secondary schools start Year 7 with a topic where children talk about themselves and their family. Children in care, in families where the police are regular visitors, or perhaps have a family member in prison, want their privacy. School is the one place where they can get away from their family, but teachers think they are doing the right thing by bringing home life into the classroom.

When children are under pressure, they can find it easier to clam up or behave badly than to find an acceptable version of their story to tell others; once they get a reputation for being difficult, they can find themselves on a collision course with teachers and classmates.

Through working with a company called Innovating Minds, people who are specialists in mental health in schools, we started to use Reflective Practice to deal with incidents in school. It is almost like a script we follow.

We ask the child to describe what happened: 'What did you say /do?', 'What did the other person say/do?', 'What were you thinking?', 'What were you feeling?', 'How did you interpret the other person's words/actions?' We then ask them to evaluate how effective their response was and to think what they could do differently next time.

It is objective and non-judgmental; after a while they start to work through this process automatically and learn to regulate their own emotions. This is the first step in developing a vital skill that will help them function in our society. This seems to be a much more productive approach than applying sanctions, fixed term exclusions or putting children in isolation booths.

Schools now routinely accept that safeguarding is everybody's responsibility; similarly, everybody has the responsibility to try to understand why children are the way they are and why they behave the way that they do.

We want all our children to leave us as well-rounded human beings who can look after themselves and their families and make their way in life. This is harder—but much more worthwhile—than being known for our good exam results.

Michelle Stephenson, former assistant head at Young People's Academy is now starting her second job in special education. Previously an English and media teacher in mainstream education, she believes that her PGCE did not prepare her to deal with the complex bundle of emotions, experiences and aspirations that each student presents.

What They Didn't Teach Me About
Understanding Inclusion

Lorraine Boyle

I completed my BSc (Hons) in Psychology and MSc Health Psychology at the University of Central Lancashire. I pursued a career in mental health until I had corrective surgery on my eyes, which freed me to pursue my passion for teaching. I have wanted to work with children with disabilities from a young age, due to the fact I was born partially sighted. I wanted to give something back and help people 'fight the system' as I had done all my life. Being visually impaired, I struggled in school—not academically, but it was often physically challenging. I had some fantastic teachers in primary school who really understood my needs. It was suggested to me in my Year 6 assessment that I go to a special school due to being visually impaired. Luckily, my mum knew this was a bad choice for me, and I am glad she chose for me to go to mainstream school. However, the SENCO support from the school was poor; this is where the ambition to help people in a similar situation as myself came about.

I didn't require a lot of support at school; I mainly needed the teacher to write in black pen, to have a note taker and sit close to the front. Sometimes these needs were not met; for example, often the teacher would not have a black pen. Sometimes I would have a note taker, but then I wasn't always able to sit at the front. Some teachers didn't understand the importance of a child both needing support and being allowed to be the same as everyone else. This would often lead me to complain to my SENCO. I would be told I was being awkward. I would also trial new equipment which would sometimes not meet my needs; again, I was told I was being awkward. I would have loved to be a teacher, even then, just to show I could do a better job than those who failed me.

After I completed my university degree in Psychology, I didn't feel comfortable teaching due to my poor sight, but I still wanted to help people. I then completed my Masters, after which I worked part time for a learning disabilities charity; I enjoyed this as I was helping people in their day-to-day life. However, I felt my passion was in mental health. I started to work at a mental health company, helping people with their transition from hospital back into the community. I initially enjoyed this job, but I gradually lost my passion for it as there was little room to progress further and use my degree as I was qualified to do. Two years into the job I was offered an operation to correct my cataracts. They told me this would vastly improve my eyesight, which it absolutely did; I no longer needed to rely on visual aids. It was while I was off work that I decided to do what I had always wanted to do: I wanted to teach.

I applied for Teamwork's SCITT and started training in September 2018. I believe my life experience prepared me for teaching in ways that doing the course straight out of university might not have. First, I am more aware of being inclusive with a wide range of children. More importantly, I am more aware as to why it may have been difficult to supply this support when I was a student. Often it comes down to resources that are available. As a child you don't realise this, but as a teacher it can be quite disappointing when all you want to do is support your children. Now being on both sides of the argument, I can support the children the best that I can with the support that I have. Therefore, I want to develop my career further and be a SENCO. I feel I have lots of experience, both as being disabled, but also working with disabled people in the past.

Working in a different field has also given me a perspective on work-life balance that I think some people on my SCITT course struggle with. I am very strict with my routine. I do what needs doing for school and anything that can wait, will wait. I focus on what is important. There are obviously times where a lot of things are important, and I do a lot of working after school. However, on a general level, work starts at 7:30 pm and stops at 9 pm on an evening. I still have lots to learn about this, but as a trainee, I think this is a good balance that some people don't have.

Lorraine Boyle is an NQT in a school in Bradford. She is passionate about inclusion and would like to complete her SENCO training in the future.

What They Didn't Teach Me About
Childhood Trauma

Mike Armiger

Trauma is not what happens to you, it's how something affects you. It is a very individual and nuanced topic that needs reflection. Many of us have experienced adverse events in our lives—often as children—but it's the perception and resources we have available to us throughout the experiences that can make a difference.

I always remind people that if we knew the context and impact of some children's experiences, we would often see their reactions as completely understandable. Sadly, we are often operating without this context; however, this doesn't prevent us from beginning to work in a more informed way that will help support all our young people.

Trauma can involve believing that the world can be unsafe and unpredictable. Living with children in care throughout my childhood taught me that young people who have experienced traumatic circumstances often experience them in places where we should all feel safe. This is such a fundamental invasion of someone's physical and psychological safety, trust and capacity to believe adult's intentions are true. We know that the resulting impact on a child's development can be profound. I am all too familiar with the 'they are not engaging' response from services and external agencies when young people can't access the therapies they have waited months to receive. We have been told that unless young people are able to talk to someone about their stress, distress and trauma, that there is nothing we can do. But that's not true. Although it seems difficult, a focus on regulation is one of the more hopeful pieces of this jigsaw.

Throughout my time in education and health, I have seen many young people unable to access interventions because their experiences and adaptations make it difficult for them to articulate their thoughts, needs and trauma. These changes are not ones they choose. Too often, these young people are placed into settings without any understanding of how their brains and bodies work. For us to begin working successfully with these young people, we first need to understand the need to support their capacity for regulation.

Regulation and understanding the need to work on a physical level with the whole body often go under the radar. Our attention can lean more towards cognition, articulation, emotional literacy and much more, but we forget that trauma and shock can be stored in our bodies. For many young people who have experienced trauma, their nervous systems have been adversely affected, and they adapt to survive their circumstances. These adapted nervous systems can be a real challenge for many young people; they often find it challenging to identify and regulate their physical and emotional states.

Young people who have experienced trauma can struggle with self-regulation; executive functioning is often impaired for them. Some of the best strategies I can suggest include: routines involving movement; doing a 'job'; building physical, relational and psychological safety in the learning space and wider school building; and, plenty of breathing and co-regulation with an emotionally available adult. Growing a child's ability to self-regulate involves co-regulation. The two have to co-exist. Although these children's experiences can break our hearts, and although our heads might hurt from wondering what we can do when things seem so difficult, and despite the time we will possibly spend wondering if we are what that child needs, there is hope.

Every piece of research and study I have read—and my own experience on this topic—points to the power of relationships. Safe relationships mitigate. It might not be now; it might be later. But those valuable, safe and healthy relationships will be what a child needs at all ages all through their adult life. I have seen many people go on to live healthy lives despite trauma. But if there is to be a better tomorrow for these young people, we must give them reasons to believe that, through our hopeful actions, profound understanding and courageous compassion.

Without doubt, my life would not be as rich without the young people, parents, colleagues and communities I have worked in. They have shaped me, supported me and taught me many valuable lessons that I will hopefully pass on to others.

Hold on to every kind act, word and achievement, for when I feel like the world is an overwhelming place, these are the times and moments I revisit to make me feel hopeful again. Educating young people is an act that will change their realities—and in turn the world. Thank you for creating those ripples.

Mike Armiger is a school improvement and mental health advisor with a focus on trauma, SEMH and suicide prevention.

What They Didn't Teach Me About
ACEs

Bretta Townend-Jowitt

As a teacher who completed a PGCE, and having mentored PGCE students and NQTs, I am well aware that training and learning about Adverse Childhood Experiences (ACEs) and trauma is woefully inadequate. As a trainee teacher in charge of a class for the first time, we often beat ourselves up if the children are not learning and/or behaving as we'd expect them to. We might ask questions of ourselves, such as 'why am I no good at behaviour management?', or 'What am I doing wrong?' We need to stop, think and remember this great mantra: all behaviour is communication.'

Instead of focusing on the behaviour ask, 'what happened to them?' Think of the behaviour in terms of the story or emotion causing it; for example, 'What is the feeling behind the behaviour?' We need to recognise that with behavioural issues, it is often 'not that they won't; it's that they can't'. If the child has a threat or perceived threat, this is triggered in the brain stem—they go into the fight/flight/freeze response that hunter-gatherers needed for survival (something we still do). The problem though is that when this is triggered, it shuts down the rest of the brain—especially the frontal cortex, which is used for thinking. Adrenaline and cortisol are released, which gives you energy; this is why pupils who have a perceived threat behave as they do: running away, fighting and feeling very strong, hiding under a table, hurting others, for example.

Trauma impacts and fragments the memory; pupils who demonstrate behaviours as communication due to stress, anxiety or trauma often cannot remember what they have done, and certainly not why they did it. We do not often know what their triggers are—it could be a sound, smell, taste or word. Feeling fear is normal; feeling terror is not. The children who have experienced trauma have felt terror and have a feeling of powerlessness.

So, adult approach and mindset are vitally important. Think about why the child is demonstrating the behaviour: are they anxious, stressed, upset or angry? Why have they such a strong feeling? Children are not born badly behaved and they do not want to behave badly; there are reasons they do so and it is always a form of communicating. The question is to identify what they are communicating to us: an attention 'seeking' child is actually an attention 'needing' child.

Pupils who experience trauma, such as neglect, abuse, being witness to domestic violence, exposure to drug abuse, or parents with mental health problems, have had times when they feel powerless; they want to be in control and that manifests in their behaviour by them refusing to work, hurting others, running away, or refusing to eat, for example.

In schools, we have children for whom co-regulation, for whatever reason, has not been consistent—therefore we need to provide it. Pupils may be chronologically above the age of five, but emotionally not able to self-regulate due to a lack of co-regulation when younger. Self-regulation can only happen after repetitive co-regulation, and it is important that pupils with ACEs have the opportunity to build good relationships with adults in school for this to improve. It takes time, patience and perseverance, but it is worth the effort—and sometimes heartache—involved.

Bretta Townend-Jowitt is the headteacher of Kingham Primary School, Oxfordshire. She is a member of The Advisory Board for Teacher Toolkit and Learner Engagement Board, Oxfordshire County Council, an Advocate for The Chartered College and the Maternity Teacher Paternity Teacher Project. Bretta is passionate about staff well-being (holding a Gold Award from Teach Well Alliance) and coaching by being a coach for Women Leading in Education.

What They Didn't Teach Me About
Codes and Labels

Emma Betts

Nothing prepares you for that moment when you shut the door to your classroom and you become a teacher for the first time. It can be overwhelming as you realise that you have to remember everything that you have ever heard or been taught; I remember that moment quite vividly, even though it was 15 years ago. And no one alludes to the amount of paperwork you are overwhelmed with: class lists, seating plans, schemes of work, lesson plan templates, assessment data, baseline testing, behaviour paperwork, reward paperwork, and it goes on… and they certainly don't tell you what to do with it!

It turns out that educational paperwork comes with its own language that has to be decoded for it to make sense; no one said I would need a translator.

What is even scarier is the SEND label, or that of EAL; how do I know what to do to differentiate for those students? The ocean of SEND codes seems never-ending: ADD, ADHS, ASD, BOSS, CAMHS, EHCP, EP, EWO, HI, IEP, MLD, MSI, OT, PD, PMLD, PT, SALT, SEND, SENDCo, SLCN, SLD, SpLD, and VI; enough to make anyone feel like they are drowning.

Labels and codes are nothing to be concerned about; labels are for clothes not children! The labels and codes just provide an identification that should inform you about a child and assist your planning and differentiation and general relationship and behaviour management of a young person. However, no amount of training or reading will be as powerful as getting to know the young person for who they are, regardless of their label. A label/code does not define a person and should not hinder their access to the curriculum; it should also not be an excuse or used as a barrier to try.

So, when you get a class-list with codes to subcategorise your students, please do not automatically assume that this is a reason for low expectations or poor behaviour: it is not! It just means that these students may need to be dealt with in a slightly different way to engage them or to support them or to nurture them. Patience and time are what these students need rather than being branded or treated differently to their peers.

My final comment would be not to fear the codes, but to embrace them. Take time to build relationships and take an interest, and help build those bridges to help the students succeed!

Emma Betts, BEd, has recently taken the roll of Literacy Lead at Cockshut Hill School, Birmingham. She is passionate about improving literacy and reading standards, especially for low attaining students and SEND. Emma worked at an MLD school before starting at Cockshut Hill and has always had an interest in helping SEND students be successful.

Chapter 4

What They Didn't Teach Me About Growing as a Professional

As you complete your PGCE (or another route into the teaching profession) and find your first job, it will be important to think about how you can grow and develop as a professional. The world of education changes rapidly, and it is crucial to keep up to date with policy directions, examination specification updates, curriculum changes and emerging research that shapes who we are as professionals and what we do. With limited financial resources and pressures on releasing staff due to cover constraints, many schools may find themselves in a situation where there is a strained relationship between providing opportunities for staff to develop their CPD and managing tight budgets (Weston, 2014). The Teacher Development Trust released data in 2017 highlighting that in excess of twenty thousand teachers work in educational establishments where no budget exists for CPD (Teacher Development Trust, 2017). The report also indicates that, nationwide, a mere 0.7% of schools' annual budgets are being invested into growing and developing educators (Teacher Development Trust, 2017). It is really important, therefore, for teachers to take control of their own continuing professional development (CPD).

Although it might not feel like it right now, it probably will not be long before many of you are seeking your first promotion into a leadership position! In this chapter, authors share their tips and experiences about how they have developed their own CPD.

References

Weston, D. (2016). Analysis of CPD Spending in England 2014-15. London: Teacher Development Trust. http://TDTrust.org/benchmarking

Weston, A (2009) A rulebook for arguments. (4th edition) Cambridge: Hackett Publishing Company

What They Didn't Teach Me About
Developing Your Professional Identity

Dr Deborah Outhwaite

When you're doing your PGCE, it's not necessarily clear how promotion works. I was aware that there were Head of Department roles and other selected opportunities for women, but probably not senior leadership ones—an interesting thought to look back on now in the days of @WomenEd and at a time when we are actively working to promote wider routes into leadership. It was only when I got to university (where our programme leader was a woman, studying at that point for her own doctorate) when it was pointed out to us that female careers were different to men's, and as a result, your professional identity had to be owned by you, to save it from being swallowed up by your wider personal and family commitments.

When I was doing my PGCE, I knew that I wanted to do a Master's, and so I strategically took a 12-month maternity contract for my first job. I knew that this way I couldn't get sucked in to a school, and would definitely go and do my MSc; although I was sad to leave after that first year, I knew I was doing something that I wanted to do for myself. After completing my Master's, I applied for a Head of Department role. I knew that I wanted to do a doctorate, but probably part-time as I couldn't afford to give up my salary. I had colleagues tell me I needed to be older and more experienced; my response to any of you who experience this now is please ignore them! If you want to do a PhD/EdD, go for it!

I switched to a fractional role when I had my children, despite being told that I needed to be in school full-time to avoid missing out on promotions. I remember crying when I went for a UPS role, when my youngest child was three, where part of the feedback was that I could do a Master's if I wanted to develop my professional learning. I had mentioned wanting to do a doctorate in the interview, but the Head of School hadn't even looked at my CV; he just knew that I had done Leading from the Middle (the old NPQML). I knew that I had to own my professional learning, and no one else was going to do that for me, so I enrolled in the part-time doctorate anyway—these days this is better role-modelled for us through the range of #edutwitter chats and @CharteredColl publications. As a university lecturer, I have also had opportunities to present @BELMASConf and work with my @ BELMASOffice Research Interest Group (RIG), this costs around £5 a month, and I would have loved to have known about these publications back on my PGCE!

Dr Deborah Outhwaite, Director, Derby Teaching Schools Alliance (DTSA).

What They Didn't Teach Me About
Developing My Teaching Persona

Claire Nicholls

In the first stages of my career, it wasn't unusual for me to cry at work on a weekly basis. Looking back, I don't think I was always unhappy. I certainly wouldn't have stayed in the profession for more than a decade if I didn't enjoy it. What I did often feel though was a sense of frustration, inadequacy and, at times, hopelessness. I'm now a happy, successful teacher and senior leader. I'm proud of my career and how far I've come, but when I look back, it is sometimes tinged with a sense of regret that I didn't realise how to be both happy and successful sooner: I should have just been myself.

My Primary PGCE was a whistle-stop tour of teaching. On a year-long course with three teaching placements, there simply isn't the time to devote more than a couple of sessions to subject knowledge and pedagogy in subjects other than English, Maths, Science and your chosen specialism (French, in my case). There certainly wasn't much space for critical thinking and debate. So, we were taught the 'right way' to do things. Once in school, it was much the same. As a Newly Qualified Teacher (NQT), I replicated the teaching styles and working patterns of my peers. We planned together, collated resources and pooled expertise.

The thing is, as an NQT I needed to learn from my colleagues. So, I learnt their ways of doing things. I mirrored their schedules, replicated their work-life balance and worked to their rules. I even taught lessons they'd planned. When they didn't work for me, I felt that I was the problem. I was a brand new teacher, so perhaps I just needed more practice, more experience, more time. But despite gaining that time and experience, I was still unhappy. Whilst I never missed a deadline, I was constantly being asked if I wanted someone else to complete my share of the resources, as they'd already done theirs. When I received an 'inadequate' judgment in a lesson observation, I became convinced I just wasn't cut out to be a teacher.

Something had to change. I decided to do things my way and started to be more secure about my own abilities. Whilst still keeping school policy, curriculum and current educational research in mind, I began to teach the way which worked best for me and therefore for my pupils. They weren't going to learn best if I was trying to be someone else. I became more stubborn about my work-life balance; as long as my work was complete, what did it matter to anyone else when I left school?

It takes a while to develop your teaching persona, and you will undoubtedly need the support of others along the way. Don't feel that you have to be someone else though; no matter how great the teacher in the next room, that other school or online is, that doesn't mean it'll work for you. Find your own way and believe in you.

Claire Nicholls is a Bristol-based Special Educational Needs Coordinator. She has been teaching for 11 years across primary and secondary, in both mainstream and special schools and is a Specialist Leader of Education for SEN. She is a representative for the Maternity Teacher Paternity Teacher project and writes about parenting, identity and authenticity.

What They Didn't Teach Me About
Investing in My Own Subject Knowledge

Ruth Luzmore

At school I was a competent, but not confident mathematician. Despite being consistently put into the top set and managing to scrape an A in GCSE, I was always surrounded by other pupils who knew what the problem meant and could get to the answer faster than I could. I can remember the exact moment I truly believed that I would always be inept at maths. When I was in Year 10, my school was having a weekend open day and my maths teacher wanted help to promote the department to prospective parents. Ending the lesson early, she read out a list of names of those she wanted assistance from and asked everyone else to leave. The humiliation of being the only one in the class to stand up and leave confirmed at that moment that my self-doubt was justified.

So, when it came to my PGCE, I had a real internal battle to win around whether I would have the aptitude to teach maths. To their credit, the lecturers and tutors on my PGCE did an excellent job in this regard. I graduated with a newfound respect for a subject which was in fact rather beautiful; something to be enjoyed rather than feared. I convinced myself that as a twenty-something, I would be more than capable of coping with the demands of the primary curriculum I would be teaching in my NQT year.

And so, it came to be that I was given the top set of pupils to teach—35 ten-year-olds. While I was concerned about the number of the pupils, senior staff reassured me that, because they were all top set, it would be easy to teach them.

But it was like turning back time. These pupils were fast and I was not. They were quick: they not only completed the lesson work I set for them faster than expected, they were also faster than me in solving problems that we worked through together during the input. They were faster to see my mistakes and each other's mistakes. And faster to see that I was not adequately prepared to teach them. Those first few weeks were an absolute nightmare for me. Not only did I have 35 books to mark each day (none of that 'no marking' back then), but I needed to find enough work to keep them busy for the full hour, which then would need to be repeated. It was becoming an unmanageable, cyclical hell. It quickly became clear that I needed to learn more about the curriculum they had covered and where it was I could extend these pupils if I was going to be effective.

So, what did I do? Well there was really only one solution. I needed to swallow my pride, put on my humility pants, and accept that I needed to do some work to get myself up to standard. For example, my recall of number facts needed to be a lot quicker; I'm not proud of this, but I only really learnt my times tables properly once I was teaching. And I learnt them because I had to.

It turned out that, despite my love of all things in the humanities and arts, maths became the subject I loved—and still love—to teach the most. I love teaching those who struggle, ensuring that in their learning they don't feel humiliated, but also pushing and motivating them to absolutely master what they need for the next stage. I also love teaching the most able. There is a joy of working with pupils who think they know everything and then throwing them a curve ball of a question or teaching them something entirely new and watching both the delight and frustration they feel unpicking it, examining it and manipulating it.

It was the best lesson I had—investing in my own subject knowledge.

Ruth is a headteacher in an inner city primary school. For over a decade she has worked in education as a teaching assistant, class teacher and held a variety of leadership roles. She is a director of New Voices and she is currently researching for her PhD. Ruth is currently writing about pedagogy for the TES.

What They Didn't Teach Me About
Acronyms

Hannah Wilson

Starting out as a teacher is like learning a new language. Teachers speak in acronyms, and these acronyms can vary from school to school. The codified language of schools, especially when you are talking about SEND and identifying characteristics of different learners, can make your head spin!

Some schools now have glossaries to help new staff and governors decode what is being talked about. You will need to get your head around them quickly, so I would recommend starting a notebook as a glossary—even better, start a google sheet and share it with other trainees. You can then gift it to beginner teachers and new staff the next year to help them navigate the new language.

Don't be embarrassed to put your hand up in meetings to ask. You might get an eye roll suggesting you should know it already, but it's always better to know rather than guess. Also, the more we choose to speak in full words, the more we might help others from feeling confused and isolated. Remember what it felt like when you arrived at your school, and don't fall into the same trap.

Hannah Wilson is the Head of Secondary Teacher Training at University of Buckingham (former Executive Headteacher of two start-up schools in Oxfordshire) and Co-founder of #WomenEd.

What They Didn't Teach Me About
Always Learning

Emma Turner

I wish someone had told me that teaching would be about learning—*my* learning. That I'd learn how it doesn't matter how tired you are, or how awful your commute, or how much your own life may be fraying at the seams, once you turn around to see those faces, some grinning, some chattering, some worryingly quiet, all else would be forgotten.

I'd learn about the chaotic home lives some children lead, or have my eyes opened to family dynamics which would restore my faith in humanity. How I'd learn about how resilient children are when faced with life's tragedies or how small gestures and hand scrawled notes of 'yoo are the best teecher' would melt my heart. I wish I'd been told the pride I'd feel when a child with multiple, complex learning and behavioural needs played the part of the handsome prince in the school play, and I wish someone had told me how much this would mean to his mum who would hold my hand, hug me, cry and thank me for believing in him and letting him have a go. I wish I'd been told that I'd fall in love with subjects I used to loathe myself at school, simply because of the joy it brought to see children delight in finding solutions and in their own achievements. I wish someone had told me that some lessons I'd laugh so hard with my class that I couldn't breathe and would have tears running down my face.

I wish I'd known—and therefore could steel myself to finding out—that sending some children home on a Friday would mean they'd have to wait until Monday until someone was kind to them or gave them a smile again. I wish I'd known how storytime under a tree would be as magical as the literary world about which we were reading together, and that seeing a child realise they could read was one of life's treasured moments.

It turns out that every day in school is a learning day, and that's before you even include the children's learning. So, yes, I wish I'd been taught many things in my teacher training—but learning from the children, education's greatest teachers of life's most important lessons, makes it all worthwhile.

Emma Turner FCCT the research and CPD lead for Discovery Schools Trust and Affinity TSA. She is a former co-headteacher at a primary school in Leicestershire and is the founder of #NewED. Emma is also a contributor to the TES.

What They Didn't Teach Me About
Racism, Equality and Equity

Bennie Kara

I grew up in a predominantly Asian area, so I didn't notice any issues with racism while I was at secondary school. There were a handful of young Asian teachers, so there was an element of representation. It was at sixth form college, which was far more mixed, that I understood what racial divides were. I remember going into the canteen and realising for the first time in my life I had to choose which side of the canteen I was supposed to stand in—white or Asian? It was a system where the two groups didn't mix, and no one thought that was odd.

During my teacher training I was placed in a school that was predominantly Pakistani-Bangladeshi. I didn't even think about the racial connotations of the discourse around poverty and cultural capital. We were all told that kids from poor socioeconomic backgrounds needed the best teachers. They were the urban, inner city kids. I gave careers advice, university advice, and training advice to the older students without any consideration of how the world might treat them differently. Looking back now, I was completely unaware of what it meant to be an Asian teacher. I understood that I looked different, but no one in my training mentioned that I would go through my career with my Asian identity front and centre.

As the years have passed, I have had to teach myself about what it means to be an Asian teacher. The more I have read, the more I understand that all teachers have to be taught racial theory—and most importantly, what the difference is between equality and equity. So many teachers make the mistake of thinking that all children have to be treated the same. But this isn't true. Children have to be catered for according to their social starting point. This is equity. I think teachers are pretty good at understanding equity when it comes to social class, but not race. When we teach children about racism and discrimination, we should help them all to understand equity. That's pretty difficult if the adults in the classroom don't know what it means.

I wish I had been taught theory and reality before being told I was a role model for children from diverse backgrounds. I would have been better equipped to be that role model.

My best advice now that you've started this journey is to read about critical race theory. It won't matter what the demographic of your classroom is—being informed about how society creates barriers for minority groups will be an invaluable tool in creating fair citizens of the future. Be frank with your students about equality versus equity, about unconscious bias, about power systems and structural racism. It's a gift to them and the world they live in.

Maybe then they will be equipped to challenge the status quo and to question fiercely if they ever walk into a room that is segregated by race.

Bennie Kara is a Deputy Headteacher specialising in Teaching and Learning. She has taught across London and in Oxfordshire in roles where she was responsible for curriculum, assessment, whole-school literacy and English. She is an advocate of grassroots organisations such as WomenEd, LGBTEd and BAMEed, often speaking at events on diversity in the curriculum and leadership development for all.

What They Didn't Teach Me About Privilege

Penny Rabiger

I started teaching having been desperately let down by both the education system and the adults in my life. My reason was thinking that I could be a more reliable, trustworthy and therefore powerful adult influence in the lives of those I teach. Throughout my teaching journey, I have always known that taking the time to reach out to each and every one of my students is the best way to ensure that they are seen, felt and heard as the important individuals they are. I have always had a strong moral purpose to not only teach my subject well but also to see my students as valuable beings, and help them to release their true potential. My approach was mainly about the individual, and my understanding of the huge influence of class, race and gender was probably minimal throughout my time as a teacher. I knew it was important, but I wasn't taught anything about this as part of my training and neglected to think about this in any great depth until later in my career.

Much of the narrative in the education sector, when looking through the lens of race and gender in relation to our students, seems to deal exclusively with attempts to close the gap of disadvantage for certain identified groups progressing through the education system, or entering into the world of work. The issues of class-based, gender- and/or race-related discrimination and systemic bias are not clearly taught in the depth required during initial teacher training courses, let alone openly discussed with the aim to dismantling them in our own institutions.

The pervasive discourse seems to be that there is a need to 'treat' the student through targeted interventions or selected enrichment activity, rather than to examine the structural and systemic sexist, classist and racist mechanisms that call for additional support in the first place. One of the key drivers for many teachers wanting to work in deprived areas, for example, is around addressing a 'deficit in social capital' in our students. In actively engaging in a more politically alert and socially committed attitude to teaching, it should be mandatory, especially for those of us who are white and middle class, to consciously understand how we occupy a given position of power and influence. But what if we could go further than this? What if we could go about dismantling the notion of luck, hard work, and meritocracy being the guiding factors before we metaphorically 'send the elevator back down' for a student? Could we openly examine what the subjective barriers and enablers were in the students' and the teacher's journey to date, and identify what may lie ahead on the onwards journey? How exciting it could be if each of us was to expend time and energy within the bastion of our own institutions and circles of influence on understanding and dismantling the systems which create this 'social capital' imbalance in the first place. Is it enough to send the elevator back down, when we could act to re-route it?

In recent years, I've been on a journey reading and thinking about identity; I realised that, as a profession, we seem to have lost sight of the idea that teaching is a political act. As a white, straight, able-bodied woman, the notion of teaching and schools has several layers of complexity for me. I believe that we have lost our way in how we educate our teachers, and it is our responsibility to have courageous conversations and deliberately acknowledge and investigate the influence of race, gender and class. We need to examine what we truly understand about how these influence not only teaching and learning experiences, but also young people's ability to reach their potential in a system which rewards privilege while simultaneously peddling the lie of hard work in a meritocratic system as the key to success in life. Our job as teachers isn't enough to change a system where a student from a disadvantaged background who gets a 1st from Oxbridge is less likely to land a job in the elite professions than a student from a privileged background with a 2:2, but we can make a difference. We must agree to move the narrative from merely helping a student get the grades to go on to the next stage in their journey through that biased and unfair system , to a bold commitment to curing the systemic and institutional ills which create these conditions in the first place.

To this end, we should ensure that learning about privilege is central to teacher training. This could then progress to a personal exercise to examine context in more depth—the structures and restrictions each teacher may or may not have faced in their professional journey, and an understanding of the political, social and structural context within which we operate as educators. Arising from this should result a commitment to work to understand these in context, as well as actively participate in work to call out and treat bias, direct and systemic discrimination and systemic discrimination within our own practice and our own organisational structures and practices.

Penny Rabiger spent over ten years working as a form tutor and an English teacher. Penny is Chair of Governors at a Tottenham primary school and a Trustee on a multi-academy trust board in South London. She is a Fellow of the Chartered College of Teaching, a steering group member of the BAMEed Network and on the advisory board for the Teacher Toolkit. She blogs at https://tenpencemore.wordpress.com and can be found on Twitter @Penny_Ten.

What They Didn't Teach Me About
Gender Equality

Carly Waterman

Not only did no one tell me about gender equality during my PGCE, no one has ever really told me about it in my life so far. In some ways, this was a blessing. I grew up largely unaware and unhindered by the knowledge of institutional gender inequality. This meant that I always felt like I was Queen of the World. I felt able to take on anything. Nothing was beyond my grasp. In my first ten years of teaching, this remained generally true. I was promoted to Head of Department after two years, Assistant Principal after six, Deputy Head after seven and then something in the universe shifted and nothing was ever really the same again. That something was the revelation of #WomenEd. I understand, finally, that just because something hadn't affected me personally didn't mean it wasn't true, or important, or worth fighting for.

Now, after becoming a #WomenEd regional leader, analysing England's leadership data and hearing the stories of so many women who have been underestimated, overlooked or ignored, I am more informed and more equipped to support women into educational leadership and to ensure gender equality is a priority for me as I forge forward with my numerous roles in education as a leader, a governor, a trustee, a researcher and a blogger. It is incumbent on me, as a person in power, to be the change I want to see, to be acutely aware of unconscious bias in others and to challenge inequality whenever I see it.

What pains me is that I could have been contributing to gender equality from day one—but I didn't know it needed me. Sure, there's only so much you can squeeze into a one-year PGCE, but my fervent belief is that something this big, this important, should be talked about much more often, especially to those entering the profession. Through #WomenEd, thousands of teachers and potential leaders of both genders are carrying the torch of equality and making it part of their narrative. That excites me. It has opened up a new world of knowledge and empowerment for new teachers, making them far more informed and up for the challenge of creating a new and improved version of our profession.

The funny thing about equality is, like learning, it represents a long-term change. You can't 'unknow' it and you can't stop seeing inequality in the world around you. Via #WomenEd, I have had my eyes opened to racial inequality, disability inequality and inequality for the LGBTQ community. And I'm just talking about within the education profession; merely a microcosm for the injustices in the world around us.

In the end, education is about change. As an educator I am here to change the world. You might think that's egotistical, or futile, or irrelevant—and that's fine. I wish I realised twenty years ago, when I started out as a teacher, that my own sense of agency can really make a difference. It's not just about teaching children; it's about so much more.

Carly Waterman is the Headteacher of Lodge Park Academy in Corby. She is a regional leader for #WomenEd., a trustee and Governor in three Northamptonshire schools/Trusts, an organiser of #EducatingNorthants and a supporter of teacher-led, grassroots movements to create change in education.

What They Didn't Teach Me About
Racial Inequality

Halil Tamgumus

Do not smile at the kids. I'll never forget being told those words as we all sat there sparkling with excitement at being the next generation of teachers on a PGCE course. You probably had the same advice, as I am sure many others did before me. It is complete rubbish by the way! Smile. Make them laugh. Show them humanity. After just two weeks of having me as a teacher, my Year 4 children would do anything for me. Give some of yourself to your children and you will receive a loyalty that will transcend the time they have with you.

The humanity part of teaching is vital, yet we are not really taught about the complexities and sensitivities that some children live with in courses such as a PGCE—well I was not anyway. This is such a contradiction of sorts; teaching is all about the development of the human race, but we are often not told about the potential difficulties young people in our schools face on a day-to-day basis.

You have probably been told about the mechanics of how children learn. You have been shown the best way to pitch work at the correct levels. You have been told about how to keep children safe in education. But were you ever told about how inequality, especially racial inequality, would be such a big barrier to learning? I never once was. Did you know for instance that black Caribbean children are almost three times more likely to be permanently excluded from school than white British children, which means that their life chances severely deteriorate? Gypsy/Roma children are almost four times more likely to be permanently excluded and Irish Traveller children are almost five times more likely.[1]

As a teacher, what can you do to help level the playing field so that all ethnic groups have equal access to education? The following ideas are based on my experiences and observations, and I believe that they go some way in helping children buy in to the education system and make them feel like it matters to them!

- Bring your background to the foreground. Give yourself to all of your children. Do not be selective with whom you share and how you share.
- Think about what you teach the children—who is it aimed at? Find texts that represent your children, as you will have an array of races, ethnicities and backgrounds in your class. Think about your planned topics—do they allow children a chance to shine or give them the opportunity to find out more about who they are?
- Develop your cultural sensitivity—there have been many situations where I have heard people make sweeping statements about what are seemingly small things. There have been times where I have allowed my own understanding of the world to guide me in making blanket assumptions about people. The important thing is that we learn from it; we need to expand our knowledge in order to give children the best possible opportunity, regardless of where they are from, what they believe or their skin colour.

At the time of writing this there are presently 21,356 headteachers in England—guess how many are black? Just 277. As educators, we have to ensure we inspire all of our children in order to allow them all to have equal chances in life.

Halil Tamgumus is currently a headteacher at a school in inner city Leicester. Prior to becoming a headteacher, he worked in primary schools as a teacher, maths lead, Year 6 lead, behaviour lead and assistant headteacher. He has also worked as an LA writing moderator. Halil is passionate about making the primary curriculum as racially and ethnically inclusive as possible.

1 https://www.ethnicity-facts-figures.service.gov.uk/

What They Didn't Teach Me About
Asking for Help

Andrea William-Jones

These days I'm a mentor and professional tutor with almost 20 years' experience, and I always start my first session like this:

> *Teacher training is rather like learning to drive! Learning to pass the driving test is different from learning to drive on the roads regularly, and training to teach is very different from thriving and surviving in your NQT year. Treat them as two parts of the same process—and never, ever stop learning!*

It's the little things that make a difference and the little things which help or hinder your day, your week and your term. A long-retired, eminent colleague once told me, 'It's not what you can plan for in teaching which makes it the best job ever... it's what you can't!' And he was right!

You've done the basics: you've developed the essence of planning and delivery, learned how to take registers and assess students, sat in on parents evenings and experienced the joy of being a Form Tutor... now's the time to make it your own!

You have to accept that some things will happen:

- You will catch a cold once a month for the whole year. It comes with working in a germ bath.
- You will meet students whilst out with your family or out shopping, or even on holiday. Nine times out of ten they'll be overjoyed to see you and will wave and chat.

- You will be tired, and you will long for the holidays; make sure you enjoy them because you've earned it.
- You will need time to get used to being in a new school, with a 90% timetable, and a full school calendar.
- You will feel overwhelmed at times, but that's okay!

As I look back as a Fellow of the Chartered College, I wish there had been as much help and support available for early career teachers as there is now. Use the help that's there for the taking!

- Join the Chartered College and access their networks.
- Join a Union.
- Get to know your department, year group or team.
- Get to know the other NQTs in your school or Trust
- Join #Edutwitter.

I grabbed opportunities to ask for help as I saw them; after all, you can only benefit from them, and you'll also know you aren't alone in how you feel. There are bound to be things you wish you'd known. For me, it was stuff like learning to conduct (I am a music teacher), or writing on a whiteboard (these days you might have a visualiser too!). And sometimes it's the small things that it might help to know, such as the best ways to store your lunch or where to lock up your bike.

But most of all it's about finding your way and working alongside the support that's available through departments and teams. Teachers are essentially 'people persons' and yes, they're busy, but they also understand the beauty of collegiality and support.

I was too afraid and in awe to ask—please learn from my mistakes and ask!

Andrea William-Jones is an Assistant Headteacher, Musician and Mum based in North Bristol. She is passionate about developing teachers at all stages of their career and empowering them to be the best they can.

What They Didn't Teach Me About
Joining the CCT

Rebecca Nobes

As an NQT, now is a great time to get on board and be a part of your professional body, The Chartered College of Teaching (CCT). At the time in your career when you've just stepped away from all the support your university/training provider has given you and into your own classroom, the Chartered College is there for you. The Chartered College is there to put the latest in educational thinking in your hands via the Impact journal, to connect you with other teachers and to recognise your expertise with Chartered Teacher status or Fellowship when the time comes. I've just completed the Chartered Teacher Programme as part of the pilot cohort; it was the best CPD I've ever had the opportunity to benefit from. I'm so pleased to be able to continue contributing to the development of the programme and the College.

Joining the Chartered College of Teaching is about becoming part of a network of like-minded individuals who all want the best for the teaching profession and the young people that we teach. Teaching shouldn't be about survival, as it is commonly seen. As a body, we can work together to raise the status of our profession, giving teaching the reputation it deserves. I wish the Chartered College had been around when I was an NQT; then I wouldn't have had to try and find the way myself.

Rebecca Nobes is Head of Spanish at a large, comprehensive school in Chelmsford, Essex. She founded and still frequently hosts #MFLChat on Twitter and is a committee member of her local branch of the Association for Language Learning. She completed an MA in Education in 2017 and has just completed the pilot of the Chartered Teacher programme from the Chartered College of Teaching. She continues to contribute to the College as part of the elected council and enjoys attending and occasionally speaking at events such as ResearchEd.

What They Didn't Teach Me About
Becoming a Chartered Teacher

Sandra Clinton

I have recently been awarded Chartered Teacher status by the Chartered College of Teaching. I was part of the pilot cohort for this qualification; it's been an exhilarating and stimulating fourteen months. I started teaching in 1996, and for the first ten years of my career, I constantly engaged in opportunities for professional development beyond my own classroom. In the last ten years, the increased workload of being a Head of Department has changed my focus to developing others, and so I was excited to see a new qualification to sink my teeth into.

This intense, flexible and engaging course enables teachers to reflect honestly on their teaching practice and to select specific areas for improvement. The programme is suitable for teachers of all subjects and age groups; it features a well-balanced curriculum that has common core content while allowing for flexibility, so you can tailor it to your own teaching experience, settings and interests. The assignments range from online debates to written exams, simulated scenarios and written reports. There is even an assessment on assessment! Teachers on the programme are encouraged to network and to develop a strong sense of belonging to an education community, sharing ideas and supporting each other. Through use of the excellent software, we were given windows into each other's classrooms by recording clips of ourselves teaching, which we then shared with our peers. This was a key part of the course for me. Once I got over how I looked on camera, it was fascinating to watch myself and my students in action—and a real privilege to be able to see colleagues from other institutions at work in their own classrooms.

A key component of the course is the personal development plan, which is written and refined by the participants in consultation with their mentor. At regular intervals during the programme, you revisit this plan and reflect on your progression against the professional principles. Throughout the 14 months it runs for, we had contact with several experts in their field through face-to-face training, webinars and even a phone interview with a leading academic. This rare opportunity to receive expert advice really makes you feel valued as an education professional. I was genuinely amazed by the amount of interest they showed in my work and it was really motivating to have their support.

The final assignment of the course is an action research project of your choice, for which you pose a research question, complete a literature review, collect baseline data, carry out an intervention and then test if it has had an impact. This whole project is written in a fully referenced research report and also presented as a poster. I chose to set up a journal club at our college; this has now become part of our staff inset programme for next year.

I have met so many committed and enthusiastic teachers and education professionals through taking part in the programme. My interest in pedagogy has been reinvigorated, I've attended (and spoken at) a ResearchED conference and written articles about my experience. Studying to become a Chartered Teacher is challenging, hard work and requires ruthless time management—but it is never boring! The course is underpinned by the principles of evidence-informed practice, and I have found that these principles have permeated my own decision-making and practice. I have become much better at writing within very strict word counts, revisited referencing skills not used since university and spent enjoyable evenings of my summer holiday reading research articles.

This was without doubt the best training I have ever had. The combination of flexibility to meet your needs and core course content makes it relevant to teachers at all points in their career and from all sorts of institutions. It has been a rich and valuable experience, and I'm excited to see what happens next for Chartered Teachers.

Sandra Clinton is Head of Chemistry and Physics at Brighton, Hove & Sussex Sixth Form College and has been a classroom teacher for more than 20 years. She is passionate about giving all students taught in her department the best learning experience possible. She has taught chemistry (and science) in an 11–18 school and a sixth form college, is a Founding Fellow of the Chartered College of Teaching and has completed the Chartered Teacher programme. She also conducts a youth brass band with players ranging in age from 5–18.

What They Didn't Teach Me About
Being an NQT

Sam Strickland

Welcome to the best job and the best profession in the world. Rarely will two days, two lessons, two minutes, two seconds ever be the same for you during your career as a teacher. No other job will reward you intrinsically as much as teaching—but equally, no other job will be as demanding and taxing.

I am sure you are chomping at the bit to get stuck in with your pupils and inspire, inspire, inspire them. No doubt you will have been trained in an array of lesson strategies, with a real focus on varying lesson activities, using lesson objectives and planning, planning, planning. No doubt a mantra that you will have come across is that if you plan a really good lesson, the pupils will behave.

I would like to share with you my thoughts and tips to help you navigate your way through your first year in teaching. A small health warning before I do. With the exception of your training year, your NQT year is probably the toughest. I nearly quit the profession multiple times as an NQT because I hit the teaching equivalent of the runner's wall. Fortunately, things get easier and, by your third year, you will feel like you can walk on water. Every day you will have sensations of feeling like you are sinking, swimming and surfing and your emotional bandwidth will reach peaks and troughs you never thought possible.

Here are some key tips:

- Planning endless lesson activities does not always mean that the pupils behave. Planning endless activities will mean that you are working late most nights and are too tired to teach as effectively as you can. Ultimately, this is the fast track to burning out and leaving the profession.

- If your school does not have a series of classroom-based routines, develop some that work for you. I would suggest standing at your class door, meeting and greeting the students as a starting point. Give your pupils an instant engage task; this can easily take the form of a five or ten question quiz, which promotes students to recall knowledge you have already taught them.
- Unless forced to do so, do not waste hundreds of hours writing lesson objectives and making pupils write them down off of PowerPoint slides or the front board. This approach is, at best, white noise and, at worst, a complete waste of time.
- Hinge your lessons around a big question. There is a lot out there on this.
- Remember that the teacher is the expert. Pupils come to school to be taught by you, not their peers, not by Google. You are the one with the degree and the teaching qualification. Do not fall into the trap of limiting your teacher voice.
- Join a subject community, join #EduTwitter, attend ResearchED conferences.
- Follow the school's behaviour policy and approach.
- Do not be frightened to ask for help, support, advice and guidance.

Finally, and most importantly of all, make sure you carve out time for yourself to do something that has nothing to do with work.

Sam Strickland has worked as a Head of History, Lead Practitioner and as a subject lead for the North Beds SCITT Consortium before becoming an AP, Director of Sixth Form. Sam then progressed to VP and an Associate Principal at Brooke Weston Academy, with results receiving commendation from the DfE, Nick Gibb and the SSAT. Sam has also served as a lead facilitator for NPQSL, working for Inspiring Leaders and now serves as the Principal of The Duston School.

What They Didn't Teach Me About

My Safeguarding My Digital Footprint

Ceri Stokes

What they didn't tell me about at university was to make sure that I protected and safeguarded my digital footprint—mainly because Wi-Fi hadn't been invented. But times are changing, and we need to keep up.

While at university, your social media account, Twitter, Instagram or Facebook was probably the expression of your social life. You planned the next event, reminisced about the good old days and probably laughed (liked) the silly jokes (some of which could be considered inappropriate). Unfortunately, those comments or photos might come back to haunt you!

Much like how famous people have skeletons in their closet and are criticised for being bad role models, as a teacher you will be judged in exactly the same manner. The only difference is that you don't have the money that comes along with being famous. So, you need to start considering your options.

You can lock everything down and try to make it as private as possible. The problem is that you may not have had control over what you were tagged in. That fancy dress party that you went to dressed as the character from the Rocky Horror Picture show, or the time your friend took a picture of you tipsy doing cartwheels down the high street, might be saved somewhere that you are unaware of. Or the person who has tagged you might be the uncle of one of your students who follows them. So there never really is a completely private account that you can control. So, then you panic and consider deleting everything. You suddenly remember that Tinder account that you opened as a joke. Did you ever close it? Can you close it? The challenge is that it isn't all bad; social media can be an amazing tool. It can help with your wellbeing: you are human after all and need to have a life, and there is nothing wrong with that. And social media can be amazing CPD; teachers can be fantastic at supporting and sharing. But restraint and good judgement must be exercised. For example, perhaps you wrote blog posts about your experiences, which you are worried could hinder your future job applications. This makes you realise that your digital footprint is so much more than just social media. Have you ever googled your name? It is worth doing. You may not be able to remove things, but maybe you could move the not-so-good stuff onto the second or third page. Are there things that you would rather be known for, like running half marathons or charity work? If so, proudly promote these accomplishments.

So, what about starting a professional account? This could be a good idea, but it still raises some interesting questions. Should you post pictures of students' work? What about posting good or bad examples, funny things they said, annoying things the school has made you do, the joys of report writing? At this point my advice would be to check the school's Code of Conduct or Acceptable Use Policy for ICT. They should have advice and clear boundaries. Not all schools or SLT are tech savvy, so you may have to help them with this; it is almost certain though that you won't be the only one who will be considering these points. It is good safeguarding practice to protect yourself, which in turn will to help protect the children.

Ceri Stokes is a Designated Safeguarding Lead at an independent boarding school. Ceri is passionate about the need for good PSHE, including helping with Mental Health, e-safety and healthy relationships.

What They Didn't Teach Me About
Engaging with Research

James Tomlinson

Research is becoming an important feature in teacher training—and it is about time too. In this narrative I share my belief that through open dialogue between educational researchers and teachers, we are establishing a set of exciting buzzwords across the profession. To save you hours of time planning high-input (design and delivery) yet low-impact (student outcomes) lessons, you need to know about cognitive psychology.

Cognitive psychology seeks to understand the mind through studying mental processes, such as attention, perception, memory, thinking, storage, retention and retrieval. Put more simply, cognitive psychology seeks to understand and explain how we learn. So why are so many teachers still in the dark about it? After all, you would expect us to design effective instruction to support effective learning. Well, Weinstein and Sumeracki (2019) state quite accurately that very few Initial Teacher Education (ITE) courses feature cognitive psychology; this results in many teachers delivering instruction based on their own experiences as a learner, which can be detrimental. I hold my hands up here and admit to being that teacher. During my PGCE and NQT years, I spent hours creating lessons that looked great at surface level—colour, fancy fonts, images, the lot—which seemed engaging to the pupils, yet based on what I know now, they did not support the retention and storage of knowledge. I also thought my teacher explanations were pretty spot on. How wrong I was! I often made connections between topics, but I did not model this as well as I should have done or make it explicit enough. I didn't know I was supposed to. It came naturally to me—after all I knew my subject and the ideas or area I was connecting it to—but it does not come naturally to pupils, and I did not recognise that at the time.

We don't need to know exactly what goes on in the brain to do our jobs; we're already told that we make more decisions in a day than a brain surgeon does. Nevertheless, we should know that as soon as we experience new information, we almost instantly start to forget it. This is something to remember when you're next teaching Dickensian times in English, Pythagorean Theorem in maths, tectonic plates in geography or body language in drama. Every time you teach a new idea, concept or process, you are creating a memory.

You should deliver new ideas, concepts or processes in chunks, ideally between four and seven. Why you might ask? Memory consists of many components, but the ones you need to know about are the working memory and the long-term memory. The working memory consists of what you are holding in your memory right now; the last two paragraphs you have read for instance. In teacher terms you might describe the knowledge you are teaching for that particular lesson to be that which is contained in the working memory. It is our job to get this knowledge into the long-term memory so that it can be retained and retrieved later. Easier said than done. It is not achieved by teaching strategies such as re-reading or highlighting information, using multiple worksheets, discovery learning or using keyword mnemonics. We need to make sure that what goes in (what we teach) is remembered, and this is best done both by making connections or building schema and by allowing pupils some time to forget it. Dunlosky et al. (2013) found that learning (and therefore teaching) strategies to support memory include elaboration, distributed practice, interleaving and practice tests. This allows us to reconstruct memories (or information we have been taught in the past).

Memory attempts to reconstruct what we try to retrieve. Take for example, a PGCE student planning a lesson on the threats to the tropical rainforest. The first time a student teacher delivers the lesson it may be staggered and lack clarity, because the knowledge is very much still in their working memory and therefore is difficult to explain. However, after teaching the lesson to five different classes, the main ideas have transferred to the long-term memory and are easier to retrieve; they therefore become easier to teach. The fifth class do not get the same experience as the first class because the teacher has changed their memory of the threats to the tropical rainforest; they have removed any boring bits and made connections to other topics such as climate change. Eureka! That's how memory works, and engaging with research teaches us about it. I'm not going to explain what elaboration, distributed practice, interleaving and practice tests mean in teacher terms, it's your job now to go and engage with the research on it. The publications by Weinstein and Sumeracki (2019) and Jake Hunton (2018) are great places to start!

What should you take away from this? Well, all teachers should have an understanding of how we learn. Teachers should aim to build memory by limiting the demands in the working memory to between four and seven chunks of new information and teach students to connect this to information in their long-term memory, creating knowledge. It should be noted that the long-term memory is not a computer or a library. Memories are reconstructed when we attempt to retrieve them and so teachers should use effective teaching strategies such as elaboration, distributed practice, interleaving and practice tests.

My closing comments would be don't overthink lesson planning and don't spend ages making worksheets full of colour, fancy fonts or images. Keep it simple: create worksheets that get students to think by asking themselves what, where, when, why and how and make connections to previous learning. Allow pupils time to forget what you have taught them—you can't test learning at the end of a lesson, but you can test it a few lessons later in the style of a practice test. That builds memory.

References

Dunlosky, J., Rawson, K., Marsh, E., Nathan, M. and Willingham, D. (2013). Improving Students' Learning With Effective Learning Techniques. *Psychological Science in the Public Interest*, 14(1), pp.4-58.

Hunton, J. (2018). *Exam Literacy*. Carmarthen: Crown House Publishing.

Weinstein, Y. and Sumeracki, M. (2019). *Understanding how we learn*. Oxon: Routledge.

James Tomlinson, MCCT, is the Curriculum Leader for geography at MEA Central in Manchester. He has previously led a department to achieve the Secondary Geography Quality Mark. James is passionate about curriculum design and improving teaching and learning through effective teacher behaviours and cognitive psychology. He is currently completing his MA in Leading Learning.

What They Didn't Teach Me About
Questioning the Research

Dr Jess Mahdavi-Gladwell

I came to primary teaching by way of an infrequently trodden path. After my first degree, I wandered deeper into the world of academia by embarking on a doctorate. My subject was Psychology, but always with a focus on children and schools. My research focus was school bullying. From very early on my PhD journey, I went into schools and completed questionnaires with classes of children in both primary and secondary. I was lucky enough to be invited and welcomed into a variety of schools and to see many dedicated and gifted teachers allow me to use their teaching time to further my research. I didn't truly appreciate the gift they were giving me.

After more research, diving into the world of parenthood and even more research, I decided that this was the time to qualify as a Primary Maths Specialist. I enjoyed every minute of the training—well almost every minute—but certainly all the minutes that involved research. I was bright-eyed and bushy-tailed in my unshakable belief that research could change things. It would change educational outcomes, school experience—even life in general—for the better. I had read the book, and written some articles, and now it was time to wear the t-shirt. The wrinkles that appeared included the following:

- They didn't tell me that people might not read the research.
- They didn't tell me that, as a teacher, I may be faced with a choice of reading a research paper or reading my child a bedtime story.
- They didn't tell me that research findings can be extrapolated beyond where it is right to do so, and may then become the 'truth' which is taught to the next generation.

- They didn't tell me that two headteachers would tell me that learning styles theory was true, and that it didn't matter if research suggested otherwise, they were both visual learners and so it must be real.

Initial teacher training did not prepare me to be the person who could be an advocate for research-evidenced practise in school. (Chartered College did that, but that's a different chapter.) Initial teacher training didn't teach me, or my peers, the skills we needed to take the research and turn it into impactful classroom practise; lessons that would be a true and fitting translation of the huge number of research hours (and blood, sweat and tears) invested into trying to make a difference. Neither was I prepared to work within a framework that might be informed by, 'How it's always been done'.

You know the hindsight being 20/20 adage, but that's the point of sharing with you. So, what do I wish I had done back then? I wish I was that person who made staff meetings run over because I thought discussion in that forum might change something. The one who wanted to effect change to a system that felt like it was working to those already in it. The voice of perceived criticism of the status quo.

What do I wish I had known back then? That research is an excellent and valuable tool to inform practise. I wish I had realised that research isn't just published information to be used as a hammer and that experienced voices are a different kind of research. They may not be backed up with numbers and percentages and beautifully presented graphs, but what really is impactful is the interplay between critical reading of research and the maturity to pick apart how it is relevant to the setting, the challenges that implementation that will bring and the need for a balance between outcome and the input required to create it.

Proud to be British-Iranian, Jess left her native Barnsley for Goldsmiths in 1997, completing her degree, PhD and Post Doc there. In 2013, Jess decided to enhance her experience of researching bullying by becoming a primary school teacher (IoE). Awarded CTeach (pilot cohort), Jess's passions are evidence-based practise and not-wasting-teachers'-time.

What They Didn't Teach Me About
Planning

Aditi Singh

Yes, you're going to groan at this one and think it mundane. But I remember being an unqualified teacher for six months, having landed an unexpected opportunity in secondary special education, and worrying each night at the thought of planning for 'those SEMH kids again'.

To me, planning was consulting those year plans and trawling TES for any resource that fit. And once I landed and adapted what looked like a meaty resource, I'd collapse into fitful, disturbed sleep. Lesson starters were not a thing, getting through my meaty resource preoccupied my thoughts, I dreaded the days when they needed 'something else' and plenaries were not a word in my lexicon. I did exactly what teachers are told not to do; work from one activity to the next, frustrated by my own lack of ability to 'tell stories about science'.

Because this is what they didn't tell me about planning: lessons are stories, and that like all good stories, they have starts, middles and ends. You need to introduce ideas, then develop them, and conclude your lesson so that your students are almost left wanting more—don't omit teaching what you need to, but leave them excited about digging deeper. Lessons could be analogous to a short story—somewhat terse and contained, but quickly effective—or to a novel—heavier and more detailed, requiring multiple reads or time to appreciate the information—but either way they must be engaging. For me, some were frustrating and went nowhere, and my pupils and I bonded over our shared disillusionment. Others were unexpected delights, when a new technique was learned and was quickly internalised, and we celebrated by being mutually engaged.

As I trained, my internal narrative about planning started to change. Each new piece of information that I needed to teach became a puzzle piece which begged the central question: which part of tomorrow's story is this? And slowly, planning became less of a 'task' and more of my everyday background chatter in my head. Every new video, resource, topical article and writing framework started to arrange itself visually in my mind, and resources constructed themselves around the linear narrative in my head. I even popped a '1, 2, 3, 4' menu on my whiteboard, signposting each phase of my story against a recognisable structure. And then, my story wasn't just mine, it was one that I shared with my pupils every day; and one that they began to modify with me, in time.

They said that sometimes you couldn't win with SEMH pupils. Turns out, if you tell your best story, sometimes you can.

Aditi Singh is a biologist and science teacher who is also an Assistant Principal at an SEMH school in London. Aditi's job is all kinds of adventurous, but even on days when all is bleak, her classroom keeps her going. She likes to hike and draw when the teaching hat gets left at school.

What They Didn't Teach Me About
Your Influence in the Classroom

Kathryn Callaghan

I was very fortunate to have had a wonderful PGCE lecturer who was incredibly forward-thinking, introduced us to many ideas that were not yet part of mainstream education and had some fantastic contacts, ensuring that we had wonderful guest speakers each week educating us on a wide array of pedagogical issues. However, something that was only mentioned in passing was what I refer to as 'the weather'. We were taught to encourage a positive learning environment, and to ensure that we met the needs of all types of learners in our lessons, but after almost fifteen years of teaching, I now feel that more emphasis should have been placed on discussing the environment, or the atmosphere, of your classroom.

I knew from age four that I wanted to teach. I vividly remember sitting playing school with my dad; from then I have always had a passion for education, so I always try to convey this passion right from the second the pupils arrive at my classroom door. As the class teacher, it is I who has the most control over the atmosphere, or 'weather' if you will, of my classroom and of the lessons. I greet pupils at the door using their name and, as I am a Modern Foreign Language teacher, I greet them in the target language. This accomplishes two things: immediately they know that we are ready to work from the moment they arrive at the classroom door, and they also put their language skills into use, greeting me or answering simple conversational questions in the target language.

Pupils very quickly pick up on the atmosphere that the teacher's attitude creates. Your attitude will dictate how lessons progress, as pupils gauge if you have enthusiasm and passion for what you are teaching, if you feel that they are capable of achieving and if you have high expectations of and for them. You must try to overcome issues such as being tired or having a bad day for some reason; otherwise they could lead to a poor atmosphere in your classroom, resulting in a poor experience for both you and your pupils.

So, what atmosphere do you wish to create in your classroom? What sort of teacher do you want to be? If you treat pupils with respect, they will treat you with respect. If you have high expectations of your pupils, they will have high expectations of themselves. If you show kindness and tolerance, the pupils will understand that this is how they too should behave. As a teacher you are a role model and with that comes great responsibility to enable your pupils to develop their abilities and talents in preparation for their future lives. Your influence can make the classroom environment an enjoyable place for you and your pupils!

Kathryn Callaghan is a Modern Foreign Language teacher at an all-girls, Catholic, all-ability secondary school in Northern Ireland. She completed her Undergraduate degree and PGCE at Queen's University, Belfast before completing a Diploma at Ulster University.

What They Didn't Teach Me About
Staying in Control

Paul Wassell

Being both a control freak and a teacher is hard—every single day the job springs up surprises that you had no idea were coming: the child throwing up at the back of the classroom; the unscheduled fire alarm; the Year 7 that has managed to get completely lost in a maze of corridors and ends up in your classroom by mistake. But effective planning means you can expect the unexpected as much as possible.

When putting together a lesson, it's about considering every eventuality and looking at stimuli through the eyes of your students. Would I understand that word? Does the question I'm asking really get me to think about this topic? What else would I need to think about? Making your resources accessible, engaging and relevant will mean you can expect your students to understand, to make progress and develop their skills in the process. Rushing your planning or not taking into consideration the multitude of factors that can impact a lesson means you increase the risk that you cede control to outside forces.

It means taking time to decide what you want the students to actually learn and how you are going to guide them through their own journey. It means looking at what students have written, what they have said (to each other and to you) and making a judgment on where, as a class, your priorities need to lie for the next few lessons. It means getting to know your students, and what works for them as learners. Every class is different and every student an individual—what might work for one group could fail miserably for another.

Amongst teachers and educationalists there are always endless debates about the best ways to teach, as if one particular method trumps them all. There are those that advocate getting students out of their seats, encouraging physical activities over deskbound learning, and then there are those who think essentially lecturing to students is most effective. My advice is to be a magpie—take little bits from everywhere and use your own knowledge of your own students to decide which approaches are best at which times. Lessons need to have engagement, they need to make the students enjoy themselves, but they do need substance as well. When planning, never repeat yourself unless you know a particular approach works well for your students. Try different things, get yourself on Twitter and Facebook and see how others plan. Don't be afraid to experiment and mix it up.

If, like me, you're a bit of a control freak, take control of as much as you can through your planning. That means investing time to research, time to prepare and time to reflect on every lesson. If you get that right, you'll still be in total control, despite what surprises the day may bring you.

Paul Wassell is a former teacher, Head of Department and Assistant Headteacher of 10 years. He now designs online resources for English teachers.

What They Didn't Teach Me About
the Child with No PE Kit

Louise Flatters

Picture the scene. You've come to the point in the day when it's time for PE and you've asked everyone to go and collect their PE kits. Tom and Sammy come back to tell you they can't find theirs. So you send them off again to look properly. Tom reappears with his PE kit. It was on his peg. Sammy eventually returns just as everyone else is nearly ready saying that she still hasn't found it. So you chance leaving everyone else alone in the class to go and locate the missing item.

'Would you mind keeping an eye on the class for a minute?' you ask a busy TA who is trying to work with a small group in the corridor. You walk purposefully and quickly to the cloakroom with Sammy, and another student, Jo, (remembering not to run as you must set a good example).

There, on the peg beside Sammy's, is her PE kit. You ask her to take it quickly back to class and start getting changed. On top of those types of—often daily—occurrences, Jo's PE kit has been missing for weeks. So, yet again, you quickly rummage in the spare kit box, only to discover nothing except a small pair of shorts and a red swimming costume. You decide you'd better get back to class to work this one out, and return walking even quicker than before (but still not quite running) with Jo—who's looking a little concerned that you may actually make him wear the red swimming costume for PE.

Needless to say, the noise coming from the classroom is embarrassing, and you spot the headteacher coming down the corridor; you quickly say in an over-loud voice 'Goodness me, you're usually so quiet when we get changed!' and smile at the headteacher as she decides not to stop on the way. Then, you ask everyone to line up, after wondering to yourself why they couldn't have put their clothes into their PE bags while you were in the cloakroom. Knowing the strict school policy on everyone wearing proper kit for PE, a sudden wave of bravado sweeps across you, and you quickly whisper to Jo that he can do PE in his uniform, but he should take his jumper off first.

Finally, everyone is in line and water bottles are collected. Tom's hand shoots up, 'But Sammy's not ready!' Sammy is sitting on the floor, reading a book in just her t-shirt and pants, with her PE bag being used as a book rest. You quickly help her tug on shorts and plimsolls and she joins the end of the line. Hopefully no one will notice the one child without a PE kit; there are only 20 minutes left of the PE lesson now after all.

The Serious Side

You may have found this slightly amusing, and in many ways, it is. But I have deliberately painted a scene where it would have been easy to make a different snap decision. I'm sure you can think of reasons why Jo doesn't have a PE kit in school, and I hope you'll realise that there is very little Jo can do about it.

Please don't exclude a child from PE, or any other activity because they don't have the right equipment, even if it's just a one off. Please don't embarrass them or humiliate them by telling them off about it. Sometimes having the right kit just isn't the most important thing; better to do PE in uniform than not at all. Aren't we usually quite happy for them to roll around in their uniform at break times?

If you knew Jo well, you might decide to speak to his parents/carers, or you might realise this would be futile. You might decide you need to pass on your concerns to the Designated Safeguarding Lead.

If you were really organised, you'd stock up on spare PE kits, or ask the SLT to help with this in the light of the strict PE uniform policy. You could even make Jo up a bag to keep in school. That would be one less thing for you and Jo to worry about.

Louise Flatters started a career in education in the 1990s and has since worked in eight primary schools and for five different local authorities, specialising in EYFS and KS1. She is currently headteacher in a small village school in North Yorkshire. Louise is a parent of three and a passionate believer in inclusion.

What They Didn't Teach Me About
Preparing for Leadership

Jon Zeb

My PGCE year was probably the most tiring, terrifying and inspiring year of my life. I studied PGCE in history with an optional module in PSHE. My cohort was the first to undertake a trial numeracy test. We were told not to worry though, as it was expected to be a 'one off that wouldn't catch on'.

In considering the question 'What they didn't teach me on my PGCE' I had two options: either behaviour management or leadership. Considering behaviour management is arguably the bedrock of teaching and learning, we spent very little time on this area during PGCE. It was something we were supposed to 'pick-up' during our placement. The second area, leadership, was an area not mentioned at all. I decided to explore latter in this narrative.

My second placement during PGCE was really successful, resulting in the school wanting to offer me a position. This role, however, was as a Head of Subject—a subject that wasn't actually taught at the school at that time. As the new Head of Business Studies (my second subject), I had to navigate my NQT year, alongside leading a subject, creating schemes of work and resources, and managing two other members of staff. To say it was challenging is an understatement. During the next three years, I decided pastoral leadership was for me, becoming a Head of Year and Head of PSHE. I remember my first ever piece of leadership advice from the retiring Head of Year. He said, 'Jon, always carry a notebook and pencil. When someone starts to complain to you, nod intently, pull out the notepad and make copious notes, and when they have gone, don't look at it again. If it's important, they'll come back to you'.

Over the following 20 years, my career included: being part of an SLT taking a school from RI to Outstanding; being Vice Principal within an outstanding, academy-chain assisting in the establishment of a £24m 'national flagship' free school that attained 'World Class' status; and, being an educational advisor for the Education Department of Jersey, Channel Islands.

Throughout this whole period, I had never actively sought to develop my understanding of leadership, or sought recognition for it, until I met the curator of this book, Sarah Mullin. Through conversations via social media, she inspired me to develop my understanding of leadership and be recognised for the knowledge, skills and experience I already had. This included enrolling and achieving my NPQH (National Professional Qualification for Headship), being named as a Founding Fellow of the Chartered College of Teaching, a Fellow of the Institute of Leadership and Management and a Chartered Teacher of History by the Historical Association. This year, I also enrolled on an MA in Educational Leadership.

So my advice on leadership is to be the air conditioning unit. You create the climate in which all other stakeholders thrive. 'The real role of leadership in education… is not and should not be command and control. The real role of leadership is climate control, creating a climate of possibility' (Robinson). Ensure there is a good balance of opposing ideas and creative tension, relentless routine and spontaneous creativity, guarding the culture and rituals whilst culling that which hinders innovation. Convert doubt into enquiry, problems into solutions and stress into positive outcomes. Invite people to be part of the creative process and the journey. If they are involved in the creation, they will be emotionally attached. Share your vision and values, be a role model. Never forget where you have come from, why you are there and where you want to take those who are looking to you as their leader.

Reference

Robinson, K. (2013, April). Ted.Com. How to Escape Education's Death Valley. Available at: https://www.ted.com/talks/sir_ken_robinson_how_to_escape-education_s_death_valley. (Accessed 26th November 2019).

Jon Zeb, PGCE, NPQH, FCCT, FInstLM, CT(Hist), Senior Vice Principal, White Rose Academies Trust

What They Didn't Teach Me About
Leadership

Dr Jill Berry

When I started my teaching career, I had no clear idea of how my professional journey might develop over time. I loved my subject and wanted a job which would allow me to share my enthusiasm, use all I had learnt so far (about English, in my case) and continue to learn and build my experience and expertise in my subject area. But I don't think I looked beyond that initially.

Over time, I began to recognise that a teacher leads learning in their classroom: you support and challenge, motivate and inspire, model and lift. The skills you are developing are leadership skills, as you focus on doing all you can to get the best from others. In due course, you may decide you want to stretch yourself further, and, while still continuing to get the best from the young people you teach and care for, you are also keen to make the most of your leadership skills to support, challenge and get the best from your colleagues too. In the process, of course, you are able to make a difference to the experience of more pupils by working with and through other staff.

You may have the opportunity to take on an academic leadership role, such as a subject co-ordinator or a Head of Department. You may have the chance to experience pastoral leadership, as a year group co-ordinator, Head of Section or Head of House. In time, you may wish to consider a senior leadership role, which will give you the opportunity to make a whole-school impact, using the leadership skills you have honed so far to make a difference on a wider canvas. You may decide in the course of time that you are ready to take on headship, both a considerable responsibility and a great privilege, as you now have the capacity to make a difference on a scale unlike any other you will have experienced. If your leadership journey develops beyond this point, you may find you have the chance to take on a role which has impact beyond one school, allowing you to enable others across a number of institutions to achieve their personal and professional best.

I loved my career: I was a teacher of English, a Head of English, Head of Sixth Form, Deputy Head and Head. Headship was the most joyful and rewarding of all the jobs I had across a thirty-year period. I had no idea when I trained as a teacher that I would have a professional life which was so stimulating, varied, energising and satisfying. You don't yet know how your career will develop, but my advice to you would be to consider the leadership skills you will build on and strengthen from the very beginning, leading learning in your classroom—and don't underestimate where they might take you! Good luck!

Dr Jill Berry is a former head teacher and is now a leadership consultant.

Chapter 5

What They Didn't Teach Me About Teaching and Learning

'I never teach my pupils. I only attempt to provide the conditions in which they learn.'

— *Albert Einstein*

As teachers, we know that our primary role is to impart our knowledge and wisdom to the children in our classroom. It is also important for us to nurture our own knowledge, skills and mindsets so that we can understand teaching and learning processes in greater depth. Many schools provide a comprehensive training and CPD programme for teachers centred around academic research that shows high impact outcomes in the classroom. In this chapter, authors share their advice and reflect on their experiences as they have grown and developed as practitioners over the course of their careers.

What They Didn't Teach Me About
Rosenshine's Principles

Sarah Mullin, on behalf of Tom Sherrington

The fundamental elements of responsive, instructional teaching should be at the core of any PCGE or ITE programme. My admiration for Barak Rosenshine is largely informed by my experience working with teachers in many schools and colleges where my aim has been to engage teachers with research in order to support them to improve their practice. I find Rosenshine's Principles (Rosenshine, 2012) to be the most clear and comprehensive guide to evidence-informed teaching for many reasons, not least because it resonates for teachers of all subjects and contexts, focusing on the aspects of teaching that are generally universal: questioning, practice and knowledge-building.

Rosenshine makes a direct link between research and practice, linking classroom observations to student outcomes, with examples providing a strong understanding of the real things teachers do. This gives his paper a teacher-focused authenticity. There are four strands that permeate Rosenshine's principles: reviewing material, questioning, explaining and modelling and practice. Whilst the paper is best read in its entirety, a succinct summary is presented below—this is something that may not be taught as part of your PGCE.

Rosenshine's 17 Principles of Effective Instruction

(Rosenshine, 2010)

1. Begin a lesson with a short review of previous learning.
2. Present new material in small steps with student practice after each step.

3. Limit the amount of material students receive at one time.
4. Give clear and detailed instructions and explanations.
5. Ask a large number of questions and check for understanding.
6. Provide a high level of active practice for all students.
7. Guide students as they begin to practice.
8. Think aloud and model steps.
9. Provide models of worked-out problems.
10. Ask students to explain what they have learned.
11. Check the responses of all students.
12. Provide systematic feedback and corrections.
13. Use more time to provide explanations.
14. Provide many examples.
15. Reteach material when necessary.
16. Prepare students for independent practice.
17. Monitor students when they begin independent practice.

Review

Daily review is important in helping to resurface prior learning; this includes as recently as from the previous lesson—students are not likely to remember everything immediately. Reviewing the learning is a powerful technique for building fluency and confidence. Weekly and monthly review involves longer-term retrieval practice, which continues the process of building long-term memory that supports future learning.

Questioning

Ask more questions to more students in more depth. Rosenshine provides a range of examples that teachers can ask students. He also reinforces the importance of process questions—asking students how they worked things out, not just asking them for the final answer. Rosenshine stresses that the use of questioning provides the platform for teachers to obtain feedback about how well we have covered the subject content, allowing us to check understanding to ensure misconceptions are addressed.

Sequencing Concepts and Modelling

- It is important to break down our concepts into small steps, with practice opportunities at each stage.
- We need to provide lots of opportunities for modelling worked examples, including the importance of the worked-example effect to reduce cognitive load.
- Scaffolding is needed to develop expertise. This is a form of mastery coaching, where cognitive supports are given and then withdrawn gradually. The sequencing of this is key; for example, stabilisers on a bike are really powerful aids to learning and confidence building, but eventually they need to come off.

Stages of Practice

Understanding the difference between guided and independent practice is important, as they are both essential in the art of teaching.

- Guided practice requires close supervision and feedback, with teachers monitoring students' initial attempts to make sure that they are building confidence and not making too many errors.
- A high success rate in questioning and practice is important. Rosenshine suggests the optimum is 80%.
- Rosenshine states that students need lots of time for successful, independent practice in order for the skills and knowledge to become automatic.

This narrative has been adapted from a blog on the website, teacherhead.com, and the book *Rosenshine's Principles in Action* (Sherrington, 2019). Tom Sherrington's advice for training, early career and experienced teachers is to embed these principles into your practice; they are not intended to become a tick list. The ideas of practice, modelling and questioning have meaning only in the context of curriculum content.

References

Rosenshine, B. (2010). Principles of instruction. Geneva: UNESCO, International Bureau of Education. Retrieved from http://www.ibe.unesco.org/fileadmin/user_upload/Publications/Educational_Practice s/EdPractices_21.pdf

Rosenshine, B. (2012). Principles of instruction: Research-based strategies that all teachers should know. *American Educator*, *39*, 12–19.

Sherrington, T. (2019). *Rosenshine's Principles in Action*. Melton, UK: John Catt Educational.

This narrative was written on behalf of Tom Sherrington, a highly regarded educational consultant, author, teacher trainer, blogger and founding Trustee of the National Baccalaureate Trust. Tom is an experienced former headteacher with over thirty years of school experience. Tom has written a number of texts including The Learning Rainforest, *a model for great teaching in real classrooms and* Rosenshine's Principles in Action, *which inspired this narrative.*

What They Didn't Teach Me About
Silence

Dr Janet Goodall

One of the hardest things to learn in any teaching situation is the value of silence. Particularly early on, one thinks that there must be someone talking all the time—either you as the teacher or the students interacting with you or each other. All too often, it appears, new teachers fear silence. They ask a question and rather than allowing students time to think about what the answer might be, they wait just a few seconds and then jump in with the answer themselves, or some other explanation. Or they ask students to work with each other, and then continue talking, forcing students to either not talk to each other or ignore the teacher.

Don't fear the silence. I don't mean that classrooms should be silent all the time; rather, I mean silence is a tool like any other, and can be a very powerful one.

If you ask students a question, let them think for a minute—don't rush in. You're not a bad teacher because they don't know the answer instantly; in fact, you may be a very good teacher who's asked a question that's challenging your students to think new thoughts!

If you ask students to work with each other, let them do that. Don't talk over them, don't keep interrupting them—you probably don't like being interrupted at work and neither do your students.

Teaching is one of those things where you're always getting a little bit better, always tweaking your practice, always learning something new; using silence is part of that. Examine each situation. Is it a productive silence? Are people thinking? When have the group discussions moved off-topic (or better yet, when are they about to do so)? Remember that silence doesn't equal doing nothing.

Dr Janet Goodall is an Associate Professor at the School of Education, Swansea University. Her main area of research is parental and family engagement with children's learning.

What They Didn't Teach Me About
Powerful Explanations and Modelling

Dr James Bullous

As a trainee, I was encouraged to spend a lot of time planning lesson activities, managing behaviour, using assessment for learning techniques and all the other plates we have to spin. If I could go back and do it again, one thing I would understand the importance of is the power of a great explanation!

A thoroughly planned and carefully-crafted explanation, that made use of several different well-developed and timely models, would have saved me so much time and effort. My main error, and one I see many trainee teachers make today, is I assumed that as I knew the content, I could teach it to a group of thirty 12-year-olds. A very naive thought indeed. Einstein is quoted as saying, 'If you cannot explain it simply, you do not understand it well enough'. I have a PhD in chemistry and thought I fully understood it at a KS3 level—that is until I stood in front of those students!

I also cannot stress enough how simplification is not 'dumbing down'. Instead, simplifying is taking a difficult concept and chunking it in to manageable pieces for your students to follow the narrative of your thoughts. A great explanation and well-planned modelling allows teachers to do this very effectively and eliminate misconceptions as they arise.

Now when planning a lesson, or any new learning, for Year 7 to Year 13, I sit down and think, what do they know already? What new knowledge do they need to gain? How am I going to introduce this in a manageable amount to ensure they are able to construct new memories on top of prior knowledge? Once I have established these facts, I prepare an explanation that takes the students on a journey. Sprinkled in are concrete models, via live modelling on a visualiser, and physical models to illustrate theoretical ideas. This process takes time and subject knowledge to prepare but is well worth it! Once you have planned these lessons, strategies or approaches, you can often remember them and use them over and over again, probably improving them each time. This is a skill I now recognise in experienced teachers—but it isn't obvious at first to a trainee, so it would be helpful if someone had pointed it out.

With my trainees, we now focus on explanation as part of the planning lessons teaching standard, and we work together to write down the clearest and cleanest possible explanation, including what models are required. Modelling can include live modelling, deconstruction of students' sample answers, worked examples and partial examples, and is most effective when students understand the links to a problem or concept clearly.

This has resulted in improved behaviour, fewer misconceptions, more rapid progress by students and much happier teachers.

Dr James Bullous is a Vice Principal and Director of Science across the City Learning Trust. James has mentored and coached a number of Initial Teacher Training teachers and Newly Qualified Teachers. He is a Subject and Professional Mentor for several different university providers.

What They Didn't Teach Me About
the Critical Importance of Psychology

Andy van Terheyden

What's the most important thing a teacher can learn during their training? English, maths, or science? I'd argue not. Behaviour management or pedagogy? Again, I'd argue not—but we're getting warmer. For me, it's psychology. Because it's only by really trying to understand our children's minds that we can decide how to get the best from them.

Psychology within education has certainly risen in prominence over the last ten years. The concept of 'growth mindset', for example, has gone from largely unknown to widely popular (though there is much debate about whether it has been truly understood). Despite this, I believe that psychology remains the most undervalued aspect of education, and thus, almost inevitably, of teacher training.

I want to be clear that—because psychology encompasses a lot, and can mean a lot of things—I'm talking about the study of the mind. This means both thought and emotion, and encompasses both neuroscience and metacognition. So, what's important to know that you may not have learned during teacher training? Let me focus in on 'mindset'. Here are my top five tips:

1. **Mindset is everything.** What your students believe about themselves—about their abilities or potential—is, in my opinion, more important than anything else. As Professor Carol Dweck suggests, a student who believes that they have the ability to improve, is more likely to take the steps necessary to do so by listening to your teaching and feedback. By contrast, if

a student who believes that their intelligence is already set in stone, what's the point in listening at all? No listening means no learning.

2. **You first.** To change pupils' mindsets, you have to start with your own. Mindset is a spectrum, and no matter whereabouts you begin, work at moving along it as much as you can. If your children see you embodying that journey, they will follow. Read 'Mindset' by Dweck and research as much as you can. Realise where your mindset is weaker and consider why. Chat to those more experienced in mindset theory about how you can improve.
3. **Teach it!** Teach mindset to your students, including discussing any misunderstandings you may have had yourself. I've seen this done successfully with children as young as four. Tell them what you thought about your brain before and what you've learned now. Teach them the difference between growth and fixed mindsets, going back to the neuroscience (there are plenty of resources out there to help), including *why* it's so important for them to know.
4. **Model and encourage.** There are many ways to do this. Here are a few:
    - Always discuss the learning process. Whether talking about hobbies you are currently doing outside school or describing how you learned the current topic under discussion when you were young, let them hear your journey.
    - Show that you love and value challenges (and therefore mistakes), including praising effort and mistakes over correct answers.
    - When it comes to your (current) weaknesses, avoid statements like 'I'm no good at art'. If you do find yourself (or one of your pupils) using one, add 'yet'.
    - Avoid displays that only celebrate perfect work. Instead, put up edited pieces as a celebration of improvement.
5. **Repeat, repeat, repeat.** Mindset isn't something you do at the start of a year, before getting on with learning. In every display,

every discussion, every piece of marking, repeat and repeat your message. Your ultimate goal is for growth mindset to pervade your whole practice; if you do that, it will seep into your children through every pore.

Word of warning 1: Beware the myth that perseverance will eventually lead to success; this is neither true, nor is it what growth mindset means. Growth mindset is about believing improvement is possible—see that as the gateway which allows the possibility of success. After that, you still need deliberate practice to make improvement; trying hard isn't enough itself.

Word of warning 2: Some people simply don't subscribe to mindset theory and its supporting studies. As with most theories, read up and make your own informed decision.

I've seen first-hand how the above steps—if carried out with unrelenting commitment—can transform children and open them up to progress you never thought possible. Good luck!

Reference:

Dweck, C. (2012). *Mindset*. London: Robinson.

Andy van Terheyden is a deputy headteacher who has worked in areas of deprivation within London, Slough and Luton. Andy is founder of the educational podcast, Classroom 101, in which teachers banish unhelpful practice.

What They Didn't Teach Me About

Starting a Lesson Positively

Fiona Ruck

During my PGCE placement, I remember seeing a member of staff who would stand at the door at the start of every single lesson with a noticeboard. On that noticeboard was a list of three instructions for the pupils to read on their way in to enable them to complete a piece of bell work. This has stuck with me ever since, because what this enabled him to do was to greet and interact with every pupil on their way in. The pupils all had some form of dialogue with him and they all started to work the moment they entered the room. I won't pretend that I have a noticeboard ready at the start of every lesson, but what I do consistently and without fail is to have a piece of bell work ready to hand out at the door as my pupils enter. This gives pupils a focus and enables them to start thinking and being productive straight away and gives me just a little time to talk to each of my pupils individually. It may only be a smile and a simple 'good morning' or a little 'how are you?', but it's important; this may be the first interaction with an adult that some pupils have had that day.

In school, we have adopted a very simple strategy that fits my mantra perfectly. At the start of lesson one, every day, and with every pupil, the teacher meets the pupils at the door and greets them with a handshake. Not revolutionary, I know! However, it has really caused a stir. Research has suggested that it could improve punctuality, yet, more significantly for me, it acts to extend that relationship building where high expectations of each other are key. If only you could have heard some of the grumbles in the staffroom, the fear of germs, the outrage that we actually have to touch the children, or been witness to the vast amounts of hand sanitiser being bought into school each day, you might wonder why we did it! Yet, in the 'real world' post-school bubble, they will be expected to meet and greet with a handshake. Let us embed that now, from the offset. Let us interact with them on a level where we make them feel like responsible citizens, like young adults, capable of taking ownership of their learning and their decisions. Unbeknown to all of us, we might be the first person to acknowledge them that morning, to ask how they are, to genuinely show an interest in their wellbeing. Because what they didn't teach me on my PGCE is that not all of my pupils have the same upbringing as I did. Many of these children, these young adults, have had to endure or are still enduring daily personal challenges that even I, as a 32-year-old woman, would struggle to comprehend. For many, school is escapism, a place where they can be children for six hours a day. It is so important to acknowledge and converse with every single one of them. This can be difficult in every lesson, which is why starting a lesson positively is such an important strategy to show pupils that they are valued and that you care.

Fiona Ruck, BA (Hons), PGCE, Med, is second in geography at a Catholic School in Birmingham. She is passionate about engaging and enabling students through teaching and learning strategies, as well as developing positive relationships through effective behaviour management.

What They Didn't Teach Me About
Technology-Integrated Learning

Lauren Knussen

Technology-Integrated learning (TIL) is the use of technology to engage students and help teachers transform students' learning, incorporating skills that will help them beyond their school years. Some technologies are more useful than others for learning. For example, the use of video in the classroom to help students understand a topic or content area is common. But we do need to ask ourselves to what extent does that help students achieve deeper learning? And does it make much difference whether a video is used or an engaging text? We need to critique how technology is used in the classroom. What are most valuable are technology-based tasks which incorporate 21st century skills like collaboration and creativity.

So how can we use technology to engage higher order thinking skills? Well, a model which represents different 'levels' of TIL and can act as a guide is the SAMR model, developed by Dr Ruben Puentedura. The stages of SAMR are presented below, with some examples of how technology can be used in the classroom.

Substitution: This is when technology is used to replicate something students might do in a non-digital format; e.g., typing up a document on a computer, or create a presentation using software such as PowerPoint. These tasks are good builders of basic computer skills and/or good ways to engage students in a topic initially.

Augmentation: This is when technology is used to improve on the delivery of content or the way students might carry out a task; e.g., incorporating multimedia in a presentation, or the use of interactive stories online to augment the students' understanding of a content area. These technologies improve the learning experience, rather than just act as a substitute.

Modification: This is where technology is used to redesign the task significantly to allow for collaborative work. Students often construct knowledge as a group and produce a technology product to show their learning; e.g., students create a multimedia brochure which incorporates students' own video work.

Redefinition: This is where tasks are completely redesigned to reflect the full affordances of the technology available in the classroom; e.g., students use Google Maps to 'visit' locations in literature and to produce a documentary in groups detailing the look and feel of the region or the creation of videos of students' slam poetry which incorporate images and video which help create the atmosphere of the poem topic.

The above descriptions are included here to act as guidelines, not to ask you to consider in depth how to classify your technology-based learning activities. But hopefully they will help you to think about how you can think about using technology in new ways. A quick online search for SAMR activities will provide some further examples.

Developing your skills with technology-integrated learning

There are some things you can do that can help you along the TIL path:

1. Get to know a few useful types of digital tools really well, rather than getting confused by the infinite number of apps that are out there. Some good ones are:
    - *Padlet*, an app for mind-mapping activities.
    - *Poplet,* an app for students to contribute their ideas on the interactive whiteboard.
    - *iMovie*, great for any kind of movie or video production. Students can get really creative. The *MovieTrailer* option is great for video book reviews.

- Augmented reality apps for creating augmented reality images and video attached to documents (students love these—they work like QR codes). These can be used to add commentary on a poster.
- If you have the hardware, robots are great for maths and science, but can also be used creatively to depict characters in stories.
- *Minecraft Education* is good for students learning about 3D shapes and general design work, such as town planning activities.
- *Code.org* can help you get to grips with coding, and it has activities for students designed for different age groups.

2. Think about what you want the students to achieve and if there is a way you could transform the task and learning experience by integrating technology.
3. Try to ensure the technology-based learning activities have a critical role to play in the programme you have designed. This way, you can be sure your use of technology is integral to the learning process, rather than just existing to add some 'bells and whistles'.
4. If you think about the programme you want to create first before you search for TIL activities, it will help you to hone in on relevant lesson ideas, without being bamboozled by the thousands of possibilities that are out there.
5. Give yourself time to build your skills gradually, and have fun!

Integrating technology can be a daunting task for teachers, and there will not necessarily be much support in schools. Still, expectations that teachers integrate technology are high. If you think about what you want to achieve with technology, develop an understanding of some key technologies and give yourself time to develop your skills, you will have every opportunity to become a confident user of technology in the classroom.

Lauren Knussen, Research Associate, School of Education, University of Technology Sydney (UTS), Australia. Lauren has worked as a teacher of languages other than English and of English as a second language in Ireland and Australia. She has also been a college director and has led professional learning for teachers in technology-integrated learning. Lauren is currently a research associate on an Australian government-funded research project on teacher design practices and is in the final year of a PhD in Education. Her doctoral research focuses on early career primary school teachers' design of technology-integrated learning.

What They Didn't Teach Me About
Differentiation

Nina Rogers

My first foray into using differentiation was with my Year 7 group. My PGCE mentors taught us to differentiate for all, and stretch the most able, which I agree with—but I also had a belief that no child should be limited in the level of work they can achieve.

In my lessons, when it was time for independent work, I would plan the main task but also have work on the screen that was a stretch and label it as 'challenge'. I asked the pupils to complete as much work as they could in the ten minutes.

Sometimes the pupils would say, 'Miss, the challenge is hard. I can't do it', and I would give them a bit of guidance to get them started. I actively told them we have to work at things that seem hard and if we do then we find that we can achieve success.

When we went through the answers—and they found they had got the answers right—I could visibly see the joy on their faces, as they had succeeded at something which initially they thought they couldn't do.

Over time, the pupils really looked forward to the challenge questions and tasks that I set and sometimes even encouraged each other to have a go at it. It was really lovely to see children who may not ordinarily be designated as being the most able, having a go at challenging work and achieving success.

Nina Rogers, BSc (Hons.) is a secondary teacher in Birmingham, UK. Nina is dedicated to providing pupils from all walks of life with opportunities to achieve success and build self-confidence.

What They Didn't Teach Me About
Connections-Based Learning

Barbara Anna Zielonka

In 2007, I graduated from university and started my teaching career. It is not a surprise that my first years of teaching were challenging; it often felt like I was walking on ice. However, I have always believed that no matter what, I would be able to fall in love with teaching in a way I never imagined once I started exploring effective strategies in education that promote meaningful learning and go beyond discipline boundaries. I wish someone mentioned these strategies while I was studying, but unfortunately, I noticed very early in my career that things we were taught at university and the things I needed to focus on were worlds apart.

One of the approaches that has totally changed my teaching and learning has been connections-based learning (CBL). It is a pedagogical approach where teachers connect their students to experts, communities and organisations so that they can learn from each other. We live in the 21st century, and connections play a very important role in our lives. We need to take advantage of the connected world in which we live. Connections-based learning gives my students real-world experience that cannot be recreated in any other way. In the beginning, I talked to my friends and asked whether they knew someone who could present a short talk about topics we had discussed in class. These days, I tend to reach out to speakers via social media networking sites—usually Twitter or LinkedIn. Most of the people I contact are willing to be guest speakers, and it does not take long to arrange an online session during which they offer insight into their field and answer my students' questions. Technologies like Skype, Zoom, Microsoft Teams and social media platforms mean that our world is more connected than ever and can present amazing opportunities for education. By connecting students with experts from different fields, we can create a network around students that helps them to understand how the world works and how to pursue meaningful careers and experiences.

By incorporating connections-based learning in my classroom I can offer interesting and exciting classes, during which my students develop their oral skills and soft skills and have the opportunity to participate in the process of establishing and using one's own network. Learning is no longer limited to the four walls of the classroom. So next time you plan your lesson, think about guests from all over the world whom you can invite to your classroom!

Barbara Anna Zielonka is a full-time high school English teacher, global educator, educational technologist, teacher trainer, writer, project manager, judge in international educational competitions, lifelong learner, catalyst for change and reader. In March 2018, Barbara was named one of the top 10 finalists of the one million dollar Global Teacher Prize. In May 2018, Barbara became the laureate of the 'Outstanding Pole in Norway' contest in the category of science.

What They Didn't Teach Me About
Setting Cover Work

Nimish Lad

What they didn't tell me about setting a cover lesson was the specificity required to get it right. Let me start this by stating that the only way to get this to work is by trial and error, and when it does go wrong, it is no one's fault whatsoever! It takes time to learn how your classes adapt to cover work and how they try to complete the work set in your absence. Put yourself in the shoes of the teacher covering your lesson; they may have just come from geography, then PE, then English, and now your science lesson. Add to that the fact that their specialism may be in art!

A few handy tips to ensure a productive cover lesson include:

- **Be very specific**—have clear instructions for what you would like the pupils to do and learn about, preferably as a list on a PowerPoint slide.
- **Set high expectations**—don't underestimate the amount of work that the pupils will cover within a cover lesson. Make sure they know (by making it clear on your list) where you expect them to reach on your list.
- **Pre-emptively thank the pupils**—write your PowerPoint slide list like you are communicating with them, and let them know in advance that you are thanking them for their co-operation and hard work.
- **Resource the cover**—make sure that you have adequately resourced the lesson with resources that are easy to find within the

room, be that with a textbook, a video or a set of questions (and answers) for the pupils to answer.

- **Copy in your head of department or line manager**—they will be able to provide support to ensure the lesson runs smoothly, either by talking to the member of staff covering in advance or popping in to check that everything is okay.
- **Don't do a one-off lesson**—the class will feel that the learning taking place is not worthwhile as it is not fitting into their current learning sequence, which will mean the lesson will get off to a poor start, making it difficult for the cover teacher.

Tasks that I have found work well as part of a cover lesson include:

- Reading through a text as a class and then answering some questions based on what they have read.
- Creating a summary of a larger piece of work.
- A short ten-question quiz, with answers, based on recently taught work.
- Think, pair, share activities
- Dedicated silent working time

This does seem like a long list, and it is difficult to set cover when you are not well. However, the problems caused by picking up after poorly set cover lessons increases your workload in the long run. When cover has been productive, the next lesson can begin with a 10-minute review of the work that the pupils should have completed, allowing the learning to move on rather than spending the next lesson going over the work which should have already been completed.

Nimish Lad, Senior Leader at Wrenn School in Wellingborough. Nimish has worked in teaching for over 13 years as a science teacher, head of science and senior leader in multiple schools. He has often supported teams when cover has needed to be set to ensure continuation of curriculum and learning.

What They Didn't Teach Me About
What Makes an 'Outstanding' Teacher?

Matthew Walker

I love my job, with all it entails; I simply have a need and love for helping others and freeing them from worry, concern and negative thinking. It is a love and need that comes from my mother, who unfortunately passed away when I was eighteen. She helped shape my worldview and modelled the secrets of what an outstanding teacher is and should be; extraordinary given that she was paralysed by low self-esteem and low confidence. Her outstanding emotional intelligence and teaching ability helped me overcome these same challenges, which is what I want to share. For me, this is her legacy.

I believe that every teacher comes into the profession to help students achieve their very best. I believe we are all outstanding teachers. Over the last few decades the accountability system has clouded our definition of an outstanding teacher.

To unpack this problem, I suggest we must go through four key steps: dissecting, understanding, applying and embedding what an outstanding teacher is defined as.

Step one: Dissecting

We must dissect and eliminate what an outstanding teacher is not, which is the first step that leads us to truly knowing what an outstanding teacher is.

We cannot define a teacher simply by a grade or a colour.

Step two: Understanding

When we understand our why for teaching, we can collectively shape and instil our vision of what an outstanding teacher truly is.

We cannot learn to teach from a book; the learning is out there, in our classrooms, in our corridors, in our schools. When we teach with our hearts, no one can go far wrong.

Step three: Applying

When we apply our own why for teaching into our practice, we will inadvertently create more joy and happiness for ourselves, and, more importantly, for our students.

A teacher's mission should not be to just teach facts and figures, but to also improve the quality of life for their students. When we teach a subject, sometimes we win, sometimes we lose, but when we teach a student, we are guaranteed to win every day of the week.

Step Four: Embedding

After we have dissected, understood and applied what goes into making an outstanding teacher, we need to embed that construct into our societal mindset. If it exists and is celebrated from the bottom up, it is heard loud and clear. This is when true change will happen, and it will reach beyond our classrooms and schools.

We have a national crisis now. In the last two years, more people have left our profession than come into it. We must not and should not ignore this: we must celebrate this wonderful profession and highlight all of its beauty!

To do this we must unpack the myth and belief of what an outstanding teacher is and is not. When we look again, this will lead us onto the right path of building this profession from the ground up.

Matthew Walker, Assistant Headteacher of Teaching and Learning and full-time dyslexic. Matthew has been a lead teacher of teaching and learning and head of PE in Manchester. Mathew is interested in reigniting the sense of purpose that drives all teachers.

What They Didn't Teach Me About
the Storyform Engaging Emotion

Dr Gillian Judson

No one encouraged me to think about my practice in terms of storytelling; shaping content in ways that would leave my students feeling something about the topics we learned.

Some people think that educating people is easier now because there is a wealth of knowledge readily available on the internet. I disagree. Access to knowledge is not the greatest challenge that educators face. Making knowledge meaningful and memorable to students is. After all, *how often have you spent time 'surfing the web' only to leave with absolutely nothing learned? How often have you read something and, soon after, completely forgotten about it?* If we want to encourage meaning-making, we need to talk about how to emotionally connect with information and ideas. No one told me that.

Our role as educators is to help our students to form an emotional connection with fractions, photosynthesis and forces. We need our students to *feel* something about cell division, citizenship, censorship, civil war. Or dinosaurs, division, drama, (I could go on and on with this alphabet game). When topics are shaped in ways that leave students *feeling* something about them, teaching becomes storytelling. And the storyform—the narrative—is one of the most powerful learning tools human beings have.

No one told me this.

Dr Gillian Judson is member of the Faculty of Education and Executive Director of the Centre for Imagination in Research, Culture and Education at Simon Fraser University in Vancouver, B.C., Canada. She's interested in the role of imagination in all learning contexts, imaginative and ecological teaching practices, educational programme design, educational change, educational leadership and imaginative online learning. Recent books: Imagination and the Engaged Learner: Cognitive Tools for the Classroom (2016), and A Walking Curriculum (2018).

What They Didn't Teach Me About
Progressive and Traditional Education

Jozef Butterfield

Imagine being a literary scholar familiar with every great novel, but who has never read a poem or play; a mathematician skilled in geometry, but with no concept of algebra; a bank clerk who withdraws funds for customers, but cannot deposit. Surely, we would consider their knowledge incomplete—desperately lacking and incapable of meeting the demands of the job?

Imagine now that I'm talking about a teacher, entering their NQT year—or perhaps fully qualified—with an incomplete knowledge of their trade, a fundamental block of knowledge absent from their practice. Shocking though this might seem, this is the lived experience of some of the newer members our profession.

My question is why? We see the growth of 'progressive' education at the expense of 'traditional' teaching methods. So, what exactly are these ideas? Far from dull philosophical positions,

Progressivism and traditionalism underpin every part of our day-to-day practice: behaviour, curriculum, even the purpose of schooling itself. For now, we'll consider the teacher-pupil relationship.

Progressivism sees a teacher's role as 'guide from the side': pupils have more control over their own learning, with hands-on tasks and group activities, while the teacher provides stimuli and direction. Critics (myself included) characterise this as inefficient, rudderless, even utopian. Conversely, traditionalism sees the teacher as 'sage on the stage', favouring direct instruction of pupils from the front, with lessons that tend to emphasise knowledge over more abstract skills. Our critics call us Dickensian, elitist, authoritarian. It should be said that these positions aren't a simple binary, but exist on a spectrum. My own school, largely traditional, holds progressive views in some areas.

My purpose here is not to convert you. Most newly trained teachers are likely familiar, consciously or otherwise, with the progressive methods that still dominate most schools and teacher training programmes. For the sake of balance, I recommend three modern texts that I believe best represent the ethos of traditionalism. For the history and need for traditional methods, read Peal's Progressively Worse. For the science behind it, read Willingham's Why Don't Students Like School? To see it in practice, look no further than the Michaela Community School's Battle Hymn of the Tiger Teachers.

I believe a re-evaluation of traditional teaching methods is essential in transforming not only our own practice, but in returning British education to its elite position on the world stage. I don't ask you to adopt my views without question. I only ask that you make yourself aware of all the fundamental ideas that shape education in our country.

Jozef Butterfield, @Jozefteacher, is a teacher of English at Michaela Community School. He passionately believes that traditional educational values best empower disadvantaged pupils. He writes about teaching and other topics on counterstrokeblog.com.

What They Didn't Teach Me About
Immersive Learning

Tom Hanlon

When done effectively, immersive learning can be a great way to capture children's interests and maximise learning outcomes. Personally, our topic work (history and geography) is my favourite subject to teach. At the start of every new topic, I aim to create an immersive experience that will hook the children in, instil excitement for the forthcoming lessons and create a learning opportunity that will be memorable and beneficial. An immersive learning environment is inclusive by nature, due to the fact that it lends itself to all of the learning styles. Therefore, it creates an opportunity for all children to engage and learn in an effective, multi-sensory way.

A key example from my teaching is an experience created for our Titanic history topic, where the children walked in to find both of our Year 2 classrooms completely decorated like the infamous ship. After they were split into social classes, they then had to spend the morning finding the answers to their questions by exploring the clues and information sheets from within the six sections: Crew Room, Boiler Room, Dining Area, Captain Quarters, Lifeboats and Bedroom Suites. While the passengers were dining at lunchtime, the ship then hit an iceberg. The children spent the remainder of the day finding out how and why the ship sank, followed by a debate. The children were fully engaged throughout the day, and as a result, learned a great deal of information that they were able to refer to for the duration of the topic. To this very day, the pupils still talk about our day and, when asked a question about the topic, they are able to recall the answer from their long-term memory.

When planning an immersive experience for a topic, a key thing to remember is the intended learning outcome for the session. Creating an immersive environment that has a positive impact on your children's understanding of a unit of work can add to your already heavy workload, therefore it would be a shame for it to simply be 'fun', with no long-lasting impact.

For every activity planned, ensure it has a purpose and, ideally, enables your children to be both reflective and active participants.

Tom Hanlon, Class Teacher, Liverpool.

What They Didn't Teach Me About

Positive Behaviour

Conor O'Boyle

When I began my PGCE, we were asked to write down our 'hopes and fears' for the course. While our 'hopes' were wide-ranging, from sharing our passion for our subjects to getting a good job, lots of us had the same 'fear': behaviour. What if our pupils didn't respect us? What if we weren't strict enough? What if our brilliantly planned lessons were derailed by pupils messing about?

You'll hear and observe and learn a lot about behaviour during your PGCE and in the years afterwards; there's a lot of fantastic advice out there (as well as some not-so-fantastic advice), and to a certain extent you need to try things for yourself and make mistakes. So, here's my advice, my one shortcut to achieving the classroom culture you want: pretend you have it already. Fake it till you make it, as the saying goes.

I know when I started out, if the behaviour wasn't what I wanted, I got more and more negative: raising my voice, telling pupils off, writing names on the board. And guess what? That only made things worse. It was only when I flipped this on its head that I started to feel I was getting a handle on behaviour; when I was looking for the positives, more and more pupils were meeting me there. So rather than berating the pupils who are turning around and chatting when they should be working, I made a big deal out of those that are doing what they should be. Even if only one or two pupils were working, I focused on them; before I knew it, it was five pupils, then half the class, then practically the whole class.

Let's face it, we all love to be liked, to be praised, to be noticed, no matter how old we are. So, create a culture where the easiest way to be noticed is to do exactly what you, the teacher, asked for. In fact, I'd even take this a stage further. Pretend every class is your favourite. Pretend you've been counting down the hours until you get the joy of teaching them again. Pretend that seeing them has just made your day.

That's not to say you lower your standards, accepting pupils talking over you, being rude or not doing the work you've set: it's really important that you follow your school's policy on all of these things (or take the lead from your mentor). But if and when you do have to apply sanctions, act like this is the last thing you'd expect.

I can't promise this'll make everything easy all the time: you'll have tough classes or lessons that don't quite pan out as you'd hoped—this is normal. But look for the positives, and you'll find they're probably already there.

Conor O'Boyle is a Modern Languages teacher. He has taught French, German and Spanish at a range of secondary schools in Sheffield and is passionate about making languages accessible to all pupils.

What They Didn't Teach Me About
Enjoying the Now

Dr Thomas Seaton

After thirty-five years serving as a teacher, curriculum coordinator, associate administrator and principal, I retired one year ago. Time has a way of moving quickly, helping one see that when there is more time in the rear-view mirror than beyond the windshield, change can be a good thing. Please allow me to share some advice from my current vantage point.

Three years before I retired, I committed to live and lead differently, so I began to dig into readings on mindfulness and living in the moment. I came to see that new insights gained can have a powerfully positive impact on how we view our work.

From the moment the first bell rings launching the new school year, until the day you are bidding students farewell on the last day, you are devoured by thoughts of the future. That's what we educators do. We are continually thinking about where kids need to be, what level they need to reach by a certain point in time and our every thought and effort goes into bringing the child along to make it to the finish line. What's wrong with that?

It is not a question of right or wrong; rather, it is a question of approach that we need to examine. We should try to live more in the moment throughout a school year, regarding the learning that takes place as a continuum of moments, a series of 'nows' that add up to the 'now' that leads us to the last day of school.

As I reflect on my career, I remember numerous data meetings where we would discuss student progress, and while we established norms to include celebration of student growth, we weren't very good party people. I wasn't very good at leading the celebrations. We continued to remain focused on where students needed to be, rather than where the student was in their progress. We had the best teacher of mindfulness, in the form of current student data, and we often failed to recognise its power. We drifted to the future and lost the value of the now, lamenting how much needed to be accomplished and in which time frame.

Why do we feel like the growth is never enough, rather than enjoy the moment and recognise that all progress is the fruit of our labour? We need to celebrate student achievement with each building block of literacy and numeracy they master, as measured by standardised and authentic assessments and teacher observation of daily functioning in the classroom. I see so clearly now that we do ourselves and our children such a disservice if we lose sight of daily progress and fail to celebrate that growth, both in the classroom and around the data table. The ability to remain positive lies in practicing mindfulness, by living in the moment. Sometimes, we can't see the forest for the trees.

You are the ones in the classroom every day, and it can seem like nothing is happening with certain students. Growth can be very slow, and you certainly have some days where instructional methods seem tedious and ineffective. But each 'now' is just as important as the last one and the one to come, so don't despair! Remember those children who 'break through' all of a sudden? We can't time growth spurts, but we surely can measure them!

Inevitably, each year new teams would meet to assess student scores, and we would lament student progress. As I tried to live more in the moment, I learned to share where the child was a year ago, or even a month ago, as a way to celebrate how much growth had taken place. This can also be a way to celebrate colleagues, rather than pointing fingers when determining the amount of work to be done.

Dr Thomas Seaton, EdD, is a recently retired elementary school principal. He worked with high poverty populations while serving as principal. In the latest chapter of his life, Tom is writing on transformation and turnaround experiences that impact educational leaders.

What They Didn't Teach Me About
Organising My Classroom and Resources

Emma Havoc

During my training, the content of lessons was pushed, but not how to manage the classroom or students. We had assignments on schemes for learning and lesson planning, but very little on the movement and flow of students around the room. I knew I wanted to foster independence in my students and didn't want to spend a chunk of my time fetching and carrying the equipment basics for them—they needed to be in places they could access. I know now that a huge part of teaching art, and no doubt many other practical aspects of other subjects, is how you organise the resources and your room. How the students move to get equipment and resources and back to their seats, or how they wash up, is almost—especially at the start—more of a triumph when they do it without incident than what they make.

So, my advice is, plan your room carefully. Work everything out in advance: work out how they will move between key points; where you will stand and where they will need to face to see you; where you will put the equipment and will they be allowed to access it freely? If it works for you, label pigeonholes, cupboards, find boxes or baskets or trays you can use to group regularly used equipment or spare worksheets for absentees and store it in a well-organised way. We can learn a great deal from the primary sector approach to accessibility of resources and secondary students appreciate the trust that comes with this just as much as their younger counterparts. As a new teacher—or a teacher with a new classroom—there are lots of decisions to make, but if you get this part right it can make a big difference to your behaviour management going forward.

Emma Havoc is an experienced teacher from the North West of England. She has worked in secondary schools for over a decade teaching a range of Art-based subjects from KS3 to KS5, particularly Fine Art and Photography.

What They Didn't Teach Me About
USB-ing a Hero

Glenn Carter

What is it to be a hero? What is it to be a hero in a primary school? Well, that all depends on whether you have the right tools or not, because, as I've found during my years as a primary teacher, the tools are the key!

But what are these tools? Well, quite simply, it's my little box of cables, adapters and bits-and-bobs that nobody told me I would need. One of the single greatest decisions of my teaching career was to go and raid the Poundland cable section—all because I needed a micro-usb cable to connect a camera at school. It was from there that I would become the knight in shining armour for many folks in a flap—no need to fear these scenarios:

- The Assistant Head needs to plug a microphone into a portable speaker outside: I've got your ¼ inch jack adapter right here!
- The projector in your room has broken and you need to bust out the old, portable one five minutes before a lesson observation? One HDMI lead coming up!
- The Nativity performance in front of hundreds of parents is about to be ruined because one of the 'wise' men stood on the sound cable from the laptop and broke the end? One 3.5 mm audio lead at the ready!

Some schools are better prepared than others when it comes to technology, so perhaps their Computing co-ordinator already has a lot of these things, but I can tell you now, nothing is more satisfying than realising that *you* can solve the problem because *you* have the tools.

Being a hero isn't always about doing something bold or brave, it's about having the tools and resources to help those in need when they need it.

So be the hero, dodge defeat and look embarrassment straight in the eye. Go to Poundland and grab every type of cable that you can find: USB, audio, HDMI and iPad!

And trust me, when the time comes, it won't be a picture of Superman flying over the school... it'll USBe you!

Glenn Carter currently teaches Year 5 in Stockton-on-Tees in the North East of England. He is the History co-ordinator and is part of the Promethean Advocate programme. He has an MA in History and has written pieces for the Historical Association. Glenn loves using technology in the classroom and finding different ways to engage children.

Chapter 6

What They Didn't Teach Me About Pastoral Care

Personal, social, health and economic education (PSHE) is essential to each school's curriculum and to meeting schools' requirement to promote pupils' wellbeing. The Department for Education (DfE) has made it clear that schools should make provision for PSHE, drawing on good practice. PSHE is a planned programme of learning through which pupils acquire the knowledge, understanding and skills they need to manage their lives now and in the future. As part of a whole school approach, PSHE develops the qualities and attributes pupils need to thrive as individuals, family members and members of society. In this chapter, authors share their advice and experiences as they explore the ways that teachers can address pupils' direct experience and preparation for their future.

What They Didn't Teach Me About
PSHE

Kay Kempers

Imagine you lived on a tiny island in an archipelago, and every day a school boat came and ferried you to your school on another tiny island. There, you learned to read and write, to do mathematics and all about the many wonders of the world. Then, on your final day, you were all led down to the island dock where an assortment of small boats waited. Most boats were simple rowboats or sailboats; some were clearly sturdier than others and all had a student's name on the side. There were a couple of motorised speedboats and a few that were little more than old planks strapped together.

'Go out and explore the world! All the jobs and homes are on other islands', said the teachers. 'But I don't know how to sail!', some students answered. 'I think my boat is leaking', muttered others. Even those lucky few students who had the fancier speedboats were looking confused, as they didn't know where to get the fuel they needed. A couple of students shouted out, 'we found a guide to sailing online. It's not the same type of sailing but it's the best we can do'. The students complained to the teachers, asking why they hadn't been taught to sail or how to read the ocean currents. One teacher shrugged, 'It's not my subject', another answered, 'well your parents should've taught you that'. Some hid around the back as they weren't sure their sailing skills were that great either and they didn't think they'd be any good at explaining the bits they'd picked up along the way. One brand new teacher looked nervously at their timetable where 'Boating Skills' was down for the Monday morning tutorial time.

Some schools call it 'Life Skills', some call it 'PSE', a lot don't call it anything at all. Personal, Social, Health and Economic education (or PSHE for short) is the art of sailing and the maintenance of boats in this metaphorical scenario. All the skills young people need to get on in life are taught in PSHE: how to apply for a job, pay bills, rent a flat, understand a pay slip, deal with interpersonal conflict, form and maintain safe consensual relationships or make sense of what they see in the media. In short, as I usually sum it up to students:

> 'PSHE is everything that's important to know about being a person in the world that isn't covered by one of your other subjects.'

And make no mistake about it, PSHE is a subject, and just like any other it has a recommended curriculum, good practice guidelines, example schemes of work, and a professional association (aptly named the PSHE Association). Unfortunately, many schools do not follow the best practice guidelines of having timetabled lessons taught by a subject specialist, and they try and cram PSHE into tutorial time or off-timetable days with brought-in 'experts' of variable quality. There's a good chance that as an NQT you might, as I was, be given a bunch of PSHE lessons—mainly because no one else wanted to do them. Unlike many though, I had an enlightened Deputy Head who sent another colleague and I on the PG Cert training course to become PSHE specialists—The National Certification in PSHE; I can't recommend it highly enough! I've been a PSHE specialist for over ten years now and I am more convinced than ever that good quality PSHE is vital to the wellbeing of our students. Every time I see another news report saying that we should teach 'character education' or 'life skills' or 'inclusion', I know that it's already there in PSHE. Or maybe it's fairer to say that it could be there, if only more schools would give it the time and staff it needs to be done well. So, assuming you start at a new school and you find some variation of this subject on your timetable, here are some tips:

1. Join the PSHE Association, https://www.pshe-association.org.uk/. They have resources, schemes of work, training, advice and membership. Any topic you want covered, they have your back.
2. Assume that your students don't know half as much as you think they do, and what they do know is likely inaccurate.
3. Topics like relationships and sex education and mental health are part of PSHE, but work your way up to those, especially if you've never done PSHE before. Start with something you feel more confident about, like budgeting from a minimum wage job, and read the best-practice guidance and get some support from more experienced colleagues.
4. Relationships and sex education is minimally about the mechanics of pregnancy, contraception and STIs. It is much more about understanding what it might feel like to be in love, about how to communicate with kindness and honesty, how to tell the difference between friendship, 'fancying someone' and a more lasting kind of love. It's about inclusion and diversity, safety and responsibility. It's about active consent. It's about resisting social pressures and waiting until you are ready. It's about accepting your body as it is and understanding that what you can find online is not realistic. It's understanding that everyone finds relationships a little bit scary at first, even the seemingly more experienced older students who laugh it off.
5. Use inclusive language. You will have some LGBTQIA+ students; they need to know you are including them too. It's easy to modify your language without being really obvious. Just use 'partner' or 'the person you are with' instead of 'boy/girlfriend'. Equally, some students will have family situations you are not aware of, including serious mental illness, addictions, domestic violence, etc. That is easily managed if you use inclusive terms; e.g., 'We can all experience mental distress and some people will need help'.
6. You will never feel as embarrassed answering a question as a student may feel in asking it. As the teacher, you model what is shameful by your reactions. Use correct terms, not euphemisms,

and don't engage in armchair diagnosis. Your students may be giggling, but they still genuinely want to know the answer and you are a better safer source than playground gossip. If it helps, after ten years at this there is virtually nothing that will embarrass me now!

7. Expect difficult discussions and painful disclosures. Good practice includes 'no names' ground-rules. My favourite is 'I know a person who has done/said/thinks....' It allows everyone to have the conversation safely. You will get more disclosures during or after PSHE lessons than at any other time, so know your school's procedures and chat with your Safeguarding Lead if you are unsure.
8. PSHE done well is often the lesson that students remember most and will use most often in adulthood. It needs to adapt to the needs of your students; if you ask them what is important to them then you will get to know how best to meet their needs. For you as the teacher, find other people to talk to. I've had both my most hilarious and my most heart-wrenching moments in a classroom during PSHE lessons, and I know that I have needed to be able to share those with colleagues who understood.

In short, PSHE is the best thing that your PGCE never taught you about. Whether it was the moment a class looked at how much an average teacher had left after tax and bills and said 'Aw Miss, that's not fair, I get more pocket money than you have left!' (we all laughed), or the shocked surprise when they understood what compound interest was on a credit card, or when a quiet teenager came up to me after a series of lessons on mental health and disclosed that she was hearing voices that scared her, or when I overheard one of my class intervening when another pupil was making inappropriate comments about a gay student—I could go on and on with examples—I have never felt so grateful or privileged to be a teacher as in those moments.

Kay Kempers is a teacher, researcher, psychologist and PSHE specialist. After twenty years in the classroom, Kay is now completing Doctoral Research into test anxiety and student belief at Edge Hill University.

What They Didn't Teach Me About
Student Voice

Deborah Kemp

One of the things I love about teaching is listening to young people. I love their no-nonsense, straight-to-the-point feedback; regardless of sometimes offending, students tell it how it is. It's always good to test out any new policy with student groups, and often students are ahead of the Leadership Team in their suggestions for school improvement.

The most familiar approach to Student Voice is to establish a Student Council. This needs to be an elected Student Council to give students an understanding of the democratic process. The most successful approach I have found has been to run a full-scale election, complete with manifestos and speeches and advice from visiting MPs and councillors. Co-opted students, who have a drive and enthusiasm for school improvement, can be added to the elected group to build the strength of the team. I impress two things on a new council: that they are representatives and should not fight their own agendas; and, that making change happen can be a long haul, but it is worth it. Finding 'quick wins' can give students a sense of the reward when their voices are heard, but they also need to understand that sometimes the work they do will have an impact on future students rather than their own cohort. This builds resilience in young people, and the understanding that making changes in an institution can take a lot of hard work and determination. Students need to be given clear roles within the council and given training in their responsibilities; I usually have the old team training up the new team to ensure a good transition.

I keep the council meetings focused on the core work of the school—teaching and learning. Students have powerful voices and offer very useful feedback on teaching and learning; they are on the front line of delivery and know what does and doesn't work for them. Students can have a powerful impact on their experience in the classroom—especially if their feedback is taken on board in the Leadership meetings as a standing agenda item.

Students will always want to talk about things like canteen food and uniforms, but I limit these to one agenda meeting every so often so as to not allow these issues to dominate the discussion. For these one-item discussions, I invite the Principal to discuss uniform and the Catering Manager to discuss food!

However, despite Student Councils being hugely important, these are only one vehicle and, in a school that truly embraces Student Voice, I believe it should permeate all areas of the school; in recruitment with student panels, in lessons using student evaluations on schemes of work, in student led assemblies, in student publications, whole school student questionnaires, online feedback and students speaking at parents' evenings and events in the community.

I also try to encourage a number of different student focus groups initiated by the students' own passions and interests; this means we are not just relying on a small, albeit representative, Student Council. These other student groups can be set up to represent niche interests; groups with one focus that support a particular school initiative e.g., green groups, equality groups, school prom groups, etc.

One example of a successful student group that I supported was the TAL team—named by the students as the Teaching and Learning Team. They were given the opportunity to monitor teaching and learning across the school and became a group that were commissioned by departments. The students wrote reports on areas identified by department reviews and these reports formed part of department action plans. Areas of focus/analysis were classroom environment and displays, gender balance in discussions, and homework and engagement. Students carried out observations, took photos and recorded interviews with other students to gather their evidence—and produced powerful reports. One important element to the success of this was staff being asked if they were happy to have the TAL team in their classrooms—most staff welcomed them in.

Critical to the success of Student Voice is having passionate, committed staff prepared to facilitate students running and engaging with these kinds of activities. The benefits are significant: developing students' engagement and commitment to their school, building a sense of belonging, self-worth and pride. Importantly, listening to Student Voice is not enough; we have to ensure we act on these voices and communicate how we are going to respond—and give the students the reasons behind these decisions. Effective Student Voice helps to grow active and positive citizens of the future.

Deborah Kemp has been an Assistant Principal Lead for Student Voice, Leadership and Engagement since 2011 in two schools.

What They Didn't Teach Me About
Emotional Wellbeing and Learning

Anne Gladstone

What they didn't tell me about at college (or perhaps what I didn't understand at the time) was the importance of emotional wellbeing as part of learning. I learned about equality of opportunity and individual needs, about Maslow's hierarchy of needs and also about ways to understand children's needs and to address them through getting to know them and their families—and I differentiated my teaching accordingly. When I started teaching, I did these things as best as I could. However, I soon found that there were some children who didn't really fully engage with learning, and in some cases were disruptive and even hostile, meaning that 'crowd control' tactics sometimes became the order of the day.

It wasn't until I was fortunate enough to work with some infant-mental-health specialists that I started to have a deeper understanding of the effect of a child's emotional wellbeing on their ability to learn—and that without good emotional wellbeing, learning is unlikely to take place. More importantly, I started to connect the dots between relationships—both inside and outside the family—and the effect they have on good mental health in general and emotional wellbeing in particular. I came to understand how profoundly our early experiences shape, not just our brain architecture, but our feelings and emotions, including how we think about ourselves as learners. I realised that as a teacher, the relationship I had with each child had the potential to profoundly affect not just the child as a learner but indeed their emotional wellbeing and how they thought about themselves, both as children and in the future as adults. I realised that I had a major responsibility to nurture and support their emotional wellbeing in order for children to have confidence in themselves as learners, and thus fulfil their academic potential. Everyone's emotional wellbeing naturally goes up and down—whether it's during the day or over a period of time—but if it's always low then we need to understand why and, if we can, do something about it.

So, what have I now learned that we, as teachers, can do to support children's emotional wellbeing? We can endeavour to form sensitive, respectful and positive relationships with children. This act alone will nurture emotional wellbeing, and will also enable us to pay attention to each child's level of emotional wellbeing through careful observation and dialogue with the child and their family. Armed with the knowledge these relationships give us, we can endeavour to make changes to our practice, which could raise the child's emotional wellbeing and put them in a better position to take advantage of the learning on offer. It's important to remember that we can't always 'make things right' for children; however, we can certainly make their time in the setting which might be most negatively affecting their emotional well-being the best it can be. The desired outcome here is to contribute to both good levels of emotional wellbeing and resilience, which will carry through into other areas of their life.

I believe we also need to monitor our own levels of wellbeing, as it is extremely difficult to support someone else's wellbeing when our own is shaky. Working with children and their families can be extremely rewarding, but it can also be challenging and emotionally exhausting. Everyone has experiences in their lives outside of the workplace which affect their wellbeing, and often our natural resilience allows us to bounce back and to just 'get on with it'. However, when our wellbeing remains low, for whatever reason, we need to learn to be kind to ourselves and to address our own emotional needs. This isn't a selfish thing to do, even if it feels like that, because our emotional state directly affects the state of the children and families we work with, so it is actually beneficial to others for us to do this. Being kind to ourselves can take many forms, such as learning to express our feelings honestly, not taking too much on or simply just taking a few deep breaths and relaxing when things are getting stressful. It is important for those working with children and their families to have the opportunity to reflect on both their practice and their emotional wellbeing through their professional supervision.

As I write this, I realise that paying attention to and nurturing children's emotional wellbeing is something we are much more likely to do than considering our own emotional needs. However, as people working with children, it is important to remember that children see us as role models and are especially influenced by us. This means children learn from how we behave, as well as from what we do and say, so if they see that we not only look after their mental health, but also our own, this will help them nurture good mental health in themselves.

Anne Gladstone is the Director of Anne Gladstone education and training services.

What They Didn't Teach Me About
the Weather

Ruth Hancock

Wind: You've heard the expression 'as high as kites'—let me tell you this is nothing when compared with the energy of students during a brewing storm. There's something about the wind that sets them off. Scientifically, it's probably down to the positively-charged electrons; I'm sure you can easily look this up for yourself if you're that bothered for the facts, but this won't help your overall class control at this time. A windy day will test your mettle as a teacher. I'm not sure I have a solution for you. But at least forewarned is forearmed.

Heat/Sun: Being an English specialist, I always refer to Act 3 Scene 1 of *Romeo and Juliet*: 'For now, these hot days, is the mad blood stirring' and your students 'shall not 'scape a brawl' if they continue with their incessant moaning that it's too hot to learn. Never give in when asked if you can go outside and teach the lesson in the fresh air. Firstly, it sets a precedent which your colleagues will not thank you for. Secondly, there's always one student who has a massive hay fever/asthma allergic reaction, one who gets stung, one who develops grass/nettle rash, one who gets sunburnt, and the inevitable one who takes a football with them and plays three-a-side with their mates. All of this draws attention to the fact that you're outside without permission, and none of this is on a risk assessment—because you haven't done one. Finally, and you could/should say most importantly, no learning EVER gets done.

My advice is to pin this notice on your board and crack on as best you can:

1. Yes, it is quite warm.
2. Yes, the windows are open.

3. No, I don't have a fan.
4. Yes, you do still need to work.
5. No, there is no magic 'maximum temperature' for class to be cancelled.
6. No, this is not against your human rights.
7. No, we can't just watch a film.
8. If you are working quietly we can have the door open (as a special treat).

Another head's up though: if you actually allow number eight to happen you may create a through-draft which will blow all your papers everywhere and cause the blinds to rattle so loudly that no one will be able to hear you teach anyway…

Snow: Our school sometimes closes because of this and it is a decision that is never taken lightly, not least because of the backlash it creates from all stakeholders. It seems you just can't please all of the people all of the time, or some of the people any of the time. Students will ask at regular intervals whether you think they'll be sent home, despite having being told in assembly that morning that 3 flakes does not constitute a national emergency. Parents will contact the school at regular intervals asking for updates and to discuss whether the buses will be able to get through at the end of the day (I kid you not).

Of course, if you teach MFL you won't have any of these issues. When the weather is distracting, deliberately make it a feature of the lesson and teach/revise weather expressions. Hopefully this example won't ever happen to you, but at one point when the rain was regularly *coming through the ceiling* our MFL teacher showed quick, creative reactions. The teacher made a display in Spanish at the point where it ran down the wall: it is raining; it always rains; it rained yesterday; it will rain tomorrow.

Ruth Hancock is a loving mother and teacher of English in the beautiful Yorkshire Dales. She has also held posts of teacher i/c library, literacy-lead, head of department, head of house and Key Stage 3 Progress leader.

What They Didn't Teach Me About
Pupil Burnout

Lauren McKay

I bet you've heard lots about teacher burnout. Those late nights and early starts, coupled with the stress of the job, leading to an increase in NQTs leaving the profession and a crisis in teacher wellbeing and recruitment. That is all true, and we're just starting to get a handle on that crisis. Most schools have some kind of wellbeing scheme in place to support us through the rough patches. What isn't discussed—in my experience anyway—is pupil burnout. This happens too, a lot. I notice it most when I'm standing in front of my Year 5s and they can't quite articulate what an adjective, verb or noun is, but can write a stunning setting description.

Pupil burnout happens day in and day out. Think about the amount of information we unload on them daily, not to mention the high assessment expectations we must maintain. Especially if you're working in KS2 or KS1, their brains are still developing, and aren't equipped yet to deal with information overload. So, what happens? It appears as though the information is being learned, but it isn't actually being absorbed and retained. They need brain breaks! Short, regular breaks from the learning to give their brains time to catch up and unwind. Here's my list of top brain-break activities to try with your class:

1. Go Noodle—this website is free to join and has a multitude of dances and activities; they're even sorted into categories such as 'mindfulness' and 'warm-up' so you can cater to the exact needs of your class.

2. BBC Supermovers—another free, active website; this one has songs and dances linked with learning, ideal for lesson warm-ups or plenaries to mix it up!
3. YouTube—as with the above, choc-a-block full of quick activities and dances to re-energise and refocus!
4. The great outdoors—weather permitting. Sometimes taking the children out into the playground for a quick run around can do them the world of good—it must be the fresh air! Can be either unstructured or with a purpose; for example, a daily run.
5. Good old fashioned games—we all know 'hot potato' with a bean bag, rock paper scissors, and no child is too old for 'What's the Time Mr. Wolf?'

Ultimately, a brain break is all about giving the children five minutes here and there in their school day to be children. The benefits of brain breaks include better focus, improved mood and attitude to learning and, above all, better pupil wellbeing. We're often told that a burnt-out teacher isn't an effective teacher. Well, burnt-out pupils aren't effective learners. Find opportunities in your timetable to give your children a bit of childhood in between their education; they'll thank you for it.

Lauren McKay is an RQT Year 5 teacher from Chesterfield, currently teaching in a one-form entry Catholic school in the north of Sheffield. She is the English and art leader and soon to be a SCITT mentor.

What They Didn't Teach Me About
Youth Violence

Steve Warner

Gang Education

I have worked with a number of schools, safeguarding leaders and governors to share our understanding and response on youth violence and gang culture. What is very apparent is the knowledge and understanding vacuum about the issues that draw young people towards violence and gang involvement. How can students be adequately educated, and the counter narrative delivered with any credence, when those charged with doing this are in the dark themselves?

Schools must consider all students as being at risk—all as potential victims and a few as possible perpetrators. Therefore, as schools it is our duty of care to safeguard communities and educate students on the threats to, and changing landscapes within, their communities and wider society.

The Role Schools Can Play To 'Connect the Dots'

Academic research identifies a number of factors that heighten the risk of involvement in youth violence and gang culture. The five considerations listed below will help schools identify risk factors and inform early identification—another key element to reducing risk.

A school should know:

- its students as individuals;
- its students' family history and dynamics;
- its students' influencers and peers;
- the community it serves; and,
- its own pastoral and academic data.

There are a number of key areas of understanding that are particularly relevant within a school context. When connected, a series of apparently unrelated factors can significantly point to an increase in risk. This list is not exhaustive:

1. **Community:** All schools should have an awareness of what is happening within the communities that they serve and the risks or impacts that this may have on their students.
2. **Family:** It is essential that schools have updated knowledge on the family composition of each student. Factors such as, for instance, father deficit, known family links to gangs, or involvement with police, heighten the risk factors.
3. **Peers and Influencers:** Monitoring of friendship groups for notable changes can be an early indicator of heightened risk.
4. **Behaviour:** Changes in behaviour can sometimes reflect student experiences outside school. For example, changes in boys around Year 9, such as increased defiance and aggression, could be signs of heightened risk. Within girls, this tends to manifest itself later, usually in Years 10 or 11, and can be evident through sexually risky behaviours.
5. **Marginalisation:** Some students are drawn to gang involvement in response to needing a sense of belonging and acceptance. Identifying those students who are on the margins of the school community can be an early indicator of heightened risk.
6. **Cultural Deviance:** As with marginalisation, those students who do not necessarily conform to their cultural 'norm' can also be an indicator.
7. **Possession of Multiple Mobile Phones:** Many students involved with gangs, drugs or who wish to maintain secrecy, will often have more than one mobile phone. Often the second phone, sometimes described as a 'burner', will be old and cheaper when compared to the expensive smart phones commonplace amongst many young people today.
8. **Child Sexual Exploitation:** One common feature of gang behaviour is sexual exploitation, particularly of girls and those most vulnerable. Those students who have a history of or

demonstrate risky or highly sexualised behaviours should be considered highly vulnerable and at risk of such exploitation.

9. **Attendance:** Schools are well-placed to monitor attendance. Short periods of unexplained absences could be an indication of County Lines involvement, whilst regular truancy and poor attendance could suggest a heightened risk. Beware of exclusions as these could fuel a rise in gang membership.
10. **Vulnerability:** Often those linked to gangs will prey on those most vulnerable. The close monitoring of our most vulnerable students, particularly those with SEN, is essential.
11. **Drill Music:** 'Drill Music' is said to be used by gangs to make threats towards other gangs or boast about their actions. It is often highly sexually explicit and contains racial, homophobic and inflammatory language. It also seeks to glamorise gang life through its lyrics and linked videos. Listening to this is the 'norm' for many students, but could also be a further indicator of heightened risk.
12. **Social Media:** As with 'Drill Music', social media is used extensively to glamorise gang life. Ultimately the responsibility for the policing of this has to sit from within the home; even so, as schools, we need to develop the counter-narrative to challenge this.
13. **Designer 'Gear':** As part of grooming, or from the rewards of gang activity, those at risk will receive expensive 'brand label' clothes, shoes or other designer items. Whilst often reflective of the pressures and fashions of young people, the sudden possession of such items can also be seen as a potential risk indicator.
14. **Gang Slang:** The street language used by gangs originates from the need to remain ahead of law enforcement, and as such, it is constantly evolving. Care also needs to be taken as many of the terms used have found their way into the colloquial language of students today.

In considering each of the above, I am not saying, for instance, that any student who listens to 'Drill Music' or has an absent father is in a gang. However, using this understanding as a foundation to 'Connect the Dots', it can be used as an effective mapping tool to track applicable risk factors and identify those students who are considered most at risk.

All Schools Need To Look 'Beyond the Gate'

I have encountered a number of fantastic school leaders who recognise the important role that schools can play in early identification and intervention. In some places there are wider discussions over issues such as funding and statutory guidance. Unfortunately, there are also still a significant number who remain oblivious to the threats and challenges facing young people today. They do not recognise—or are unwilling to accept—the threats to their community.

Regardless of the political debate or strategic school priorities, what is clear is that those of us in schools must consider our responsibilities. We need to be proactive in dealing with the 'here and now'. We need to ensure that we do everything we can to keep our students safe—we need to look beyond the gate.

Steve Warner, Deputy Head, St Mary's CE High School, Hertfordshire. Content adapted from 'Beyond The Gate'—A series of online blogs written by @swarnersmhs and published via @TeacherToolkit

What They Didn't Teach Me About
Pastoral Leadership

Maria Andrianova

Being a pastoral leader was never an option for me—or at least I had always thought so. During my training and further study (Masters in Educational Leadership and Innovation), pastoral leadership had never been explicitly mentioned, however the idea of becoming an academic leader was planted, watered and nourished in my conscious and subconscious mind. Being an academic leader, leading teaching and learning and academic professional development became focus of my early career. Becoming an Advanced Skills Teacher brought an incredible sense of achievement and fulfilment, which further enhanced my belief that I was on the right professional path; the idea of being an academic leader for life was now deeply rooted in my mind.

Ten years down the line I made a strategic decision to temporarily take a step back to look after my young children; with that came an inevitable change of jobs and schools. Little did I know that a few years later this simple, yet difficult step would lead me to discovering the joys and challenges of pastoral leadership. Looking back, the only regret I have is falling into the job due to staffing changes rather than having time to reflect and prepare myself for the challenges ahead. If you consider pastoral leadership at some stage in your career, take time to plan your pastoral journey. We all tend to start as both academic and pastoral leaders, leading subject groups as well as a tutor group. Although the focus will change depending on your career path, the duality of the job will always remain:

- As Head of Year, you will have an overall responsibility for the pastoral and academic development of your pupils.
- As Head of PSHE/PSHE co-ordinator, you will be responsible for the teaching and learning in your department.
- As a DSL, you will be dealing with safeguarding issues that affect pupils' welfare and academic development.
- As Deputy Head Pastoral, you will be line-managing departments, and this includes evaluating their academic performance.

Depending on the position, of course, the exact responsibilities would be different, but academic and pastoral will always go hand-in-hand in any educational context.

When planning your pastoral journey, focus on yourself first: technical skills and specific knowledge can be acquired through face-to-face or online training, through reading books, researching and actually doing the job, however personal development takes time.

- What are your values?
- What is your 'why'?
- What are your personal and professional goals?
- What are you doing that prevents you from achieving them?
- What can you accomplish that doesn't depend on others?
- Have you done enough for yourself?
- Are you prepared to change?
- What are your non-negotiables?
- What do you need most right now?

Knowing yourself better will enable you to add value to your life and the lives of others through your pastoral role, develop character strengths and lead with authenticity, which is essential to pastoral leadership.

Pastoral leadership is a great privilege, and with that comes great responsibility to serve your community with awareness, empathy, fairness, trust and most importantly, love.

Maria Andrianova is a school leader, an advanced skills teacher and a PhD student. She is also a school Governor and the CEO of Pastoral Support Ltd.

Chapter 7

What They Didn't Teach Me About the Challenging Times

Teaching is truly a rewarding profession. We have the opportunity to change children's lives. But nobody ever said that the job of a teacher was easy—it takes dedication, patience and resilience. In this chapter, authors explore some of the ways in which teachers may face challenges in their working roles, and they offer their best advice for dealing with the difficult times. It is at these times that it is important to reflect on the reasons why we became teachers; for many of us it was to make a difference to the lives of others.

Don't Quit

When things go wrong as they sometimes will,
When the road you're trudging seems all up hill,
When the funds are low and the debts are high,
And you want to smile, but you have to sigh,
When care is pressing you down a bit,
Rest if you must, but don't you quit.
Life is strange with its twists and turns,
As every one of us sometimes learns,
And many a failure comes about,
When he might have won had he stuck it out.
Don't give up, though the pace seems slow,
You may succeed with another blow.
Success is failure turned inside out,
The silver tint of the clouds of doubt,

And you never can tell just how close you are,
It may be near when it seems so far.
So stick to the fight when you're hardest hit:
It's when things seem worst that you must not quit.

—John Greenleaf Whittier

What They Didn't Teach Me About
Trusting the Process

Kate A. Aveling

Being a teacher is by far and wide *the* most challenging role I have ever taken on, and by the same token, the absolute, complete and utter best.

When thinking about our responsibilities to produce good communicators who are resilient, lifelong learners, compassionate, socially and emotionally skilled, curious, tolerant, consistent, culturally aware, innovative, critically thinking, informed, vocal, connected, empowered, problem solving, global citizens, it can be a little overwhelming. But I'm here to tell you that you are going to be great. If you feel overwhelmed by all of the responsibility, it's simply because you care. And if you care, you're doing this for the right reasons.

Trust the process.

During your training, there will likely come a point (or several) where you feel like it's all too much and that you just can't do it. I certainly did. In fact, I suffered with debilitating anxiety during my training. I had panic attacks and days where I couldn't leave the house, and it was mostly due to the overwhelming feeling that I was in over my head. And I think that being a perfectionist (and it seems that this is a quality of many, many teachers) had me putting immense pressure on myself to do everything brilliantly and made me over think things. And I was by no means a high flying student. I sweat the small stuff, and I needn't have. I just needed to trust the process.

The days I spent in class as a student teacher were wrought with fear that I was doing it wrong—not the way that 'this' teacher or 'that' teacher did it—despite me getting glowing feedback from my mentor. In fact, I not only disliked those days in class, I dreaded them. It was my insight into what teaching was going to be like, and I wasn't sure I liked it.

But, seven years later, I'm still teaching—and loving it more than ever!

I need to tell you that being a real life teacher is nothing like being a student teacher. Nothing. It's way better! You get to put your *own* personality into how you teach. You will have your *own* classroom management plans and you will have your *own* systems and strategies, and you will be great. If, like me, you are a repressed actress just bursting at the seams with Disney show tunes and interpretive dance moves choreographed to the dusky autumn wind blowing in a northerly direction, guess what? You get to put that into your classroom. Yep. I know. And if you're a brooding poet who likes to play classical music when tidying up, you can to do that too!

There will be days where you feel like you don't know what is going on. Don't sweat it. Ask around and you'll likely find that that's the case for lots of other teachers; no one really knows what's going on all the time.

There will be days where your perfectly planned lessons, with all the bells and whistles and laminated cards cut perfectly to the edge with rounded corners, will go totally pear shaped. Don't sweat it. You'll learn from it. And you'll find that that still happens to even the most experienced of teachers.

There will be days when you feel like you haven't changed the artwork or writing samples on your walls in forever, or times that all the other classrooms look so good and yours looks like a cyclone has blown through it. Don't sweat it.

For every day that you feel like it's a bit too hard you'll have days where one of your pupils calls you mum or dad by accident, or they tell you that you're their favourite teacher and draw a picture of you and them together. You'll see how that one kid who got anxious before every maths lesson is now asking really thoughtful questions, and another kid who was struggling to make friends now has their own little posse.

You'll find that where they once whined about spelling tests, they're now racing to the box with the spelling books in it. Other, more experienced, teachers will ask *you* how to do something. There will be days where a parent comes to you and tells you that since being their child's teacher, that child has come out of their shell, or has started reading at home, or is more tolerant with their siblings—and they are grateful for *your* impact. For you.

There will always be days where little things build up and seem overwhelming. No matter what. But don't sweat it. There are better days that make up for those scary days. I promise.

And like the Beatles said, 'There's nowhere you can be that isn't where you're meant to be. Its' easy.'

Happy teaching and remember, trust the process.

Kate. A. Aveling, BA Drama, BSc Specialist Drama & Dance teacher. Kate completed her teacher training in Sydney and now lives and teaches in Hobart, Tasmania. Kate has completed a writing course and is working towards writing and publishing her own children's picture books aimed at the value of performing arts for young people.

What They Didn't Teach Me About
the Importance of Positivity

Tom Griffiths

In some ways it feels like it's only been a few years since my NQT year—in reality, it's almost 10. To me, our education system has changed so much in my short career (for the better and for the worse), so my top tip is to focus on the positives of the job. As each half term continues, you will get more and more tired, so I would suggest picking a couple of positives each day. Whether it is how well a lesson has gone, or how you've defused conflict (it might not be simply the children, it could also be between staff members or parents/carers), or perhaps how a child is so proud of themselves because they've grasped a tricky maths concept. No matter how small the positive, it'll keep you going—especially during that arduous autumn term.

My NQT year was a fantastic, but exhausting, year at an inner-city school in Acton, London. I don't think you can ever forget your first class: my Year 2's were a bunch of lovely, excitable and wacky children. With SATs, I knew it would be a tricky year. I knew I had a lot to learn, so my mentality was to listen to everyone around me, get the behaviour management of the class under control first, and teach. It's not ideal to be arrogant or feel you've made it just because you've passed your degree—my NQT year was one of the hardest years of my career, but I got by through hard work, the support of my brilliant colleagues and recognising my mistakes in order to learn from them.

Being given your own class is the most exciting—and daunting—thing so embrace that. It's one thing as a teacher-in-training during your PGCE year—you're desperate for the class to respect you and 'be' the teacher—but you think differently when they are actually yours, and staff and children are asking you questions whilst parents/carers are at the door demanding your attention too! I certainly had some tricky parents that year, but I was always honest if I didn't know and stood confident when I needed to. Remember, you are the capable professional and they can't always get their own way; obviously you don't want your actions to affect your working relationship, so listening is key! If they need to vent, let them get it out and try not to let it affect you personally.

So, enjoy it! It is long hours and crazy days, but the holidays help you feel human again and the positivity and support from your colleagues will keep you going. If you're not on Twitter or Facebook then get yourself on there and be part of the groups; you'll see on those tough days that you're not alone and you'll also make some lovely virtual friends—not only that, it's great CPD too!

Tom Griffiths, LLB, PGCE is the Assistant Headteacher at Tidbury Green School in Solihull. Tom studied Law at Nottingham Trent University while working as a teaching assistant in a deprived area of Nottingham. He currently leads on Maths and assessment as well as being responsible for mentoring and training middle leaders.

What They Didn't Teach Me About
Making Mistakes

Fiona Ruck

In my first weeks of teaching, I was asked a question by an A-level pupil that I simply did not know the answer to. I was ashamed. They hadn't taught me how to deal with this situation on my PGCE, so I pretended I hadn't heard the question and carried on teaching! What experience has taught me now is that it's so important to encourage your pupils to have a go and to make mistakes. Mistakes are simply evidence that you are trying. If you are not making those mistakes, you are not trying hard enough. Use Michael Jordan as an example. 9,000 missed shots in his career, 300 lost games, 26 times he was trusted to take the winning shot and missed. But these mistakes led to his epic success. Show them that you make mistakes too. Admit to not knowing the answer when they ask you that ridiculously hard question. And then find out for them (thank the Lord for Google!). We are only human after all, and the way we learn best is by making those mistakes. Show them that this is encouraged in your lessons. Help them to feel empowered. Strategies such as mini whiteboards are great for this. They are great for assessing progress, but another benefit is that you can also encourage everyone, including your passive learners, to have a go at writing down an answer and holding them up to the class. Let's create confident citizens who are not afraid to challenge themselves. After all, if our pupils did not make mistakes, if they did not need us to scaffold their learning and inspire their thinking, if they came in knowing it all, we would be out of a job!

So, what is my advice to you? Be creative with your pedagogy; make learning a fun and positive experience. Remember that each pupil is unique and special. They all have very different lives and very different experiences. Be their consistency. Be their safety net. Be their inspiration. Be their Mr or Mrs Motivator. Encourage them to make mistakes. Be forgiving. Never ever hold a grudge. Be their cheerleader. Teaching, after all, is an act. Every lesson you are on stage in your own theatre, often with a difficult audience. The sooner you realise that that smile will be long overdue by Christmas, the better. Build positive relationships. Respect them, encourage them and inspire them—as a result, they will achieve more than they ever dreamed possible.

Fiona Ruck BA (Hons), PGCE, MEd is second in Geography at Archbishop Ilsley Catholic School in Birmingham. She is passionate about engaging and enabling students through teaching and learning strategies as well as developing positive relationships through effective behaviour management.

What They Didn't Teach Me About
Filing Away the Negative

Emily Weston

A lot of the advice you'll hear on the road to, and through, your PGCE and NQT years will vary greatly. You'll hear people say it's hard work (which it is), and that teaching is becoming an ever-increasingly difficult career with a high workload, and sometimes there are toxic environments where stress levels are increasing. But, if we think about it, these are all issues which can occur in *any* career.

If you have a passion for teaching, if you want to make a difference in children's lives and are ready to put your heart and soul into the job, then my advice to you is not to ignore what you hear, but to listen, file it away in case you need it one day, then focus on all the positives you hear. For as many horror stories that you hear about teaching, you'll hear 10x that amount which highlight all the positives that comes from it; it's a job satisfaction like no other.

I currently mentor PGCE students, and I'm always impressed by their enthusiasm, ideas and positivity. This year alone they've shown me new ways to teach angles in circles, a way of creating potions which involved science (that I never would have considered!) and an evidence-filled industrial revolution lesson. Students can take ideas you give them and turn them into something you'd never consider. It's their—*and your*—passion and creativity which helps to keep this profession going.

And all those negative stories you file away? Yes, it's true that some people will go through that experience: I was one of them. But by being forewarned, you know what signs to look for when finding a school to start your career in, such as:

- Looking at a school's marking policy.
- How their planning is done.
- What support is offered to staff.
- How a work/life balance is looked after.

Overcome the negativity you hear, see, and even sometimes experience, to become the best teacher you can be.

Emily Weston is a Year 6 Teacher, PGCE Student Mentor & Reading Lead—Swindon, UK. Emily is passionate about teacher wellbeing and mental health within schools. She is keen to raise engagement with reading within schools, through sharing a love of books and authors. Emily writes an educational blog—'Teaching Isn't Black and White'.

What They Didn't Teach Me About
Classroom Management

Helen Abbott

During my NQT year, I was in a mainstream school. We had the honour of a past student visiting us via helicopter after a lottery win and a donation being made to the school. Staff were given strict instructions not to let pupils out of classrooms for the visit. Unfortunately for me, I was in a room that overlooked the field and two of the four walls were windows. So we had the perfect view. This also meant we were able to watch a 'specially selected' group of pupils line up to watch the helicopter. My class begged and pleaded, but I stuck to the rules. So they took matters into their own hands—and jumped out of the windows! Thankfully we were on the ground floor, but at the time I was horrified at my complete lack of classroom management. Now I can laugh about it!

The absolute hardest job I've ever done was cover supervising for a year. If you can get through the heavy sense of dread when you hear a class of 30 plus cheering as you approach because they think they can skive the lesson, you can get through anything! I had to put up with kids calling inappropriate numbers on their mobiles, singing Christmas songs over and over (in summer)—and a whole class of Year 7s ran off once! I think I've blanked the rest of it out; I can't recall a lot of that year. Overall, it was a great experience and I got a lot from it in terms of managing behaviour, trying out different approaches and developing a thick skin!

Which follows on to, never take the things pupils say personally. They test the boundaries and say some truly horrible things, but they don't know you personally, so don't take it to heart. My usual reaction to such things is to laugh—it's not the one they're expecting and it can diffuse any escalating behaviour. It can be hard when they know what buttons to press and they want to lash out and cause hurt, but it's so important to remember that you're the adult. They want boundaries to be laid out, so by all means reiterate them, but don't get angry and retaliate; it just shows they have succeeded in getting to you, and you've proved them right in their expectations of you. So when I'm told 'I hate you' I respond with, 'well that's a real shame because I enjoy having you in the lesson!' It's actually quite easy—and dare I say it, quite fun seeing them react when the response is different to what they expect.

Helen Abbott, BA (Hons), PGCE, NPQML is Head of Foundation Curriculum at an Alternative Provision Academy in the North West. She is an art specialist fervently believing in the therapeutic benefits of the subject. Helen is currently working on her NPQSL, completing a whole school project on Mental Health and Wellbeing.

What They Didn't Teach Me About
Classroom Control

Imogen Thomas

'5... 4... 3... 2... 1...'

The noise level in the room hasn't changed. I am standing at the front and I might as well be doing star jumps in a gorilla costume for all the good it has done me in getting 9y1's attention. I am conscious of rule one of being a teacher: do not let them speak over you. But that was actually the third time I had repeated those 5 numbers and waited in the centre of the room for quiet. Someone else had told me if you stand in the same spot in the room they will recognise this cue as well; what they didn't do was tell this to 9y1. So now I am parsing through my options as I begin to feel the familiar hot anxiety wash over me and simultaneously regretting my choice of a light-grey shirt this morning.

I opt for writing a solitary tally mark at the top of the white board, knowing that this consequence would involve just as much punishment for me as it would for them. There is a murmur of interest from the front rows, but most remain oblivious as a moment later I add a second tally mark. That is until a shout comes from the back of the room, 'She's going to keep us at break!' This is followed immediately by an unequivocal, 'Na—she won't be able to do that!' I am not sure whether to sanction the shouting or admit that they are probably right. It is not as if I can barricade the door, and as it stands I am only one wrong decision away from a full-on mutiny.

'You must be consistent and fair with sanctions at all times to gain the respect of the class': another sound bite of Teaching 101 cuts across my inner monologue in a condescending tone. I question how I am to implement these words of wisdom in a room where the majority of students are about as close to behaving respectfully as they are to sprouting wings. Despite my deep, subconscious lack of faith in myself, I prepare a plan of action. Calling it as I see it, and as fairly as possible, I begin adding names to my sanction list on the white board. I consider a myriad of offences, from slowly tearing the worksheets I had handed out to smashing the pens (that they had borrowed) under chair and table legs to, my favourite, the more traditional disruptive technique, engaging in deep, meaningful conversations with each other as if the work in front of them and I didn't exist at all.

As more names go up, a reaction ensues; they know these names come with detention. I take the moment of attention, even if it is hostile attention, to announce my cavalry charge. I call over the disgruntled noise: 'it is clear that some of you are not taking this seriously and so I am splitting the class in half. Those who have nearly completed the activity can come to the front for the practical; those who have not will stay at the back of the room'. I reason with myself that abandoning the education of almost half the class is worth saving the dozen or so quiet faces amongst that crowd.

One student does not take my new tactic well. During the ensuing argument, and considering his previous final warning, I send him to 'on call'—a sort of time out zone for students—in a separately staffed classroom. This was apparently the wrong decision. In a move of admittedly admirable solidarity, two other students get up, pack their things and walk out. At that very moment my head of department walks into the room. There isn't time to explain myself; my composure has to withstand until the end. It is as if we are watching a horror film: we both know it is not going well, but we knew that was probable when we chose the genre, i.e., a mix of 9y1 with my minimal experience. In the end there is usually only one person standing, but it is looking less and less likely to be me.

I choose to ignore my mutineers and for the final five minutes police my now divided classroom. I help some with the practical, and try to muster the confidence to stand by my tally marks. As I turn back to the board however, in the closing moments of the lesson, I see all the names from my sanctions list have been rubbed off. With a class of 30 and infractions so numerous, it would be impossible now to document this fairly—and given the erasure of names as a parting shot, the level of student respect towards me is all too clear. All of this hits me as I see those black smudges on the board, and for the first time (but not the last), I want to quit, right then and there.

At the end of that horror lesson, the remaining students waited impatiently through their two minutes before leaving. Somehow, the wreck that was my self-confidence deepened when I heard one quiet, sincere voice say, as he left the room, 'Thank you for today, Miss'. I must have looked even worse than I felt. This was period two of a five-lesson Tuesday, and I had round two starting in exactly twelve minutes.

The 'Working Conditions' section of my teaching contract had only one box ticked: 'isolated working'. At the time of signing, I found this confusing; especially given the 30 or so students I expected to be in a classroom with me. I didn't understand that 'isolated working' meant that you are very much on your own. This includes all the mutinies and all the moments of muttered (or shouted) abuse; even one count of being referred to as 'darlin' by a student in a tone that made my skin crawl.

This may not be—hopefully is not!—the reality of early teaching experience in all schools, but it certainly is in some; quite often in areas where effective education is needed most. Thankfully, my mentors were a fantastic support system, and it helped that at times I was able to retreat into the science prep room for a quick cry and a motivational pep talk from our technicians.

My main words of encouragement are that eventually the need for such support lessens, and enduring horror film sequences like that Physics class with 9y1 occurs on a less frequent basis. And I have not quit. The reality I wasn't prepared for, and what caused the most anxiety, was not knowing when such lessons might happen, and whether I would be able to mentally re-group in time for the next one.

Imogen Thomas is a Biology teacher from Solihull.

What They Didn't Teach Me About
the Demands of the Job

Bethan Howells

Learning to teach is very much like learning to drive. I vividly remember my very first driving lesson, when my instructor, after telling me a bit about gears and letting me practice with the pedals, suddenly told me to set off. I was filled with panic. For some reason, I didn't expect to actually drive on my first driving lesson (naïve, I know). But this is the first similarity to my experience of learning to teach. Although you are fully aware you are on a course that is designed to teach you to teach, I guarantee the first time someone asks you to take a group or class on your own, you will have to resist the urge to look around expecting to see a 'real' teacher they surely must be addressing. The important thing about this analogy, though, is that even though you feel thrown into the deep end in both scenarios, you will swim in both too. It just takes time and a lot of patience.

For most people, the first time driving without an instructor is terrifying and exhausting. There is just so much to think about: getting in gear; finding the biting point; indicating; checking your mirrors; checking your blind spot; changing gear again; looking both ways; getting in the right lane. No matter how many people said, 'Don't worry, you'll be driving without even having to think in no time' I refused to believe them. How could driving ever feel like second nature? There was too much to think about! I think teaching is one of the most demanding professions because of the sheer volume of things it requires you to think about at once. Within just one lesson, there's an abundance of things to consider: modelling; setting clear explanations; assessing for learning to ascertain the children's understanding; preparing further tasks for those who need stretching; having the flexibility to explain in a different way for those who don't understand initially; setting behaviour expectations; praising children. Even then, you'll still have that nagging voice in your head, asking, 'what about the one who looks upset? What could that be about? What should I do to make them feel better without disrupting the whole class?'

Just like with driving, at the beginning teaching is exhausting and overwhelming. And it is so easy to think 'I can't do this, this is just too much and I'll never be able to do it all!' I certainly had these moments often throughout my PGCE. That is where the driving analogy kept me going. Just like with driving, people kept telling me that teaching gets easier, that some things start to become second nature. Thinking back to learning to drive is what helped me to believe them and keep going. Although it seemed impossible that teaching would become second nature, and there would ever be less to think about, I remembered how I once thought the same about driving. Yet, now, I can actually feel a mild shock of surprise to see my front door and realise I've arrived home from work—driving has become second nature. I am only in my NQT year, but already some things are also becoming more second nature. When I first started, I would lie awake in bed rehearsing for hours what I would say to teach a particular concept; now I can simply think 'Ah, I'm teaching adding fractions tomorrow', and rest calmly in the confidence that I know how to model and explain this. That is just one example where teaching has started to become second nature for me, and I am hoping more will follow (assessing writing, please?). So, what I ask of you is, in those inevitable moments where it all feels a bit too much, take some time to remember how difficult driving was at first, and how second nature is it now. Trust me that teaching is the same and you will get there, with time.

And for those of you who haven't learnt to drive—or those who are just loving the analogies and can't wait for more—here is my next one: life is like a long-distance run. This one goes for pretty much anything in life, but it particularly helps me through the tough times of teaching. And it's not an analogy plucked out of thin air, or someone else's experiences. I am not a natural runner; I can't run fast or for very long, and

I have been prone to give up in the past. But I have found running to be an effective way to combat stress and anxiety. So, in the particularly stressful PGCE year, I found myself running more and more. It was one especially long run (for me) that inspired this analogy. I set off on a 9k run around my local reservoir. About ten minutes in, I found myself thinking about how far I still needed to run… I could see the great expanse of the reservoir lying dauntingly ahead of me and I knew I had a huge hill to climb at the end. In that moment, thinking about what lay in front of me, it took everything I had not to just stop right there and give up. This feeling resonated greatly with how I often felt on my PGCE.

On a day where everything has gone wrong and you begin thinking about everything lying ahead of you (placements, assignments, presentations, projects, job applications), it can feel so much like you just want to give up then and there. Here is the inspirational part: I didn't give up on that run; I stopped myself thinking about the distance left to go and concentrated on what I had to do right in front of me. One foot in front of the other. And this is what I ask you to do on those days where the PGCE, or teaching in general, can all feel too much. Stop thinking about everything there is still to do (because that to-do list is endless and will never go away), and focus on what is right in front of you, because only in doing this did I finish that run. I even managed the big hill at the end, which (bonus analogy just for you) gave me a sub-analogy. The big hill is those really bad days, where you have some extra challenge in front of you—maybe it's a lesson observation, a child whose behaviour is extremely challenging, or a big, scary meeting. You might have to take smaller steps, or pause for a quick breather, but whatever you do, keep pushing on at your own pace, one foot in front of the other. I guarantee the sweetness of crossing over that finish line and conquering that big hill will make it all worthwhile.

Bethan L. Howells, Bsc (Hons), PGCE (Maths Specialism). Teacher at Brandwood Primary School, Bolton, UK. Bethan is a young and enthusiastic NQT, passionate about creating lifelong learners and in making mathematics learning accessible and enjoyable for all.

What They Didn't Teach Me About
Teaching Art Education in a Challenging Classroom

Dr Joachim Broecher

I came to a school in the Rhine Ruhr area to complete my teacher training. In order to engage and inspire pupils with significant social and emotional difficulties, I developed a movable layout technique. This enabled me to teach art education in challenging classroom circumstances. I invited students to arrange pictorial elements such as human figures against a selection of backgrounds such as landscapes and city scenes. Students were encouraged to work on their projects with diverse artistic means and had great success.

References

Broecher, J. (2019). Accessing art with movable layout. In J. Broecher (Ed.), Creating learning spaces: Experiences from educational fields (pp. 55-72, chapter 3). Bielefeld: Transcript, Open Access Program. http://knowledgeunlatched.org/ku-select-2019-books-libraries/

Dr Joachim Broecher, Professor and Director of the Department for Teaching Students with Emotional, Social, and Behavioral Difficulties, at University of Flensburg, Germany.

What They Didn't Teach Me About
Leaving a Toxic Workplace

Kiran Sunray

Not everyone will think like you. Not everyone will be as passionate as you. Not everyone will care as much as you.

My NQT year has been coined the 'Baptism of Fire'. But reflecting on it ten years later, it was one of the best learning curves I could have had. Now a senior leader, the lessons each and every person taught me at the beginning of my career has shaped the sort of leader I am becoming.

During my NQT year, it felt like there was a real absence of kindness, compassion and passion. These three strengths were instead seemingly replaced by contradictory behaviours and purposelessness. It was a toxic environment, but it led me to one important realisation/ lesson, one which will always stay with me.

If I wanted the easier life, I could have adapted and become like the people who spent their time kindling fires instead of supporting each other. But I didn't. I cried every morning for the first year of my career. I wiped the tears away as soon as I heard the bell ring and smiled at each and every child who walked into the classroom. My classroom was my haven—and I hope it was a haven to every child too. So I left that toxic environment and found a school that valued and appreciated me.

Kindness is a golden thread that has strengthened me, and is a part of who I am as a teacher and leader.

They didn't tell me that teaching would become a love of my life. They didn't tell me that kindness is the most underrated teaching and leadership tool. I found that out myself, so I hope my experience can help you.

Kiran Sunray is a primary teacher and English leader. She has been teaching for ten years and is passionate about how English and reading can empower learners. Kiran is a Regional Leader for #Womened and curated the @womenedbookclub. She reviews books for Just Imagine, shares practice enabled through the OU/UKLA/RfP initiative and speaks at local and national events about empowering fiction, diversity and kindness.

Chapter 8

What They Didn't Teach Me About Collaboration

European folklore widely portrays the magpie as a creature fond of spotting shiny objects and stealing them for their own nests. I would suggest that an excellent teacher becomes a metaphorical magpie, searching for excellent practice elsewhere and bringing those ideas and initiatives back to their own educational settings. There is a plethora of ways that this can be done, some examples include: observing colleagues in your own schools; attending CPD courses; joining social media networking sites such as Facebook, Twitter and LinkedIn; and joining local or national communities for teachers. In this chapter, authors share their advice as to how staff working in education can work together to grow as professionals and maximise outcomes for children.

What They Didn't Teach Me About
Working Together

Emma Stanley

Collaboration (n)—The act of working together.

To those who are new to teaching, or are soon-to-be-NQTs, you are extremely lucky. You are about to embark upon a profession that values support and collaboration, and where access to such support is available in abundance if you know where to look for it. In today's world of social media, that is easier than ever. I am going to focus on Twitter because it offers a depth and variety of support for teachers.

If Twitter has taught me anything, it is that there is a plethora of teachers out there who are willing to share their time, their expertise and their resources simply to be helpful to colleagues. It makes me feel proud to be a part of this #edutwitter community, and it is one that I happily contribute to. This community of professionals is fantastic to be a part of for many reasons, including:

Sharing of Ideas, Resources and Advice

Need an idea for how to teach equivalent fractions? Need a resource for teaching present perfect tense? Need help with planning a unit? Simply ask and there will be a number of teachers who can offer ideas, planning or resources. I'll outline more about sharing in a moment.

Keeping Each Other Afloat

Had a bad day? Feel like you're drowning? Twitter colleagues are always on hand to offer you a virtual cup of tea and sympathy. Teachers come out in force to support those who are struggling, offering advice or a listening ear. Having this support can be a real help and it lets you know that you're not alone. Teachers who have been in the profession for years still have bad days: never feel afraid to reach out.

Celebrating Our Successes

Us teachers are generally modest folk. We do amazing things day-in and day-out without feeling the need to be recognised or rewarded (what could be more amazing than imparting knowledge upon the future generations?). However, sometimes we're proud of ourselves and want to share our success with others. Taught a really great lesson? Had great feedback from a lesson observation? Share your success on Twitter and there will be teachers who are there to offer a 'Well done' (or funny GIFs of people cheering). No one will see it as showing off, so don't be afraid to share those good moments.

Laughing at Ourselves

Teachers are a funny breed... we really are. We have a second voice, known as 'the teacher voice', which we will use at inappropriate times. We have 'the look', something we use in our daily lives without realising it. We can't look at a disorderly queue without wanting to arrange everyone into single file. I could go on, but you get the idea. Sometimes our jobs can get intense and stressful and we need a little light relief. Twitter teachers are there to ease the burden by sharing anecdotes, which help us to see the funny side of being a teacher and give us a laugh when we maybe need it most.

Debating Current Issues

Education is often a hot topic and there is always plenty to debate. From changes to education, to SATS tests, to best ways to assess, it's all there on Twitter. Also, Twitter is great for 'down time' with your colleagues, a forum where you can have friendly debates on anything non-teaching related too. Brexit? European elections? The best flavour of crisps? (This was a genuine debate.) A word of caution: many teachers on Twitter behave respectfully, but watch out for those who seemingly think it's acceptable to make unkind comments. You need a thick skin at times—not everyone will agree with you, and they can be quite fierce about it.

Continued CPD

Sadly, as budgets for schools are minimal, CPD is not always readily available. This is where Twitter can be fantastic at filling the CPD gap. Many teachers have their own blogs, or offer expertise and resources freely. Not only this, but there are often events, such as BrewEd, where teachers can get together to listen to their colleagues deliver fantastic talks on a range of topics. This is also a great way to meet teachers, many of whom you may follow on Twitter.

Sharing with Others—#sharingiscaring

I mentioned earlier, Twitter can be a wonderful place for teachers to share ideas, planning and resources. Sharing takes a number of forms: emailing out resources; sharing Dropbox or Google Drive links; or sharing links to TES resources. Here are some of my top tips on sharing:

1. Teachers have worked hard to produce resources, so if you use a shared resource, a thank you goes a long way.
2. If you use or adapt someone's resource/idea, please don't pass it off as your own. Always try to credit them where possible, or at least acknowledge that the idea came from someone else. Phrases such as 'I used ______'s resource...' or 'I adapted ____'s resource...', or (if origin is unknown) 'I found this idea on Twitter and...' A sure-fire way to upset people on Twitter is to claim an idea as your own. There are not many new ideas in teaching, as that wheel has already often been reinvented, but people can still be quite protective about resources they make/ideas they share.
3. Follow Twitter pages where ideas/resources are shared. Some top ones are: @rezorztweets (general resources), @Y6Support (Year 6 ideas/resources), @Team_English1 (English ideas/resources), @_Reading_Rocks_ (Reading ideas/resources), @Writing_Rocks17 (Writing ideas/resources), @PrimaryRocks1 (General ideas/resources).
4. If sharing a resource, accept that you may not be able to protect your work. It's not uncommon to see work that has been shared freely by teachers being sold on well-known sites. However, the

#edutwitter army are quite eagle-eyed, and if free resources are being sold, they will report it and share their disgust on Twitter. More often than not, the resources are then removed from the paid sites.

All of the above illustrates how Twitter can be a fantastic resource for teachers in a number of ways. Yes, there are those who behave inappropriately on Twitter, but most teachers are kind, supportive and friendly. I can't recommend joining the #edutwitter community highly enough: I hope I'll see you there!

To get you started, here are some of my favourite people to follow:

@MrsSarahMullin (Deputy Head in Birmingham. I had the pleasure of meeting her at BrewEd Solihull)

@SarahFarrellKS2 (Shares resources for SPAG and Maths)

@TeachUsMrBlack (Shares resources, including SATs style reading tests)

@primaryteachew (Lovely ideas, particularly for reading)

@Teacherglitter (Lovely ideas and generally a good person to follow)

@MrTs_NQTs (Perfect support for NQTs)

I have my boss @RobertMorrisse3 to thank for my Twitter journey. Without his encouragement to put myself out there and share what I do, I probably never would have.

Emma Stanley, is a Year 6 teacher and English Leader at St Alphege Junior School, Solihull. She is passionate about the teaching of English and regularly supports teachers with planning and ideas. Emma is most well-known for teaching the publishing of writing using double page spreads, and for her London-Underground-style editing stations that are used in schools across the country. She has been teaching for 12 years and is currently a Lead Moderator for KS1 and KS2 in Solihull. Twitter handle: @MissStanleyY6.

What They Didn't Teach Me About
Collaborative School Leadership

Sarah Mullin

I firmly believe that there is no greater resource than the skills and experiences of each other. We would not be where we are today if it was not for the guidance, wisdom and support of those who have mentored us, challenged us and given us the opportunities we needed to flourish as leaders in education. It is our responsibility to grow future leaders by providing a range of opportunities to enable colleagues to develop skills in resilience, resourcefulness and reflection. We need to encourage colleagues to step out of their comfort zones so that they are able to challenge themselves, leading to positive mental and physical growth.

I had the privilege of working with a school to develop the curriculum for Personal, Social, Health and Economic education (PSHE). This is a planned programme of learning that allows pupils to acquire the skills, knowledge and understanding that they need to manage their lives. An early audit of the curriculum included meeting with a pupil consultation group and gathering staff feedback. It soon became clear that the existing programme would benefit from a revamp. Some pupils admitted that they did not find all of the lessons engaging, and some teachers did not appreciate the value of such a curriculum; they felt the time would be better spent preparing for examinations. Things had to change.

After some careful research, sharing ideas with colleagues, and exploring a range of widely available resources online, I delivered a training session for staff where teachers considered the merits of a PSHE curriculum, thinking about the core values of the school and their personal philosophies as educators. Teachers were encouraged to think about the tremendous power they have to enable learners to become critical thinkers, independent enquirers and to blossom into confident, articulate citizens. It was important for me to instil in teachers a sense of responsibility so that all staff could adopt a positive attitude towards the PSHE curriculum.

My next challenge was to ensure that we revised the programme, producing lessons which were carefully planned to meet the needs of all learners. I wanted the lessons to be quickly paced and engaging, with an appropriate level of challenge. Most importantly, I knew that teachers needed to feel empowered by the lessons. They needed to be enthused and passionate about delivering the key messages and moral values. I could have written every lesson plan for each of the five years' worth of the PSHE curriculum myself—I had enough lesson planning experience to do so—but this was not what I wanted for the team. I made the strategic decision to adopt a devolved leadership approach, carefully distributing key areas to each member of staff, so that every single member in the school community could take ownership of the curriculum.

There were many different reactions to my strategy. There were the self-motivated teachers who could not wait to share their ideas. There were those who could see the benefits but needed further support and coaching to help them along the way. And then there were those who were reluctant to adopt a new approach and feared the additional responsibility. Confident in the belief that a collaborative planning approach would ensure that everybody could share in its success, I gave clear guidelines as to what was needed, set timelines and offered an open-door policy of support.

After a mid-year review of the programme, the transformation was evident. Some of the staff that initially showed reluctance were openly positive about the contributions they made and pupils appreciated that their feedback had been acted upon. Colleagues were publicly praising one another for their commitment and hard work, and the culture of sharing good practice soon rippled across the staff room. There was a noticeable improvement in pupil engagement and pupil behaviour in their PSHE lessons; feedback from staff, parents and pupils was increasingly positive. As a self-improving school, the curriculum was regularly reviewed and revised to meet the needs of each cohort of pupils, but teachers continue to be empowered and motivated to play a proactive role in its development at all times.

It was wonderful to meet one of the teachers at a recent education conference who had played a key role in the implementation of the new PSHE curriculum. At an interview for a middle-leader position, they were asked to share an example of where they had made a significant contribution to the school community. They enthusiastically discussed their experience in planning the PSHE curriculum, showing their teamwork skills, creativity and the positive impact that they had been able to have on others. Needless to say, the candidate got the job—and they attributed their success to being trusted with the responsibility to try something new.

We never really know what we are capable of until we try. Let's provide opportunities for our colleagues to show us what they can do!

Sarah Mullin, CTE, CMgr FCMI, FInstLM, FRSA, FCCT is a Deputy Head and Doctoral Research Student who supports training teachers, early career teachers and aspiring school leaders across the country.

What They Didn't Teach Me About

Building Collaborative Teams

Jasmine Jackson

My wise mother always encouraged me to be a lifelong learner and to stretch myself whenever I had a chance. So, I continue to learn while trying to make a difference, participating on many varied committees and boards inside and outside of school. Every now and again, there will come a call to lead one of these committees. I believe that teachers are natural leaders, planning and making decisions that inform their teaching practice, supporting their students' learning and setting the tone for the many interactions they have with their colleagues, staff, administration and parents.

Sometimes, you just have to say 'no' when asked to lead a committee. But often when these requests are made you are caught off guard. You are busy coaching or doing myriad activities in the school. Perhaps the request is based on your interests in a certain area, so you etch out space in your calendar to add this 'learning' to your list. Or you innocuously agree to attend a meeting and bring back some information. Surprise!—the next thing you know, you are chairing a committee for perpetuity. Once you have taken over the role, it is never easy to step down. Few people are willing to take on the role of chairing. The key is to succession plan along the way, which involves picking the right people.

Assembling a team that is the right size with the appropriate mix of personalities and skills is important. No team is free of internal conflicts, be it lack of trust, friction between team members, or never being able to get to 'yes'. But the goal is to minimise these conflicts. For one of the first committees I chaired, I actively recruited team members whose skills I knew would be valuable to meet the team's goals. My committee, the first year, was eight staff members and one student, and, seven years later, it had ballooned to 14 people. With later committees and boards I chaired, I became more experienced at supporting team members and devising strategies to improve the performance of the group.

Setting the 'Norms of Collaboration' (pausing, paraphrasing, posing questions, putting ideas on the table, providing data, paying attention to self and others, and presuming positive intentions) early helped to create a safe space for team members to share ideas and feel valued. I also had to reflect on how my bias, values and beliefs may colour my viewpoint, as well as the weight my ideas had on the group. I wanted our decisions to be collaborative, with input from all members. Over the years, I learned to be an active listener—to listen more than I spoke. After all, the goal of the committee was to come up with ideas together—collaboratively—and not for me to push my own ideas through without input from the group. I was very mindful and respectful of people's time. Team members were allowed to come when they could. Keeping a virtual team file and confirming agreed-upon meeting dates and times, followed up with reminders prior to the meeting, helped reduce anxiety and ensure high attendance.

Keeping minutes helped the team to remain on track with our goals, and helped us avoid rehashing the same discussions over and over. The minutes (following a loose version of Robert's Rules of Order), were taken at each meeting, and action items listed with timelines for completion. The role of secretary bounced around according to the committee members' availability. The minutes served three purposes: they helped keep us on task, they provided a road map, and they served as a historical document of the work done and input provided by team members. The latter is crucial so that you can be specific when you want to honour individual team members' participation.

Recognising team members' efforts and showing appreciation is so important. I recall an incident where I praised some colleagues for the work they had done to help move a project forward, but I had no knowledge that another teacher had joined the sub-committee and was also a significant contributor. I was trying to be a thoughtful and appreciative leader, but felt like I failed by excluding that one person. When I became aware of my mistake, I was quick to apologise to the person face to face and to make the correction at the next meeting to the group.

Celebrate! I try to organise private get-togethers to thank team members for their participation: a lunchtime or after-school meeting off-site or in school. In addition, I would send out a detailed email and announcement outlining special thanks to the team. I have, over the years, created certificates of participation signed by myself and/or the principal. And, most importantly, I have prepared handwritten notes, which shows that you put some effort into it, making it more meaningful than the computerised generic thank you notes. It speaks volumes when a leader takes the time to send you a personal, handwritten note, not the least of which is that it shows their commitment to building a school climate of appreciation and support for teachers' extra efforts.

Being a leader like I've described, and putting effort into building collaborative teams, can take a lot out of you. The last thing to mention—and it's one thing I am still working on—is to keep a healthy life balance. Self-care is important: flight attendants remind you to put your own oxygen mask on first when a plane is in distress before helping others. I also try not to take myself too seriously, 'because you ain't all that', as my mom would say.

I could not have achieved all the great results I did without the special skills and talents of every teacher and staff member who has participated on the many teams I have had the pleasure to lead. In essence, I was just the conductor.

Jasmine Jackman, BA, Assoc. Th, MBA, B.Ed Acting Vice Principal Peel District School Board, Mississauga, Canada. Jasmine is a third-year doctoral student in Educational Policy and Leadership at the Ontario Institute of Studies in Education (OISE) at the University of Toronto. She has been a teacher mentor, a facilitator of equity and special education workshops at the school and university levels. She is passionate about teaching culturally responsive and relevant pedagogy, volunteering, and working with underserviced youth.

What They Didn't Teach Me About

Working with Other Adults in the Classroom

Louisa Sellers

During my teacher training, we attended several seminars and workshops on managing behaviour in the classroom. They were all very insightful, offering many different approaches and techniques to suit a variety of teaching styles and settings. However, what they did not teach me was how to manage the behaviour of other adults in the classroom. In my years of teaching in mainstream primary and secondary, and now a specialist SEN setting, this is one of the greatest challenges in teaching; one I do not feel I was sufficiently trained for.

In KS1, we use phrases like, 'I shall just wait until everyone is listening', or 'while I value your ideas, please wait until X has finished', when dealing with shouting out or low-level disruption on the carpet—but what about when the chatting and disruption is coming from your classroom support? In my early years of teaching, I would become frustrated by constant chatter (not even always discreetly) from other adults in the room while I was attempting to deliver carpet input. As my confidence and relationships with colleagues grew, it became easier to address. I found that giving adults a group of children to facilitate carpet discussions helped, as did giving them pre-formed questions or actions to contribute so everyone played an active role in the input.

In secondary schools, the situation is no easier. I still recoil at the memory of spending weeks promoting a love of reading with a group of challenging Year 8's, finally getting to a point where they had all found a book to enjoy from the library, only to have a member of SLT come into the lesson to give notice of detention—to be spent in the library reading! Reading as a punishment?!

I now have a team of five support staff to manage, and it is not easy. Just as students fall out, so do adults, especially when everyone is so passionate about what they do. The best advice I have been given is to remain positive, shine a light on others and don't be afraid to be bold! Enthusiasm is infectious with students and staff alike.

What has been most challenging has also been the most rewarding. Good classroom support is worth its weight in gold. I have made several friends for life over the years. On a good day, we share in the joys, on a bad day we comfort one another. A sounding board of highly skilled people who care about the students as much as you do, keep you up to date with what's going on outside your classroom, and back you to the hilt when you want to try something new, is invaluable.

In times of frustration always think—we're in this together.

Louisa Sellers is currently a SEN teacher of students identified as having PMLD and a former mainstream primary teacher and secondary reading coach/librarian. Louisa began her PGCE as a mature student after a career in finance and experience as a community volunteer and young person's advocate. Louisa has seen education from many perspectives: parent, teacher, youth worker and school governor. Louisa is committed to inclusive education and building successful partnerships.

What They Didn't Teach Me About
Working with the Librarian

Elizabeth Hutchinson

I wish they taught PGCE students about the huge amount of support and guidance that is available from their school library and librarian. Not only are they a great source of resources—from books to online—but they are also a place of support. They will help plan a topic of inquiry, they will co-teach in your classroom, they will find and guide you to the help and support you need.

So how do you get access to this amazing resource? You walk down the corridor at school and find your school library. Look for the school librarian and say 'hello'. Tell them what subject you are teaching and ask for help with research skills or your next inquiry project. It is as simple as that! Not only will you find resources you never knew existed, but a wealth of collaboration possibilities, from tech support to international collaborations.

You may, however, find that the librarian is surprised by this request. This is not because they can't help you; it is probably because they are shocked that a teacher actually knows that this support is available—they may even need a little encouragement to give you the support you need. If this is the case, ask them to show you what books are available for the subject you teach; this is an easy way to start the conversation. Ask them if they are able to order more books on request. Some school librarians have a budget and love to spend it with the help of teachers.

Ask them to show you how to find the library catalogue and any online resources that your students will have access to. If you need help navigating them the librarian will be able to show you. You can even ask them to help you in the classroom to show your students how to use these resources for the first time. Once this relationship has been established you then need to ask about research skills. Can they support a project you are planning and how can they help teach the skills your students need?

Why is any of this important? Most of your students will Google the answer to every question. They will cut and paste the answers without really understanding what they have taken and will very rarely give credit for what they find. Your students need independent learning skills and your school librarian can support this, and awareness of their expertise is the first step to amazing collaboration for both you and your students.

Some of the ways the school librarian will help you will be to:

- Embed skills that will enable your students to use quality, age-appropriate resources;
- Teach the skills needed to navigate the internet effectively;
- Teach referencing and giving credit;
- Work with you to support you and your students.

What if you don't have a school librarian? Ask your senior leadership team why.

Elizabeth Hutchinson is a chartered librarian and a Fellow of CILIP. She is Head of Learning and Development for Guille-Allés Library, Guernsey. Runner up in the 2016 LILAC Information Literacy awards, she is an international presenter, a blogger and writes for CILIP Information Professional. She is on the Great School Libraries working party, CILIP SLG national committee and runs an online book club for school librarians.

What They Didn't Teach Me About #Bameed

Amjad Ali

Who Are We?

We are a grassroots network aimed at ensuring our diverse communities are represented as a substantive part of the education workforce for teachers and leaders in education. Difficulties in recruiting diversely is not a new issue; it is not something that has never been talked about. There have been programmes aimed at changing the visible face of education and there have been marginal gains. Change is happening, but it needs acceleration.

The Black, Asian and Minority Ethnic (BAMEEd) network is an open invitation to all for action to diversify all aspects of education. The support is for the graduate seeking to make the step into teaching as much as the Deputy stepping up to Headship. BAMEed will help make the step accessible, fair and achievable.

This is an open network. We seek to learn from each other and actively include all ethnicities. Our mix of culture and identity in the network engenders the ideal that we seek to develop in education across the UK.

Why Do We Exist?

The number of schools that are able to recruit and maintain teaching staff that are as ethnically diverse as our society is very limited. While there are many underlying issues that lead to this outcome, the two most significant factors are the lack of BAME people entering into teaching careers and the lack of support to ensure progress in those careers.

This grassroots network is dedicated to changing this dynamic.

What Can You Do?

Join us for free! Sign up for our newsletter, follow us on Twitter @ BAMEEd and come along to our events. Check out our speakers profile page; get yourself added. We have also produced a resource guide on how to organise an event, along with information on how to be an ally resource—for example, printing out our poster to show and share with colleagues. This information has all been shared on the 'Resources' section of our website. Do not forget to consider signing up to our mentoring scheme, either as a mentor or mentee.

Amjad Ali is an assistant headteacher and consultant. He is also the Co-founder of #BAMEEd.

What They Didn't Teach Me About #WomenEd

Vivienne Porritt

Was the role of women educators, and particularly women leaders, in schools talked about in your PGCE? Women dominate the workplace in schools at a roughly 75% female to 25% male rate. In primary schools 85% of the workforce is female, and in the secondary sector it's 62%.

This should be a profession in which you will thrive as a woman and be influential in strategic and organisational decisions. However, there still remain gender inequalities, particularly at the senior leadership level. The situation regarding leadership by British Asian and Minority Ethnic women is magnified given that the student population is becoming increasingly diverse. Rapid change is needed. Our intent is for you to be aware and participate in bringing about the changes needed so women can—and do—lead education.

#WomenEd is a global, grassroots movement that connects existing and aspiring leaders in education, and is growing exponentially. We campaign and use our collective power to make improvements and achieve equitable balance in terms of gender and ethnicity at leadership levels across all sectors of education. As leaders ourselves, we could see that greater support was needed for women in education: the rate at which #WomenEd has grown has been reflective of how many women are experiencing significant challenges in education.

#WomenEd especially campaigns around 3 of these challenges:

- proportionate representation in leadership roles
- reducing the gender pay gap
- increased flexible working practices

Let's look at these interrelated challenges.

In primary schools, women have a 1 in 15 chance of becoming a headteacher, whilst men have a 1 in 7 chance of becoming a headteacher. In secondary schools, women have a 1 in 109 chance of being a head, whilst men have a 1 in 38 chance. As I mentioned above, in primary schools, 85% of the workforce are female, and in the secondary sector it's 62%—we can clearly see that this is not proportionate. Additionally, in both sectors, men become headteachers before women and they earn, on average, more than women; this is true in nearly every category from classroom teachers to senior leader posts, as shown by Datalab (2015).

Worryingly, Simons (2016) highlights the waste of talent due to inflexible options for women teachers and leaders who have families: 'here is a huge bulge in leavers for women aged between 30—39. In fact, around 6,000 teachers a year—27% of all leavers in total—are women aged 30—39 (who make up around 23% of the profession overall)'.

So, we aren't paying women an equitable salary, it's much harder for women to become senior leaders and we are not creating flexible working conditions to retain them. That's what a lot women often don't know as they enter the profession.

That's why we want women in schools to be part of #WomenEd as we are challenging this situation and bringing about positive change. The best ways to engage with us are our twitter account (@WomenEd), our hashtag (#WomenEd), by reading our blog (https://womenedblog.wordpress.com/), by coming to an event, having a look at our website (womened.org.uk) or by reading our book *10% braver: Inspiring Women to Lead Education* (Porrit and Featherstone, 2019). Taking on potentially challenging situations is extremely brave and may challenge you. Be braver for yourself and for one another. Together we can reshape the leadership mould to enable a different type of leader to develop, thrive and succeed in our profession.

References

Education Datalab. (2015). 'Women dominate the teaching profession, but men are winning the pay game'. *Seven things you might not know about our schools,* 22–25. Retrieved from https://ffteducationdatalab.org.uk/wp-content/uploads/2016/02/EduDataLab-7things.pdf

Simons, J. (Ed.). (2016). The importance of teachers: A collection of essays on teacher recruitment and retention. Policy Exchange. Retrieved from https://policyexchange.org.uk/wp-content/uploads/2016/09/the-Importance-of-Teachers.pdf

Vivienne Porritt is the Vice President of the Chartered College of Teaching, the strategic lead for #WomenEd and she is also an education consultant.

Chapter 9

What They Didn't Teach Me About Self-Evaluation and Self-Improvement

As teachers, we are always monitoring and evaluating our work. We may be reflecting on a lesson during the journey home from school, we may be discussing what worked well and what could be improved with our colleagues in the staffroom, and we may have coaching and mentoring sessions with our line managers where we reflect on our practice. In this chapter, authors share their individual tips, strategies and experiences, exploring how they have used the outcomes of reflective evaluation to grow and develop as a professional.

What They Didn't Teach Me About
To-Do Lists

Alexandra Hastings

I am a lover of to-do lists. I feel as if they help me to collect my thoughts together in one place and keep me on track when I inevitably want to run off on a tangent. I've tried plenty of different ways of tracking the tasks I have waiting, but in the last year I've reverted to good old pen and paper.

Throughout my PGDE, workload was a big topic. As new teachers we were getting used to the different demands that we were going to face daily, and learning which were priorities and which were more wants than needs. However, it wasn't until I became an NQT that I really felt full force the pressure of a seemingly endless to-do list.

At first, I reverted to the techniques I'd been taught during my training. I tried to sort the tasks using Eisenhower's Decision Matrix, and tackle those that were both important and urgent first. Whilst in my training this method had proven to be helpful in organising my working life: here it seemed completely useless. I entered my NQT year with little idea of how to prioritise the tasks I was being handed; every email request seemed to highlight itself as both important and urgent. I struggled every day to work out which tasks would be vital to me reaching the end of the day feeling successful, and which would simply be a bonus. I felt overwhelmed, and it resulted in much of the practice I considered vital in my classroom being left by the wayside in favour of admin tasks, data drops and extracurricular duties.

I made it through my NQT year and, with the help of a change of school, I began to manage my workload much more efficiently. Moving schools helped me to feel confident resetting my own expectations of myself for classroom practice, and to feel like I was putting effective teaching first again. A few different strategies helped to do this:

1. I stopped labelling tasks as urgent/important, and instead focussed on what was vital for me to feel like a success by the time I left each evening.
2. My school had a staff calendar which identified each data drop and CPD session at the beginning of the year. I checked this regularly, so I never felt surprised by a task I hadn't planned for.
3. I learnt to be more effective at recognising which email requests were essential and which could wait.
4. I accepted that not every lesson I taught had to be exciting and innovative if students were learning and making progress. Dropping the idea of a 'perfect' lesson from my expectations meant I could instead focus on doing the very best job I could for myself and my students.

My to-do list is still long, and there are still things which inevitably drop off the end. I now know that in the grand scheme of things, these things weren't essential to me or my students. Now when things get left by the wayside, I know I haven't failed—I've just made the best choices I can.

Alexandra Hastings (@geoghastings) is Head of Citizenship and a Geography Teacher at Leeds West Academy in Yorkshire, as well as working across the White Rose Academies Trust as Innovation Lead. She completed her PGDE at Birmingham University in 2016, and last year returned to complete her MA in Teaching Studies.

What They Didn't Teach Me About
Planning

Doug Wise

They didn't teach me that learning can't be reliably and neatly compartmentalised into single lesson units.

When I look back, I'm struck by how much time I used to invest in planning. I found it a real struggle; in fact I could rarely organise my resources more than a day or so in advance. I remember being totally focused on making sure that students were visibly occupied for every moment of each lesson. That was paramount for me. My primary concern was in making sure that I had planned enough tasks to last the hour; I rarely stopped to consider what my students might learn from them. In short, I got things the wrong way around.

My planning was also particularly inflexible. I didn't deviate, and I can't ever recall revisiting aspects of the curriculum except during rushed revision sessions at the end of the year. Once again, the misconception that learning happens in discreet one-hour blocks was part of the problem. I thought that when I'd taught a lesson on, say, a poem by Seamus Heaney or a chapter of *Lord of the Flies*—covered the curriculum, so to speak—I could move on; after all, I'd gotten through what I'd intended to and the students in my care had dutifully done plenty of work. I wasn't aware of so many things: that engagement is a poor proxy for learning, that students forget a lot (like, loads), that students are usually pretty good at mimicking the behaviours we want to see—and so on.

Looking back, I don't think that a shared bank of departmental resources would've been that helpful to me. I had access to quite a bit of stuff from various online platforms, so even more one-off worksheets and presentations to choose from probably wouldn't have made that much difference. However, what I do think I'd have benefitted from is more opportunities to co-plan whole sequences of lessons. I needed a guiding hand to help me become clearer on the body of knowledge that students need to acquire over time, and not just in single moments. Quite possibly, for my first year, scripts to follow—direct instruction style—would've been beneficial for at least some of my lessons.

Finally, I think it would've been useful for me to spend a bit more time watching my Head of Department teach. He was brilliant. And he was brilliant because he appeared to do very little. He read aloud a lot and took the time to listen to the views of the students in his care; he also worked them really hard. It's clear to me now that he was doing it right. I think, perhaps, I thought at the time that he was bit old-fashioned and too set in his ways to change or consider doing things a bit differently. I know now, however, that he was actually really clear on what he wanted his classes to know and he knew the approaches that worked best. Above all, he was confident and experienced enough to take his time—unlike me.

Doug Wise is an English teacher and assistant principal from Bedford.

What They Didn't Teach Me About
Learning, Reflecting and Adapting

Mal Krishnasamy

Teaching is much like learning to drive. At first, you are concerned with what you are doing: changing gears, co-ordinating your hands and feet, steering, getting used to looking in mirrors—and you haven't even looked out the windscreen yet! Your first lesson may seem overwhelming, and you may feel you will never remember everything. Then, those things inside the car start to become natural. You may not even realise you are changing gear, checking mirrors and signalling. You can then concentrate on the road, road signs, pedestrians, hazards and be able to deal with them effectively because the other things are automatic. Likewise, when you first start teaching, you tend to worry about what you are doing, then you start to look at what the class is doing, then you begin to look at the progress each individual is making. The most important thing is to learn, reflect and adapt.

Mal Krishnasamy is a former history teacher and senior leader who is now the now founder of MalCPD Education Consultancy and Coaching.

What They Didn't Teach Me About
Celebrating Your Achievements

Sarah Mullin

In 2015, I established a social media marketing strategy for my school which aims to share the wonderful things that happen at school with our parents and their families. Our Facebook page is filled with images of our children playing happily in our beautiful grounds, information about the exciting daily events which take place at school, outstanding pieces of work, individual pupil achievements, and news about our community events.

But it is not just the children whose successes should be shouted from the rooftops. Use the school's marketing channels to celebrate wonderful lessons you have taught, initiatives you are leading or awards/recognition you have achieved. Celebrating your academic or career achievements allows you to build confidence, enabling you to reach for your goals. Be proud of your achievements; it's great marketing for the school as well!

Sarah Mullin, CTE, CMgr FCMI, FInstLM, FRSA, FCCT is a Deputy Head and Doctoral Research Student who supports training teachers, early career teachers and aspiring school leaders across the country.

What They Didn't Teach Me About
the Beautifying Trap

Emma Stanley

You've completed your PGCE and have secured your first teaching post. You're about to embark upon a career in a profession that is both rewarding and exhausting. Therefore, it is important to be prepared in the 'right' way—but no one really tells you how to do this. Twelve years ago, I was an NQT myself, and no one told me how to prepare for teaching, besides 'make sure you've planned your first week'. Now, as an experienced teacher, I can appreciate how important the 'right' advice would have been to me.

Getting your first teaching job is exciting. Of course you should be excited: teaching is a very rewarding profession. You're not simply walking into a 'job', but a career as a professional in charge of the future generation. Preparing for your new role as a teacher is crucial, but all-too-often excitement takes over common sense and NQTs 'prepare' by falling into what I call the 'Beautifying Trap'.

What is this? The 'Beautifying Trap' involves spending an inordinate amount of time preparing your classroom and not focusing on what's important. Your classroom is your blank canvas: Instagram and Pinterest are your inspiration, and you set to work turning your new space into a show-home. You will spend money on beanbags, cushions, inspirational posters, table baskets and an array of coloured folders. Trips to IKEA will become a part of your summer holiday and, when you're not out spending, you'll be 'popping in' to school excitedly putting up and arranging all the lovely items you've bought. You'll laminate. Endlessly. Then, after numerous days of beautifying in your classroom, you'll step back and admire your handy work, proud that you're well-prepared. Soon, the summer holiday will be near its end. You'll glance over what you'll be teaching in your first week, plan for those lessons and spend what little time you have left relaxing. However, is this really what being prepared looks like?

The answer to this is no, not really. Beautiful classrooms are lovely. I have one myself. If you were to walk into my classroom you'd see colour and attractive displays, but this is something that is built upon over time. At the beginning of the year, my displays are clear, ready to house worked examples and to celebrate children's work. What I'm saying is don't waste time creating a ready-made classroom when what really matters is the bread and butter of teaching.

What is the 'right' way to prepare?

1. Look over the teaching objectives for your year group. Do you understand them all? If not, ask. Ask your year group partner. Ask Google. Ask teachers on Twitter (I highly recommend this).
2. Look over the assessment expectations for your year group. The more familiar you are with what you're due to assess, the better.
3. Become a part of the teaching community. Twitter is a fantastic way to connect with teachers, and is a very supportive community of professionals who are more than willing to support you through your first year.
4. Ensure you know your school's routines, rules and policies. This will really help you to hit the ground running.

Once in the job, you'll realise how busy you'll become. Preparation is key. Get this right and your first year will be much easier.

Emma Stanley is a Year 6 teacher and English Leader at St Alphege Junior School, Solihull. She is passionate about the teaching of English and regularly supports teachers with planning and ideas. Emma is most well-known for teaching the publishing of writing using double-page spreads, and for her London-Underground-style editing stations which are used in schools across the country. She has been teaching for 12 years and is currently a Lead Moderator for KS1 and KS2 in Solihull. Twitter Handle: @MissStanleyY6.

What They Didn't Teach Me About
Getting Involved in School Life

Julie Fleming

During my training year, I was always seeking additional ways to help me 'tick off' another of the teaching standards; I offered to present assemblies, helped out on trips and always went along to the staff social events. In my NQT year, I continued to attend student camps, fundraise for school projects and sell tickets for a school play, but I started to feel that my teaching practice and student relationships were suffering as I became stretched too thin. I did not want to give up the extracurricular activities: I wanted to actively contribute to school culture, and I appreciated the benefits of seeing students from another perspective and using this knowledge in conversations with students. However, I had now been promoted: first to head of subject, then, within a year, head of department. I knew it was no longer sustainable when my own children began to complain that they got less attention than my students. Faced with this dilemma, while on a training course I asked the trainer, a retired and highly experienced headteacher, how could I assess which areas to let go and which to keep in order to maintain a good work-life balance. Kindly, she gave me the best advice I have been given—and my mantra still today as I approach ten years of teaching. 'Ask yourself this', she said, 'what impact will what you are doing have on student outcomes?' I wasn't quite sure initially what she meant. However, she further explained, that doing a good job would be about improving student outcomes, whether in attainment or their self-belief.

The key to choosing what activities I do now is thinking what difference it makes to my students. Faced with a choice of planning an improved lesson or attending a concert, it makes it easier to ignore the choice that does not make the most impact. I now never feel guilty for missing a staff social as long as I make that decision with students' interests foremost in my mind; additionally, an internal discussion goes that I will be a happier teacher tomorrow if the previous evening I spent quality time with my children. And don't be afraid to take short-cuts. Why spend hours writing a scheme of work from scratch if a colleague (whether in school or virtual on Facebook or Twitter) has already taken the time to do it. It's better to edit it for your specific needs and spend that additional time supporting or mentoring a student that needs a boost!

My final point would be to pay attention to our own advice: we often tell our students that 'there is no such thing as a stupid question', so if you are feeling unsure or that you think you might need a career direction reset, then find someone you trust and ask for help. There are so many good practitioners out there that would be happy to help; who knows—their advice might become your career mantra.

Julie Fleming is a teacher of business, law and economics. She champions vocational education in schools.

What They Didn't Teach Me About
Self-Theory and Growth Mindset

Lynne Fernie

How we view ourselves as learners has a major effect on our self-belief, motivation to learn and resilience. This is known as self-theory. Think about the following statements:

- Are we born smart or is intelligence a skill that develops over time?
- Are we born good at sport or do our abilities change as we practice and utilise strategies?

If you are thinking, 'yes, we are born smart/sporty', then there is a good chance you are an entity learner (fixed mindset). Alternatively, if you are thinking, 'of course we grow and develop our abilities', then there is a good chance you are an incremental learner (growth mindset).

Growth and fixed mindsets were termed by Carol Dweck (2000). Dweck's research highlighted that someone's mindset profoundly affects the way a person leads their life and can determine behaviour that has significant consequences. A growth mindset is the belief that your qualities and abilities can be developed and improved upon through one's own effort. Having a growth mindset supports seeing failure and setback as a learning opportunity, engages with issues to problem solve and means you are able to try alternative routes to success.

A fixed mindset follows the belief that one is born with particular qualities and these are not changeable. It is the belief that people are born smart/sporty, that failure causes distresses and disengagement or avoidance, and results in putting in less effort and an unwillingness to try new strategies to persevere. We can change our mindset by learning to hear our fixed-mindset voice and recognising we have a choice in how we respond, taking growth-mindset action. It is also important to recognise that we may only have a fixed mindset about some aspects of life, and that is ok if it isn't causing it distress or limiting our potential.

To support a growth-mindset approach in our classes we need to look at the strategies we support children using when responding to setbacks, the feedback we give our children, and the language we use. Modelling a positive response in class to setbacks—such as positive self-talk—is useful for children to reinforce the importance of seeking challenges and valuing learning from making mistakes.

The way we praise children has a large impact on their effort and learning, so changing from person praise to process praise is key. Person praise is praising the person, whereas process praise praises a student's effort, struggle, persistence despite setback, strategies, choices, choosing a more difficult task to challenge themselves, learning, improvement—the process. Thinking about our thinking (metacognition) and having an understanding that our language tells children what we believe and what we value is so important in teaching. Encouraging mindset language, such as adding the word 'yet' when a child cannot yet do something and engaging in daily learning discussions are other important approaches. Teaching children and young people how our brain grows and changes, and scaffolding strategies, is key in promoting optimal learning environments for our classes.

Reference

Dweck, C. S. (2000). *Self-theories: Their role in motivation, personality, and development.* Psychology Press.

Lynne Fernie is a practising Educational Psychologist in Scotland. Paisley born, BSc (hons) Psychology at Glasgow Caledonian University, MSc in Research methods (Child development) at Stirling University, and MSc Educational Psychology at Dundee University.

What They Didn't Teach Me About Developing as a Teacher

Sara Jayne Lewis

I'm not going to lie to you: teacher training is hard, and can be extremely testing to even the most resilient of students. Having a support network behind you is key. I was lucky enough to have a supportive family, friends and partner behind me throughout. The PGCE can take over your life if you let it, and in fact the library on the weekends did become my best friend. One strategy that helped me is that I am a list lover, with dozens of lists (essay deadlines, schoolwork, school deadlines) in my notebook; it felt endless at times, but the feeling of ticking an item off the list is highly satisfying.

A PGCE does not always prepare you for the classroom, with many trainees being thrown in at the deep end, especially in inner city schools where there is a high EAL prevalence as well as many SEND pupils in mainstream classes. I was fortunate enough to have experience in a SEND classroom before training to become a SEND trainee teacher, which gave me knowledge of behaviour management, differentiation and delivering creative lessons. I would highly recommend going to visit a special school for a few days; the routine and setting is completely different to mainstream and it is such a valuable CPD opportunity.

No one will be the perfect trainee teacher in a year; it takes time to develop yourself as a teacher and to put your stamp on your learning environment. The best way to learn is through reflecting on yourself as a teacher, observing other teachers and—perhaps most important of all—being yourself. The pupils want to get to know you as a person, as well as a teacher. Let your personality shine through; that's what engages the pupils. Pupils love a teacher who has a sense of humour, is happy and is always willing to go the extra mile for them. When I'm in my class, you'll always catch me smiling, cracking a joke or two and wanting to do my job and teach!

The role of a teacher will encompass so many other roles, including a social worker, parent, carer, friend… the list is long! But what you'll realise is how attached you will become to the pupils in your class. They become your family—you will eventually refer to them as 'your own children'. You grow very attached and protective very quickly. It helps that the children are also hilarious and will make the day go by quickly. They say the most amusing things without realising, and you'll find yourself wanting to write a sitcom by the end of the year!

It will all be worth it in the end. As a teacher, you will never stop learning. Take all the opportunities you can and enjoy the ride. It's a great career!

Sara Jayne Lewis, OA. Dip, BA (Hons), PGCE,.is an NQT SEND Teacher in Bristol, UK. Sara is passionate about supporting and teaching SEND pupils. Sara has extensive experience in outdoor playwork and supporting pupils with SEND and EAL. She has worked in SEN schools for 7 years and specialises in challenging behaviour, Autism and Down's Syndrome.

What They Didn't Teach Me About
Timing

Glenn Carter

During your time learning how to become a teacher, you'll have no doubt been told the importance of setting periods of time for each part of your lesson. Most likely, during observations, you'll have been scrutinised on your timing—you either spent too long or not enough time on a certain part. And it's because your timing… well… it 'SUCKS!' But what does that mean? Well simply, it means your timing is: **S**crewed **U**p '**C**os **K**ids **S**hift.

In the real world of teaching, you won't be scrutinised in every lesson over your timing, and it's important that you don't have that rigidity that's probably been drilled into you; you need to teach without worrying about not moving on fast enough or that you did move on too fast. The reality is that however well planned your sessions might be, there will always be times where you need to spend longer on something because there is a fundamental piece of learning that has not yet been embedded. To ignore that fact and move on anyway, 'because I gave myself ten minutes for the introduction and I've hit that ten minutes', makes for poor teaching. Providing questions and mini-assessments during inputs will allow you to decide on whether you need to move forwards or to reiterate a certain teaching point. Allowing yourself some fluidity in your lessons will only serve to make you a more adaptable teacher, and give the children more chance of understanding and progressing.

You've got your maths lesson plan: you're doing number bonds to 100. You start the lesson by revisiting number bonds to ten because that's a fundamental skill in number bonds to 100. But you find that they can't do it; it hasn't been embedded. You have two options: carry on and let them try the work to see if they manage it; or spend an extra 10–15 mins practising those number bonds so that they do understand it? Your plan states that they should have finished ten questions in 30 minutes, but if you took that extra time working with them to embed better comprehension then they may have only answered five in 15 minutes instead. Which do you think is more valuable? Likely answering most of the ten questions wrong—probably just guessing at half of them just to get them finished—or getting all five correct because you spent that little extra time going over it?

There have been times where I have completely abandoned a lesson during the input because they hadn't learnt the previous fundamentals of a concept that I was showing them. At that point, I needed different resources and a new set of tasks to help embed that. I could have limped on and been stressed about trying to work with most of the class to help them understand, but that wouldn't have done any of us any good. Pulling back, regrouping, slowing down, and pinpointing the areas of greatest need helped us progress.

It might take some time to feel confident enough to deviate from the timings on lesson plans, but adapting to the situation is what makes every lesson different every time that you teach it. You may have taught the same number bonds lesson any number of times, but I bet that the outcome of each time was ever so slightly different with each group of children. What you thought they knew, they didn't, and what you expected them to struggle with, they grasped. Have a plan and timings by all means, but keep it fluid and don't hesitate to stop, progress, or even abandon a lesson, if you know that it's the right thing to do. The children will thank you for it.

Glenn Carter currently teaches Y5 in Stockton-on-Tees in the North East of England. He is the History co-ordinator and is part of the Promethean Advocate programme. He has an MA in History and a background in museums. He has written pieces for the Historical Association.

What They Didn't Teach Me About

Planning, Preparing and Being Prepared

Uma Tadema

The importance of lesson planning and preparation was drilled into our heads throughout teacher training. Therefore, in my early years of teaching my ratio was 2:1 when it came to preparing versus teaching. I walked into class with every minute planned out and with a strange mixture of confidence—I was completely prepared—and nervousness, because I wanted to cover everything on my plan. Very quickly I realised that my real world students didn't conform to my plans, and there were times when nothing worked out the way I had so minutely planned at home.

While I do not want in any way to disparage lesson planning, I would like to focus on Plan B situations. Let us take a typical example: the lesson consists of audio-visual material and some piece of essential technology doesn't work. I get hot and bothered and try to figure out what to do for the next hour or so. I definitely don't want to have a labourious discussion session, especially with a large class with no preparation beforehand about what to talk about. For situations like these, it is useful to have a back-up plan; this could be something as simple as story cubes or board games. Story cubes focussing on different topics, like verbs, holidays or adventures, are compact and not too expensive. Language board games or customisable board game templates could be copied and laminated so that they can be used many times.

Each teacher has a different style of teaching, so I would suggest selecting an activity or two to keep nearby, something which suits you and your students. Important factors to keep in mind are that the material needed for the activities should be something general or versatile, light and compact so that they can be left in your bag all the time. In case of unexpected glitches, or even on days where your students just aren't into the lesson you have painstakingly prepared, you therefore have an educational and engaging activity for them to do. Moreover, at the end of the session you and your students feel that the session wasn't 'just a stop-gap' one, but one that looked at an alternative—but focussed—learning goal.

It is good to choose something that *you* like, because, in my experience, if you are passionate about something you convey that authenticity more effectively, and infuse your students with enthusiasm. In my case, since I like speaking and listening activities, I have a few laminated board games with dice. I also have a packet or two of story cubes, and a packet of story cards which can be adapted to review various grammar points or vocabulary. What we have also done in the past is to adapt a game like 'Name, Place, Animal, Thing' (where learners choose a letter of the alphabet and write down nouns which start with the specific letter for each category); for example 'Noun, Preposition, Adjective, Verb' to revise vocabulary. As you can see, the possibilities are endless.

Even after more than a decade and a half of teaching, just the thought of having activities such as these as backup materials makes me feel more relaxed, because I know that if something doesn't work as planned, I don't have to rack my brain at that already stressful moment to come up with a fun and useful alternative. I wish I had known this at the beginning of my career, which is why I would like to share it with you.

Uma Tadema, BA, PG Dip, CELTA, Cert TEB, MEd. After having worked in the service industry in India, Germany and China, Uma qualified as an ELT teacher in 2002 and has since worked in the field of education in Germany, India and Australia. Uma is interested in technology and agency in the classroom. After gaining her Master's and becoming involved with Cambridge exams, she is currently teaching in Germany.

Chapter 10

What They Didn't Teach Me About the Funny Times

Tales from Twitter

Your teacher training will prepare you for many things, but there are some events that we can neither predict nor plan for. We are working with children and young people after all, which can unpredictable. In this chapter, authors share their laugh out loud teacher experiences—and the common theme permeating each narrative appears to be: expect the unexpected!

Your teacher training will prepare you for many things, but there are some events that we can neither predict nor plan for. I asked the wonderful world of Twitter:

What is the funniest or most disastrous thing that has happened to you as a teacher?

I hesitated for some time about whether to include some of these stories, but after lots of coaxing, here they are in their raw form. I must warn you, some of them are not for the faint-hearted. Thank you to the following people for contributing your hilarious, unfortunate and sometimes painful experiences:

@Geo_Debs, @MrCartwright26, *@_mrmorgs, @rdkrdk, @jamesymcc,* @headley_miss, *@missc58, @MrsSingleton, @MissTurnerChem,* @HecticTeacher, *@EDR_man, @misslteaching, @russell_suter, @ SamanthaStockha, @hthesmaller70, @hsc_fe_teacher, @wonderwomanLH, @j0c00p3r, @LouisaW87686207, @MissStanleyYr6, @ Karbee10, @wayrf, @MidgetPope, @lkm_eng, @jennysteeple, @*

hannity24, @SamLEAF_Ed, @carolelhww, @GordonsGerman, @FRTeaches, @pepe_hart, @ChloeLiddiard7, @_mrDBu,@GymraesY, @LauraL_CHS, @KASMsHewitt, @FeDuncs, @MrHtheteacher, @MsWarner4. @MrSamPocock, @MattSPeet, @aegilopoides, @MrB_KS1, @TeachEnglishHOD, @efozzer, @MrCollard, @Oates27, @MissMermaidMel, @Headfornothing, @PEpartner_uk, @EngTeacherGeek, @MissHayre, @chipps_sci, @mxcharlier, @geolittlemiss, @mambo_andrew, @kylemarshesq, @rondelle10_b.

- I taught the same class for History and PSHE. I was being observed with this group and was due to be observed by SLT during PSHE. I taught them History by mistake. I got confused with the two week timetable—I thought it was period 3, but in fact it was period 2!
- I was walking with some students when one of them started cracking some ice with her foot. She slipped slightly and yelled for help so I ran over to help, slipped on the ice myself and ended up throwing my coffee all over myself. They still laugh about it!
- A new child brought a duck into school on their first day—a real one! We quickly set up a makeshift pen in the hall for hands on learning. The kitchen inspector only went and turned up unannounced (we still got a five star rating!).
- When I was pregnant, I was leaning over a child to mark their work and I fainted on top of the child. The rest of the class started screaming thinking I was dead.
- I was asked to go on a school trip to Blackpool. 15 minutes on the motorway when the engine blows up with a small fire! There were 40 children standing on the side of the motorway!
- Being attacked by a swarm of wasps on a school trip. This is now always on my risk assessment. It was made worse when we counted the children on the coach to find we didn't have the right number. I panicked for a minute until I realised that the extra child had been dropped off by a parent!
- I was teaching a group of girls and I just knew something was up but I couldn't work out what it was. At the end of the lesson, my mentor and myself investigated only to find a (clean) pair of pants stuck to the back of my dress!

- I had to rescue a child who had managed to lock themselves into the toilet at a wildlife park. Good thing I was a parent and knew all the tricks!
- In a phonics lesson, a child drew a circle on the carpet with his whiteboard pen to make a portal that he could disappear down because he was bored!
- At a PRU, students had hoodwinked a TA and gotten into a prep area where there were gas cylinders and very strong acids and they had barricaded themselves in. I had to bash my way through a window with a fire extinguisher to release the lock. The children loved the whole thing.
- I was reading a story to my class and they were all sitting perfectly on the carpet until they all started screaming. I looked at the door thinking there must have been a monster that entered the room. But no. There was a massive spider on my shoulder. I flicked it off… but it went straight in the direction of my class!
- I counted the children and their teaching assistant and trainee teacher onto the train whilst I stood on the platform showing our tickets to the conductor. The train doors suddenly closed and the train departed leaving me behind! I had to run for my car and meet the train at another stop!
- I spent the day in France with Year 7 who had been binging on chocolate and sweets since 7 am. It was manageable until we missed the ferry and had to sit on the coach for three hours in the blistering heat waiting for the next ferry. I can still hear the screams now!
- On a school trip to Germany we booked a trip to a swimming complex. As we were queuing, I asked my German-speaking colleague what the sign ahead of us said: 'Mondays and Wednesdays is nudist night!' We left. Immediately.
- I was once taking my class on a local walk. We crossed at a zebra crossing. Most children waved sweetly at the waiting drivers… except one child who decided to scowl and give them the middle finger!

- In my NQT year I was walking down a corridor and heard a teaching assistant say to a child who was entering the toilet 'wash your hands in the sink this time!'
- On a coach trip I stood up to tell off the children who were misbehaving. The driver pulled away and I fell backwards leaving the coach in hysterics!
- When I worked in London, we went on an excursion to Canary Wharf. The guards took one look at how the children were behaving and said 'no.' We had to go straight back to school.
- First lesson of the school year and I fell off a table whilst trying to catch the wasp that was destroying my lesson! I ended up being wheeled through the school on a wheelchair in tears—I had fractured my leg!
- A child was hysterical that they had lost their tooth down the toilet and the tooth fairy would not come. I had to put some gloves on and retrieve it!
- Falling on my back whilst shou… I mean, verbally encouraging children to stop throwing snowballs. Five seconds of silence ensued until I moved my fingers. Then everyone was in hysterics. One child mentions it every single week even to this day!
- I was stopped mid-inspection by an inspector who whispered 'Sorry Miss, but the child has just eaten a glue stick.' Cue my perplexed face. I went over to check and the child had indeed unscrewed the whole thing and had then eaten it. He was even still chewing!
- Class of Year 2 children were all lined up at the door ready to go home at the end of the day when a child projectile vomits and covers at least ten other children just as the bell went!
- I once mistakenly used a bible to kill a spider in an RE lesson. The look of horror on the children's faces was unforgettable.
- I had a student pull a tooth out during a lesson observation; a child once got all five fingers stuck in a test tube rack; during an eye dissection the eye exploded into a student's hair; a massive spider was in my room and I was petrified. A pupil got another teacher in who batted the spider at me and I freaked out!

- I was once so tired at the end of term that I fell asleep in the House Office. I would have slept through my whole Year 13 lesson if one of them hadn't have come looking for me!
- I had a pupil climb out of the window…
- Falling backwards into a large tub of water in front of 80+ Year 6 pupils and breaking my wrist in the process. This was at their leaving party and just two days before the end of the school year #fullsixweekholidayinplaster
- I was teaching a microclimate lesson on the school roof. I gathered all the children into a group and went back downstairs to the classroom only to find that one child was still on the roof, tapping on the window to get back in!
- The whole school was singing in assembly. The sound wasn't working so I turned around to flick the switch when suddenly I fell over a bench that was never normally there.
- I was delivering my first Sex Education lesson as an NQT. I was given a box of plastic penises with sticky pads to stick them to the tables to make it easier for the children to work with them. I ended up with 8 tables each with four penises welded so tight you could lift the tables. Stumps of polystyrene remained for weeks.
- I was sat in the computer room explaining the lesson tasks when I asked if anyone had any questions. One child put their hand up and asked if I realised my top was on inside out. I made a swift exit to the toilets!
- Walking out to the playground on the last day of school for summer feeling a bit sad about collecting my class for the last time. I opened the door and a football smacked me right in the face!
- On a Friday after school our netball club was short of players and so I offered to help. I went to catch the ball and a little Year 3 child came running towards me. I caught the ball, but tried to ensure I didn't fall on the child—I face-planted the ground. Bruised knees, hands and ego!

- I christened a new laptop with a little too much sodium in water. Fire alarm—kids running and screaming—Headteacher coming in to see small fires on the ceiling and desk!
- Really think carefully about open-toed sandals. Once, I decided to wear sparkly flip-flops in the height of summer… that was the day a child was sick directly onto my feet. It was thick, so when I walked away there were two perfectly formed footprints in the vomit!
- In a PSHE lesson I asked my class why they should not lie on their CV. A child responded with: so it doesn't get crumpled!
- I wrote a 'punctuate the sentence' question on the whiteboard during an Ofsted inspection. I didn't leave enough space between the words 'pen' and 'is' in the sentence 'the pen is blue'…
- I had the whole school evacuated during one of my fun science demonstrations. The children loved it. The Head… not so much!
- A pupil was standing beside the teacher when she was marking his book. He vomited all over her!
- When I asked my Year 11 class 'What major world event happened in 1914?' A genuine response was: The 1960s.
- I once marched up to a man exposing himself by the school gate. I angrily tapped on his window. He was eating sausages and chips which were placed on his lap! I ran away shouting 'sorry, I thought the sausage was something else!'
- A year 11 pupil getting stuck in a toddler swing on a fieldtrip and overhearing 'But why did you try to cuddle the pig when you are allergic?'
- It was time for English so I sat my class around the table only to find a dead mouse on the floor next to me. I do not know how I managed to stay calm!
- A student broke his pen whilst chewing and ended up with a mouthful of black ink.
- I was teaching a challenging Year 10 Chemistry class when I heard a strange clicking noise coming from a boy in the corner. I looked over to see a plume of smoke rising from his trouser leg. He was so bored he was mindlessly clicking his lighter in his trouser

pocket—and you know how flammable school trousers are! I took him straight to the Head of Year to explain himself. I found it so hard to keep a straight face whilst reprimanding him.

- I once had to untangle test tube holders from the hair of a pupil on the verge of a panic attack.
- I took some pupils to Westminster Abbey for Commonwealth day. The Queen was there and the Special Forces. One pupil managed to lock himself in the toilet attracting the attention of an agent who ended up becoming our bodyguard!
- We had a 'pet day' as an end of year treat for Year 2. One child held out a stick insect to show me. I screamed, fell over and flattened his mum, landing next to a tortoise! It was still the greatest day in my teaching career though.
- As an NQT, I played a game of Countdown with my class as an end of term activity. It was the one which revealed the best word at the end. After a horrible set of letters I hit the reveal button only for the word 'Va**na' to be printed in bold letters across my whiteboard.
- First day in my new job I was wearing a blouse. I was talking to Year 7 and realised the blouse had popped open—I now wear vest tops underneath!
- I love my job, the opportunities that we can share, the quality experiences that we can arrange and of course it's all worth it when the children, especially our younger ones, look up with those beaming eyes and smiles and say... bye bye Mr fat belly! Straight out of the mouths of babes.
- On a school minibus, a Year 9 pupil managed to vomit into a carrier bag. We pulled over and I got out and opened the bus to dispose of it. I picked it up so gingerly between my thumb and forefinger that the majority of vomit spilled out onto another student!
- I taught a tough, all-boys group and many of them were wearing electronic tags. We were studying the poem 'Limbo'. I was modelling a task on the board. I turned around and the whole class had escaped out of the window!

- Making jam tarts with Reception children. They had a go at everything including rubbing the ingredients in to make the pastry. Once the jam tarts were made and eaten one child said 'I love making pastry. I had really dirty nails but now they are clean.' I had eaten one of them too!
- When our new building was being constructed, PE lessons were off-site including water polo lessons at a swimming baths. One Year 11 boy lathered himself in shower gel and ran around the pool singing 'my milkshake brings all the boys to the yard'. I didn't know whether to laugh or cry.
- Twice when I was teaching Year 5, I had to speak to all of the boys on one occasion and girls on another to try and find out who wasn't wearing pants as a pair had been left at the swimming pool.
- On Open Evening, we decided to do a Gothic theme and borrowed a smoke machine from drama. On reflection (only made once the whole school were on the field and the source of the fire alarm had been found), maybe it wasn't such a good idea to leave two Year 9 pupils in charge of it!
- My most disastrous lesson was when a boy split his head open on a sink. There was so much blood. I was worrying about him all night. I was so relieved when he arrived at school the next day as normal following a trip to the hospital to have it glued.
- One of my very first lessons was on reproduction. I thought I had paused the video at the right part. I hadn't. The class were screaming as they watched a baby's head emerging during childbirth. I tried to blank the screen but the screen froze instead!
- A mouse suddenly appeared in a Year 11 science lesson one Friday afternoon. I had no idea what had happened until girls started clambering over desks!
- I had a child come back into my PE session having been in isolation. When I asked why he was back he replied with 'it's a one in one out policy'.
- A child got their hand stuck in a plug socket during a lesson and a different child was rushed to hospital after trying to leap frog a rounder's pole and missing it.

- My chinos split right at the bottom whilst teaching Year 4 in my first year.
- A pupil ran away in a rage whilst on a school trip to Chester because the Roman soldier wouldn't let him wear his helmet. It is funny now but was horrendous at the time!

What They Didn't Teach Me About
Eventful School Trips

Helen Abbott

School trips can be so rewarding! Enriching experiences, and so on and so on. I have definitely had my fair share of trips; some were good and some were not so good.

One particular 'reward' trip that stands out—for all the wrong reasons—was for a group of boys who had behaved extremely well in the previous term at a behaviour school. I, along with another female member of staff, felt brave and took the group to the zoo. The problems started as soon as we arrived. Bizarrely, they all ran in opposite directions as soon as we were through the gates, leaving the other staff member and I looking at each other with a very definite sense of foreboding. We split up. I found one doing a strange sort of dance on top of the otter house. Another was watching the lions before jumping out of his skin at a roar. It turned out he'd never been to a zoo before. Probably because of this, he also didn't realise the issues with touching the animals. How we managed to get out of there without a lemur stuffed in his jacket I'll never know. I had to watch him like a hawk and in the end just continuously repeated 'don't!' each time he edged closer to one. As I headed over towards the sea lions a lad appeared, racing towards me with a sense of urgency. I've never frozen like I did in that moment. 'He's in! He's gone in, Miss!' As I reached the sea lions the other staff member was already there, fortunately, pulling a boy off the fake rock enclosure.

As we rounded up the rest of the children to return home, one decided to run into a staff-only area whilst shouting expletives at another boy he'd fallen out with. We then had a thirty minute stand-off in the busy car park with him refusing to get on the bus. So my advice is to always plan for every eventuality, however unlikely it might seem—and over staff your trips!

What They Didn't Teach Me About
Making It to the Coach on Time

Danny Bullock

At the end of the school year, students who built up enough reward points received credit for tickets to Blackpool Pleasure Beach. Our principal at the time needed an extra colleague to lead a bus. 'Can you lead a coach? It will be an easy day for you...' (He had obviously not got wind of the last trip where the coach left without me—thankfully there were two coaches!) Travelling down the M62 with a few staff and 40 students, all excited at the prospect of riding some rollercoasters and no doubt eating so much junk the sick bags would be called for on the return leg, the driver began to panic. He pulled to the hard shoulder and ran to the rear of the bus and proclaimed 'Smoke, smoke, fire'. A small engine fire had caused lots of smoke from the back of the coach; thankfully it was easily stopped with a small extinguisher. The 'easy day' very quickly turned into hustling 40 students to the side of the M62 banking! The students had no real concern to the fact that cars were whizzing by; all their concern was focused on me ringing Pleasure Beach and demanding they stayed open longer! Thankfully, an hour or so later another coach picked us up, and before I knew it I was being dragged from rollercoaster to thrill ride.

Danny Bullock is an acting Vice Principal and Teach First Ambassador from Leeds.

What They Didn't Teach Me About
Starting an Exam

James Walker

SATs week can be very complicated, terrifying and stressful! A million questions need answering. What's going to be in the papers? How will my kids do? What will the pass mark be? Will we get a monitoring visit? Have I covered up all the boards properly? Will any of the kids break their arm over the weekend? Do I have enough protractors? Are they allowed tracing paper? Who gets extra time? What colour do I scribe in? Shall we have a free SATs breakfast?

Just when you think you have it all sorted, and have written up the all-important DfE school number (that the kids have been curious about all year!) and got them all revved up, you realise that it is suddenly 9:38 am and the test lasts for 45 mins. Never have I felt more under pressure to get the finish time right, as every second counts.

The kids are all looking at me wondering what the delay is. Then I start to panic! What if it gets to 9:39 am? I'll have to start this all again... It would have been so much easier to work out the finish time of a 45 minute exam if it started at 9:00 am exactly!

Finally, I pluck up the courage and plump for a time that looks right. Phew! Only to see my best mathematician pop his hand up to inform me that I am off by ten minutes... only to realise I haven't been to the toilet and the test is about to start! The problems of a year 6 teacher. Worst thing was that this was my tenth year of administering these tests...

James Walker is a Year 6 Teacher in Bristol and Talk for Writing Consultant. He is passionate about children's books and giving disadvantaged children the best education.

What They Didn't Teach Me About
Jumping to Conclusions

Ed Southall

To my detriment, in my NQT year I followed the old adage 'don't smile until Christmas' too strictly. In the last week before the winter break, I was trying to address my form group when an eleven-year-old child began interrupting me with 'Sir, Sir' and waving his hand in the air. I gave him a hard, cold teacher stare in the hope that I would need to do nothing more, and continued with my announcements for the day. His interrupting persisted, only now he had a big, smile on his face, which served only to wind me up even more. I told him to be quiet, but he remained undeterred. Finally I cracked and snapped at him. 'Right, you can stay behind after the bell and you can get your planner out so that I can tell your parents all about your poor behaviour at school'. He stopped at once and began to cry, and at that point I noticed him slowly dragging a Christmas card envelope from the desk back into his bag. 'To Mr Southall' it read.

Ed Southall is a lecturer at the university of Huddersfield. He is a speaker, author and PhD student.

What They Didn't Teach Me About
Keeping a Straight Face

Nikki Cunningham-Smith

Madness, I know, but when I went to school, the idea of not doing what the teacher told me was a completely alien concept. Don't get me wrong; I wasn't immune to getting sent out of the class when I wouldn't stop talking when the teacher was talking. Ultimately though, if a teacher said jump, I would say 'How high?'—even if I was muttering it under my breath.

And kids are funny. Sometimes when you really don't want them to be. In fact, usually when you don't want them to be. Mostly when you need to keep a straight face in order to keep control of a situation. I wish my PGCE taught me how to keep a straight face!

The first time I learnt that a pupil could ignore my basic request, infuriate me, and make me want to double over with laughter, was when I had asked a pupil to leave the room because they were being very distracting to learning.

In fairness to them, what they did I also found very funny; doing my PGCE in my mid-twenties did not guarantee more maturity.

A boy had apparently been being rather unkind to a girl at break-time, and it was spilling into my lesson; as I was about to tell him to stop, the girl, without looking up from her work, calmly told the boy that *'Your mom's so fat, the only letters of the alphabet she knows are KFC'*.

Now there is no place for 'Yo Mama' jokes in the classroom, especially when the learning objective has barely been explained. I'd like to say that I managed to keep a serious demeanour. Instead, imagine the hysteria that followed this outburst when they witnessed me turning my back on the class and laughing so much that you could visibly see my shoulders shaking.

'Look, even Miss Cunningham's laughing!'

Taking a deep breath, I calmly reassured them, 'No, I'm not guys. It's not funny to call people names—Alana, would you leave my classroom, please?', to which she evenly responded, 'Nah Miss, why should I?'.

Good question. Why should she? Gobsmacked doesn't cover it.

The worst part was, I didn't have an answer; I just wasn't ready for a child to disobey me so flagrantly, and 'because I said so' just didn't hold any weight.

Maybe I should have stopped the silliness quicker.

Maybe I should have sent the boy that started it all off instead.

Maybe I should learn how to keep a straight face!

If I was to tell you anything to get you through your formative teaching years, prepare an arsenal in your behaviour-management chest. Have some tried-and-tested responses to carry you through; don't take oppositional pupils to heart, be like a stand-up comedian and always prepare a defence against hecklers—and practice keeping a straight face!

Nikki Cunningham-Smith is an assistant headteacher, blogger and contributor to the TES.

What They Didn't Teach Me About
Expecting the Unexpected

Dr Mary Berry

No one told me how to cope with a technician opening a lab (first week of training) and announcing that the class teacher was 'stuck in a meeting, so Dr Berry will teach you about the kidney'. Unsurprisingly, I had no clue what to do, say or any aspect of how to deliver a lesson. We got through it, but I still can still remember the feeling of horror. You get used to thinking quickly and reacting to needs.

No one told me how to face a class—actually a full year group—having walked past them at the bus stop with my skirt tucked into my knickers (I was still training and had a young baby). I thought the wave from a colleague in a car was a friendly gesture—not an attempt to alert me. I had to teach the students who had seen my spotty pants. I braved it out. They forgot eventually!

No one told me that post-its, page markers, the right colour highlighter and my own stash of pens would become so important. No one told me about the sheer joy that having new stationery would bring at the start of the year or that the choice of teacher planner would become central to my happiness all year.

No one told me how wonderful it would feel when a student comes back, contacts you, or bumps into you years later and tells you what a difference you made to them. Fair warning though—all NQTs should also know teaching is incredibly hard; especially in the middle of long terms, with what seems like weekly parents' evenings, data deadlines and a class who can press all your buttons at once! But thankfully, for me the glow and warmth of the first type of interaction has always carried me through the latter times.

Remember support staff. For science teachers, the technicians are like gold! Look after them and get your orders in on time, so that when you mess up (and you will) you will be forgiven, and they will sort you out! Remember to thank everyone, including the children you teach. It really does help.

Be kind to the children you teach and the people you will work with, but also to yourself. When things get tough, find your tribe and talk to them. Remember, you have family and friends and they need you to be happy and well. If you are struggling tell someone. Most of all, enjoy teaching.

Dr Mary Berry is a Teaching and Learning Consultant. She has previously been an NCSL Senior Leader, Curriculum Leader for Science, Head of KS3 science and a Head of Biology. Mary completed her PGCE at Christchurch College, Canterbury and her PhD at University of London.

Chapter 11

What They Didn't Teach Me About Wellbeing

The media frequently tells us about the teacher recruitment and retention crisis. Teacher wellbeing is therefore more important than ever. As teachers, we often think about the wellbeing of our students and colleagues, and it is important that we do not forget to take care of ourselves. In this chapter, authors discuss some of the more challenging aspects of teaching, and offer advice and tips about how we can look after ourselves.

> *'You can't pour from an empty cup. Take care of yourself first'*
>
> *anon.*

What They Didn't Teach Me About
Self-Care

Hannah Wilson

With an increasing focus on mental health and wellbeing in our schools, we need to remember to put on our oxygen masks first. Teachers can quickly become martyrs. Yes, it is all about the children, and you will bend over backwards and give vast amounts of your time and energy to support them—but this should not be at the expense of your own health and sanity.

You need to accept that your work as a teacher is never done, so early on you need to form good habits and routines. As well as creating a daily/weekly/fortnightly schedule for your lessons, duties, clubs and deadlines, which I am sure will become a work of art, and alongside highlighting all of your school holidays, I would strongly recommend you put 'me time' in your diary.

When you are busy, stressed and feeling under pressure, the first things that go are your diet and your sleep. Next, you will begin to drop out of your healthy routines, such as going to the gym or going for a walk, and you may strip your hobbies and interests back. Then you will start cancelling on friends and family.

Life is about balance. Teaching is a great vocation but it can become all-consuming. You need to set clear boundaries for yourself to ring fence time for you, or it can completely take over your life.

My tip is to have one diary/schedule, put it all in Outlook or some other calendar program, and download the app to your phone. This way, when you are out with friends and trying to arrange socials, you have it all in one place. Then, colour code your schedule; for example,

I had blue for lessons, green for training, red for duties. Have a colour for your mental health and wellbeing, for your socials. I chose yellow. I could then see at a glance if I had enough 'me' time to recuperate and recharge each day/week.

Put in regular things that you will commit to for your physical and emotional wellbeing; for example, going food shopping on a Saturday morning, cooking a batch of meals on a Sunday night, playing netball on Tuesday night and going to the cinema on a Thursday night. This will help you get into a routine, both in and out of school.

Hannah Wilson. Head of Secondary Teacher Training at University of Buckingham (former Executive Headteacher of two start-up schools in Oxfordshire) and Co-founder of #WomenEd.

What They Didn't Teach Me About
Cultivating Positive Mental Health

Caroline Lisa

You will never be the best teacher you can be if you don't put your physical and mental health first.

The crux of this section is to encourage you to create the habit of prioritising yourself. Make time for you. Time really is all we have, so spend it wisely. By this I mean try to find the time to reflect on your own wellbeing, and consider strategies that will support you to be even more effective. Having positive mental health is more than the absence of a mental health problem; it is the ability to assess your thinking, feeling and doing in order to live your best life. It isn't rocket science; it's just about creating and maintaining positive habits. Our wellbeing is all about our ability to balance the psychological, social and physical resources we have against the challenges we face. Our balance point will depend on a range of different factors, but it's empowering to remember our emotional intelligence, resilience and psychological state can be managed, developed and strengthened by cultivating some simple, positive habits.

The **PERMA** model of wellbeing was designed by Martin Seligman, founder of Positive Psychology. These five core elements of psychological wellbeing and happiness are believed to help people reach a life of fulfilment, happiness and meaning. It is the basis of many wellbeing programs and initiatives, and it is what I base my work on now. I am passionate about this approach being used in education; everyone deserves the right to learn how to live a happy, engaging life. If we want young people's emotional wellbeing and mental health to improve, as adults we need to embody and project all that is wellbeing for them.

Positive emotions: *cultivate optimism, calm, gratitude, etc., in order to build resilience.* Mutter the word 'teacher' and you often conjure images of stress. You will meet a lot of stressed out/burnt out teachers; plan and work on how not to become one of them. We can't avoid some kind of stress or pressure—you may even thrive on it initially—but it isn't sustainable. You must manage your own emotional wellbeing, find your calm, get out of your head, run, stretch, draw, paint—just don't let life kid you that you don't have time. Interrupt what drives you mad and frustrates the hell of out of you with what you love and inspires you to keep it all in perspective.

Gratitude:—*it's a mindset gamechanger.* Left to its own devices, our minds will dwell on the negative and everything that is wrong with the world in an effort to protect you from perceived danger. Try to challenge this negativity bias; instead of starting each day with this is what I *have* to do, choose to see the good and remind yourself of what you *get* to do, what you have the privilege of doing each day at work.

Engagement: *nurture your own creativity and strengths.* When we are up against it, pressured with deadlines and barely holding it together with all the *have-to* things on our list, it is paramount you make time for the *want-to* stuff as well. Don't forget to play. Often teachers become creatures of habit, and end up living in their own world—their work world—because that's how schools and the system work. Try not to do that. Stay curious, creative and fresh. You have to enjoy what you do; if you enjoy it then you'll overcome all kinds of obstacles. Know and use your personal strengths and never let them habitually slide, make time for the things you love to do, the things which energise you and make you, you. There's so much value in play and exploration—try not to let those things go too soon. Kids need to see that play and fun equates to learning; to embed it you need to embody it first.

Relationships: *create and maintain authentic, positive and supportive relationships.* Surround yourself with people who get it: feed off their enthusiasm and share concerns and stresses about the role. Open yourself up to collaboration and be prepared to learn from everyone. At the same time, try not to be friends with solely teachers, which easily happens. Connect with people who haven't got a clue what planet you are on professionally, those who don't know their EALs from their FSMs. They will remind you of life beyond your role as a teacher and keep things in perspective so you don't get too serious. Yes, you are a role model, and yes, you have a responsible job, BUT you can still have fun and keep your authenticity—you will need it in order to connect to the kids because they can smell insincerity a mile off!

When it comes to the kids themselves, a good connection is vital. Don't dictate, and allow yourself to learn from them. A good teacher obviously needs to know their stuff and be able to communicate it, but the sign of a *really* good teacher is to be able to engage the kids by igniting their own curiosity and imagination. Your students can be so full of ideas and inspiration; in fact, they really have been my biggest teachers. Oh, and embrace the most challenging kid, for he/she is probably carrying your biggest lesson.

Meaning: *relish the sense of being connected to something bigger than just the self.* Wellbeing isn't just about cultivating positive emotions and mindsets, it extends into having a sense of purpose and meaning, something which allows us to feel we are contributing to something bigger than just ourselves. The good news is teaching can give you all that. I am kind of hoping these are the main reasons you have chosen to enter the field. Whatever you do, try not to forget what makes this job more than a job. There is no better feeling than living for a purpose, and knowing what you have done or said on one particular day has made a positive difference to someone else life—academically or personally. Hold on to those moments: post-it note them, Instagram them, Snapchat them; do whatever it is you do, just don't forget them or lose them in the vortex of teacher 'busyness'. They are your soul food and spirit ignition; have them available to relive when you need it most.

Accomplishment: *nurture self-belief and your ability to pursue and accomplish goals.* Spend a bit of time considering your career goals, become aware of your mindset and how you talk to yourself. I really do believe we can achieve any goal we wish if we approach it with the right self-talk and mindset. Teaching will bring you challenges, pulling you in different directions, one moment telling you this is important and the next telling you that is more important. You will need to decide your priorities, your focus and the type of mindset you approach each task with. With every challenge comes a great sense of achievement in fulfilling something important to us.

Challenge and achievement are an important part of building resilience and cultivating a growth mindset and optimism. Alongside this is the ability to learn from mistakes. The world will go on turning with or without that mistake you made, whether it was the data entry you inputted wrongly or the time you forgot your cover class. You will mess up, and that's okay, we all did/do; the important thing is to look for the lesson, learn from it, but then be sure to let it go.

To wrap this up, I hope your teaching career is a successful one—and by successful, I mean positive, inspiring and meaningful. Cultivate your mindset, check in with your emotions and spend time with the 'radiators'. Regularly reflect on who or what is helping you reach your goals, and don't lose sight of the reason you started. Stay curious, inspired and creative, and teach how you hopefully choose to live—out of intent, not habit.

Caroline Lisa, BA (Hons) Fine Art, PGCE, AST Behaviour Management and Creativity, RYT200hr Yoga teacher, MISP Mindfulness teacher, Founder and Director of SELF School—Personal Development and Wellbeing, Wellbeing in Education Consultant. Having worked in SEMH for most of her career, both in the UK and Australia, she founded Self School in 2016 in response to the rapid decline in young people's mental health. She is currently studying Positive Psychology.

What They Didn't Teach Me About
Being a Parent-Teacher

Emma Sheppard

Before I became a parent, I didn't give much thought to how much I would miss my teacher identity. My daily schedule was so fast-paced that I didn't even have time for such reflection until I began my first maternity leave in June 2016. In the half-joking words of my Line Manager at the time (luckily, we shared a dry sense of humour): I had one thing on my mind in the run up to GCSE exams, and it wasn't my unborn child.

When I eventually did start my maternity leave, therefore, the dramatic shift of gears took me by surprise. I was left feeling purposeless, drifting, isolated—a little unsure how to structure my day around this new small human, and yearning for the buzz of my subject and pedagogy. Being almost solely responsible for keeping a baby alive is a high calling indeed, but it simply didn't make demands of my brain in the same way that teaching did.

Founding The Maternity Teacher Paternity Teacher Project was a way to hold on to my teacher identity *and* enjoy my maternity leave in a way that suited me. Quickly, the project's focus on flexible and self-directed CPD, and visible role-modelling of parents in professional and intellectual spaces, tapped into a real need in the parent-teacher community. There were lots of teachers feeling exactly the same way as me, and celebrating each other's professional and personal development, networking in baby- *and* brain-friendly venues, and supporting each other as we returned to the classroom was hugely empowering.

It had never occurred to me to ask whether parenting and teaching were compatible roles. After all, the school holidays are a blessing that many parents in other industries can only dream of—but the early years can be difficult. A transition period occurs during which it's necessary to find a new routine, a new persona and work out how to balance your priorities—both your personal loves and your professional passions. 'What they didn't tell me' before becoming a parent-teacher was that with the right support network, philosophy and working environment, it *is* entirely possible to teach and parent happily and successfully, and to thrive in both roles.

The MTPT Project inspires, empowers and connects teachers choosing to complete CPD during parental leave. Their two-module Accreditation provides teachers with coaching and an opportunity for self-directed CPD whilst they are out of the classroom with their new babies, and as they return to work. The MTPT Project hosts regional coffee mornings across the UK, and works with schools to help them to be more 'life friendly' employers.

Emma Sheppard is the founder of the #MTPT Project. She is an English teacher, Lead Practitioner in charge of Initial Teacher Education and Teach First Ambassador.

What They Didn't Teach Me About
the 'Two-Ness' of an Educator

Iwinosa Idahor

The cleverly poignant activist and author, W.E.B. DuBois, coined the phrase 'double consciousness' in his world-renowned text, *The Souls of Black Folks*. The phrase refers to the presence of two often opposing identities present within a person. Originally written to reflect the social climate of the time, it remains relevant today as African Americans continue to strive to assimilate into mainstream culture while maintaining an authentic sense of self; a sense of 'two-ness' or duality of one's existence. As a former classroom educator, I have learned the importance of embracing and nurturing this 'two-ness'. This duality is comprised of an educator identity and an out-of-school identity, both equally necessary to establishing and maintaining a balanced and fulfilling professional and personal lifestyle.

Doe-eyed and excited about finally getting my own classroom and the chance to apply the skills and lessons learned as I prepared to work with my new students, my naiveté was apparent. The time, energy and resources that were required of my new position as a classroom educator became more evident as I agreed to volunteer for one more event or join another committee. Balance and self-care were not always at the forefront of those discussions and meetings.

Seeking opportunities to learn and grow professionally is necessary to a teacher's overall development. Too many educators work diligently in *and* out of the classroom through working with students, developing lesson plans and trying to meet the many other demands of being an educator, but there is a part of our being that also deserves to be nurtured. There is another aspect of our identity that desires to be fed with adventure, discovery, laughs, rest, exploration and love. It is easy to be consumed with guilt and fear, stemming from a lingering sense of perfectionism and a fear of failure, which can be the biggest hindrance to obtaining the balance that is essential to being an effective and fulfilled educator.

Years passed and I wish that I took heed to the countless requests from my body, heart, family and friends to simply 'take it easy'. Long hours on the job were validated by pay increases and other superficial rewards and forms of recognition. Internalised cultural and behavioural norms guided my desire to be a 'great' educator. It was easy to believe that wanting to develop and maintain a lifestyle that allowed me to grow in various areas of life—professionally, academically, spiritually and personally—was nearly impossible, and even undesirable, as a budding professional. On top of that, there was the 'if it's not broken, why fix it?' concept. If things were going well as an educator, students were growing academically, parents were content and colleagues were getting along, what was the problem? However, there was brokenness... and frustration, fatigue and fear.

Self-care is vital. Learn and remember your worth not only as an educator, but as a human being. I learned that my worth as an educator is not determined by the number of hours that I spend at school after the bell rings or how many committee meetings I participate in. It is determined by the number of lasting relationships that I am blessed to be a part of and the students whose lives I was/am able to enrich and impact through meaningful dialogue and classroom teaching experiences. I also feel incredibly grateful for, and validated by, the families that were emboldened to engage in the life of the school and by the memories that were created during school activities and events. Waiting for the time to be exactly right to begin developing and embracing your personal identity, aside from that of a pedagogue, can prove to be too late. As an educator, I learned to work smarter, not harder. Utilising technology and empowering my students to take the lead on their learning proved to alleviate a lot of the weight that came with being in the classroom. It also fostered a community where collaboration and engagement were the norm. Simply put, I had to take a step back—and I am still doing so. I realised that 'future me' deserved to be healthy, fulfilled and purposeful, and it will not happen overnight. A decision to commit to a lifestyle that allows me to continuously better myself had to be made. I couldn't be alarmed when changes don't occur overnight, and I had to remember that small progress is still progress. I decided to pursue my goals beyond the classroom, and it didn't make me any less of a 'good' educator. In fact, life is richer and your circle is expanded. Recognizing the 'two-ness' that exists within me is acknowledging the beautiful complexity that makes life truly worth living.

Iwinosa Idahor has a BS in Middle Grades Education, MEd in Counsellor Education from NC State University. Currently pursuing a PhD in Educational Leadership, Policy and Human Development. Taught Social Studies and Language Arts. Works in higher education in Student Engagement. Research interests include examining the qualities of exemplary school leadership, school discipline practices, the implementation and evaluation of equity initiatives, the experiences of immigrant and first-generation students of the African Diaspora and participatory action research. Professionally, wants to continue her work in providing students and families with an equitable educational experience.

What They Didn't Teach Me About
the Wellbeing of Myself and Others

Helen Abbott

Make friends with the cleaners, site managers, technicians. You might not come across them every day, but when you need them they will be more likely to help you. It's also about general respect and kindness; it shouldn't really need pointing out, but the amount of times I've seen teaching staff being rude to cleaners astonishes me! Why? It should go without saying you should be pleasant to everyone. Thankfully it's not something I have witnessed in my current school. It's also something we should always be modelling for the students; we can't preach respect to them if we don't follow it ourselves. Also, make time to support teaching assistants and cover supervisors. Cover supervisors have a really difficult job, so try and help them when you can!

Lastly, invest in self-care. Take responsibility for your own mental health and wellbeing. If workload is a problem, speak to your line manager and union rep. If you have a personal problem, don't be afraid to speak out about it. If you have an unsupportive school, go out and find a better one! They are out there.

Helen Abbott, BA (Hons), PGCE, NPQML is Head of Foundation Curriculum at an Alternative Provision Academy in the North West. She is an art specialist fervently believing in the therapeutic benefits of the subject. Helen is currently working on her NPQSL, completing a whole school project on Mental Health and Wellbeing.

What They Didn't Teach About the Importance of Sleep

Mark Lehain

I taught in secondary schools for 15 years and can honestly say that I enjoyed pretty much every single day at work during that time. Prior to joining the profession, I had worked in the city for a couple of years. After graduating, I really enjoyed the time away from schools and education, and it gave me the chance to grow up and mature a bit. It also enabled me to get into reasonably disciplined ways of working and managing my time, and this proved to be invaluable when I started my PGCE in September 2002.

Everyone tells you in advance how hard it is to be both a student and a teacher simultaneously, but it isn't until you experience it yourself that you know quite what they mean by it. Keeping up-to-date with Professional Studies, Subject Studies, and the associated assignments—as well as your form group, lesson planning, marking, report writing, teaching and so on—is quite the challenge. Obviously, all these thing take longer to do at the start. There will always be a tendency for them to creep into the late evening, early mornings or weekends. I didn't mind this too much myself—I didn't have children at that point and my wife is a teacher so knew the score. So I revelled in the hard work and felt well-supported by the PGCE team and peers. However, I really wish I'd learned sooner to think about the opportunity cost of an extra hour's planning in the evening. It was my wife—who'd been in teaching for a few years—who asked me at 11:30 pm one night, some point in my second or third year, 'will your pupils tomorrow be better off with you doing another hour's planning or getting an extra hour's sleep?'

It was a light bulb moment.

It's been a guiding principle for me ever since. Even as I got better and more efficient with out-of-class stuff, there were still times when I would have to work during evenings or weekends. However, I would always do a quick mental calculation as to whether or not the time taken to write those reports/plan that lesson again/check those books was a better use than just switching off or going to bed.

Recognising that a well-rested teacher might be more effective than a better-planned one is absolutely key to getting through the early years of teaching. Whether it's because you're quicker on your feet, or just more relaxed and less likely to escalate situations, a perky practitioner needing to slightly wing it is probably going to make more of a difference than a prepared, but exhausted one.

In fact, if I'm being completely honest, this is probably true for everyone working in a school—including the children. Whilst it's completely the responsibility of parents to ensure their children get into good sleep habits, reminding pupils to plan their studies so they can unwind and get enough shut-eye never goes amiss.

Mark Lehain trained as a maths teacher in 2002 and later became a Head of Department and Assistant Head before leading a campaign to open Bedford Free School in 2010. Mark became the school's Principal at the school when it opened in 2012 and remained in post for five years before becoming the Director of Parents and Teachers for Excellence, a group encouraging schools across the nation to adopt best practice in the areas of behaviour, knowledge-rich curricula, rigorous assessments and cultural enrichment.

What They Didn't Teach Me About
Using My Teacher Voice

Andrea Walker

Teacher voice! We've all done it. With friends, family—or even the unsuspecting assistant at the supermarket checkout. Forgetting that we have left the school premises, or our mind so busy with multiple 'tabs' open and running at the same time, all fighting for priority, it just slips out. We may not even notice that it has happened, or possibly have learned what the raised eyebrows mean and it has now become almost comical.

You may be standing in the classroom and your old history teacher or your mum suddenly takes control, and you are left standing there thinking 'when did I turn into....'?

Of course, when we speak about 'teacher voice', we mean things such as tone and content, what you say and how you say it. What doesn't get spoken about is your actual voice itself, or vocal health.

As a teacher—possibly even more so because I teach music and drama—I would consider my voice to be the most important tool in my collection. Yet, during my career so far, very little has ever been said about vocal health by schools, and I have never received any CPD on the subject from a specialist.

Teachers possibly use our voices in a more exaggerated way than most other professions on a day-to-day basis and, as a result, are prone to vocal-health issues. If someone has a tired or stressed voice, you would no doubt tell them to rest it and drink plenty of water; that's all well and good for some, but not necessarily when you have a class of 30 sitting in front of you and the toilet is two miles away in another block! I have taught lessons where I have barely any audible voice; rather than taking the day off, especially early on, I thought that just whispering would be a suitable communication. I learned later on that it creates more stress to the voice, so don't do it. Also, along these lines, take a couple of sips of water rather than clearing your throat.

Like with children, where we describe voices as outside or inside, we as teachers require different ways in which to speak: one to one, to the class in a small room, above a room full of percussion, or across a large sports hall. The issues arise when we do not change *the way* in which we speak; we tend to adjust the power of our voice, rather than just making it *sound* louder. Consider your posture, breathing and use a lower vocal pitch. If you are filling your lungs, the power of your voice will come from there rather than feeling that strain in your throat. If I used my classroom voice in a quiet coffee shop when talking to a friend, I would receive some very odd looks from the other customers!

Using signs rather than words for some instructions in music and drama became the norm. To stop a class in practical, for instance, I will raise an arm and students must respond and help each other respond. Each group will generally have a leader, and it is their responsibility to get focus from the group when my arm goes up. In music lessons, particularly where students are all performing as a whole class, I will often use a microphone so that I don't have to strain above the sound. Do be aware, however, that you must still project your voice into the microphone, as it does not do all of the work for you.

My intention in writing this is not to give a lesson on vocal health, as there are other clever people who specialise in this area; for example, The British Voice Association has a range of free voice care literature and the NEU has advice and links to further support. It is more to encourage you think about how you use your voice in your new classroom, and to be aware that there is a right way and a wrong way to use your voice when you need to be heard. Like the rest of your body, your voice needs looking after in order to be your most important classroom tool.

Andrea Walker is a Teacher of Music and Drama. She has been a teacher of music and drama and a head of department in Kent, Buckinghamshire, Hertfordshire and Merseyside for nearly 20 years.

What They Didn't Teach Me About
Saying 'No'

Kevin Hewitson

Teaching is a 'full on' activity. It makes emotional and physical demands on us, but we are rewarded by the energy that comes from building learning relationships and when kids 'get it'. We must be careful not to get carried away though; it's all too easy to do a little extra, stay a little longer, take something home to look at or to take on an extra responsibility.

For a while we can carry the extra load, accommodate the drain on our resources and hope to re-charge the batteries during the breaks. That can only last so long though, so be careful; if you are not fully recharged then you may not have the energy to see you through the next term or semester.

The analogy with a rechargeable battery is a good one. Just as we provide the energy in a classroom, in our relationships with the learners and with colleagues, the battery provides energy to power devices. We can recognise when a battery is running down quite easily: the lamp dims, the motor runs slower. It is the same with us, but perhaps not so obvious. Here are some indicators that I have recognised in myself, and in others:

- exhibiting less patience
- preferring routine over change
- taking longer to do things than we used to
- becoming less organised
- becoming less aware of our surroundings and what is going on around us

- 'dropping' into a chair, rather than sitting
- withdrawing socially and communicating less with those around us.

Everything on that list can make a difference to your success as a teacher, but what might be the most significant point of them all is that we stop being learners! As teachers, we must always remain learners; luckily it is one of the last stages as we begin to run out of energy and move into 'survival mode'. We can mask many of the other symptoms by keeping to routines, but it is only a temporary situation and these indicators will soon begin to manifest themselves.

So, what can we do about it when we notice things are not as they should be?

I find that teachers overall are a compliant bunch, and saying 'No' is not something they do easily. Saying 'No' is something we need to do though if we are going to find the time and opportunities to recharge our batteries. First, we must learn to say 'No' to ourselves, and then to others; admittedly it is not easy, but there are ways that avoid the fears we may have about saying 'No'.

We may feel awkward or that we are letting somebody down if we say 'No'. A characteristic of teachers is that they want to help, and so feeling as though they are letting somebody down, especially if it is a student or colleague, is not a comfortable feeling. We must, however, balance this against our wellbeing; look at the cost to ourselves of saying 'Yes' and what would happen if we said 'No'. Here are some of the questions I use to help me decide to say 'Yes' or 'No'.

1. Am I the best person to be doing this?
2. Have I the resources (time included) to do this?
3. How long will it take, and how long am I willing or able to devote to it?

What are the short-term and long-term benefits to me?

Kevin Hewitson, NPQH, BPhil (Education), Cert Ed. With over 40 years as an educational professional, Kevin has held a number of curriculum and pastoral roles with responsibility for assessment, teaching and learning and Gifted and Talented provision. Now working independently as an educational advisor, Kevin provides INSET workshops, as well as writing and speaking on all things to do with teaching and learning.

What They Didn't Teach Me About
Looking After Myself

Rosella McNally

I remember my very first lecture of my PGCE; I remember it so clearly because we were told that counselling was available during our PGCE. I remember the multiple lecturers at university telling us that teaching is hard and to get ready for the workload and sleepless nights. As I went through my placement schools, teachers that I came across always had negative things to say about a teachers' health and wellbeing. My whole time as a student, I was perplexed and wondered why every adult around me was negative about a career I loved.

Now, nearing the end of my PGCE, I can tell you that, yes, it is hard. Everyone had warned me, but this was my passion. The endless lectures of how hard teaching is did not help me; it made me feel cautious and anxious going into my placement schools. Before we even step into those schools, we must read the hundreds of different policies about children's safeguarding, children's health and children's wellbeing. We have endless lectures on how to take care of them, but no one at any point told me how to look after myself.

At first, I found it hard not going to the gym, socialising with my friends, or just being with my family. It was during my main placement when I realised that I was doing it to myself. I was isolating myself and was too controlling over my university and school work commitments. The truth is, there is always something to do—and it is okay to think about what *you* need. Sometimes you need to prioritise yourself over work.

It is so important to look after yourself; you are the most valuable tool in the classroom. Teachers need to schedule time away from school work and enjoy themselves for their own health and wellbeing, but also for their class. A teacher should never reach their breaking point, and it is up to you to prevent this. What works for me may not work for everyone, but I began scheduling times with friends, family and my partner. I write down the days I go to the gym and days that I will be able to do school work. I plan socialising events far in advance to make sure I have plenty of time to prepare and manage my workload. Working out at the gym is my stress relief, so I make sure I go about four times a week; this forces me to forget about school and focus on my strength entirely. The gym gives me strength, mentally and physically, which allows me to be fighting fit for the school day after.

Teachers need to be more open about their health and wellbeing so that we can all discuss coping mechanisms. Healthy wellbeing is an essential factor in the quality of your teaching, your performance and your productivity. Self-care is giving your class the best of you, instead of what is left of you.

Rosella McNally is a student teacher, attending the University of Gloucestershire, and has had experience in a year 3/4, year 2 and year 6 class. She has a secured key stage two role in September in a school in Swindon.

What They Didn't Teach Me About
Socialising

Andy Lewis

Some people never see their colleagues as their friends, while others will find meaningful and long-lasting friendships in the workplace—some will even find their future marriage partner! Navigating the social etiquette and norms of the school workplace can be difficult, and there is also the added complexity of virtual 'friendships' via social networks such as Facebook.

The Staffroom

It is important to make sure you visit. It is easy to spend every moment in school marking, planning and with students. Regularly take your lunch time off and sit in there. Be careful not to get sucked into negative conversations or gossip about colleagues. See if you can find a group happy to ban 'shop talk' for at least 30 minutes.

Facebook (and other social networks)

Do you want to share your Facebook profile with your colleagues? You are then 'friends' and reveal your family life, your past and what you are up to during holidays and weekends.

Regardless of what you decide, just like students, new colleagues will have a look. Check your security settings and be very careful to understand exactly what the public can see; it is important you recheck this regularly.

Be careful if you 'Like' or interact with your school page. Does that make you easy to find for students and parents? Is your profile picture suitable and is your security high enough? Also, make sure you read your school social media policy. Should you be 'friends' with students? Probably not. Ex-students? It may depend.

If you do join various teaching groups and network via Facebook, it may be worth setting up a second, professional account. This can also help with work-life balance and allow you to 'switch off' more easily.

Staff Sports

Football on a Friday can be a popular one, but some schools have running clubs, circuit training—all sorts! If it doesn't exist, once you have found your feet, help set it up; it's a great way to end the week.

Sports can be great leveller, helping break down walls—real or imagined—between people within your school; e.g., deputies can go head-to-head against the caretaker. As an added bonus, the following week there may be endless post-game analysis across all staff; a better topic of conversation that an annoying Year 9 boy!

You can unleash the week's frustrations in the game. Goals with nets are brilliant so you can release all your pressure with an ambitious shot on goal… and then make sure to celebrate!

However, watch your tackles and don't overdo it! It can be tricky for colleagues to explain to the kids that they are on crutches because you launched a two-footed slider on them. Sure, victory matters—teachers are competitive by nature, after all—but remember, it's about the camaraderie; however; it's always good to buy the losers a pint down the pub afterwards...

The Pub

The classic end-of-week celebration. If colleagues go to the pub at the end of the week, try to pop along. It can be a nice way to unwind and get to know your colleagues outside of school; it can be a good way to informally network and build up extra support too.

However, avoid talking about the students, especially by name. It could be a parent, or an aunt, or indeed anyone, sitting at the next table. Make sure you don't have a drink and then complain about, or slag off, colleagues. You have no idea what friendships or alliances exist outside of schools.

It is vital that you do not buy the first round of Jägerbombs; especially pre-5 pm. Control your drinking; your new colleagues won't quickly forget a drunken liability on the first Friday of the year!

You will end up spending more time with colleagues than with your friends—and maybe even spouse! It is important to develop positive relationships in the workplace—this can make work happier and less stressful. Just consider and manage those relationships. Have fun, but be careful!

Andy Lewis is an Assistant Headteacher in East London. He has written various secondary RE textbooks and delivers CPD locally and nationally. He frequently tweets and blogs about RE and wider educational issues. Andy met his wife whilst working at a school.

What They Didn't Teach Me About

Making Time for My Loved Ones

Bukky Yusuf

Congratulations on your choice to be a teacher! Teaching is the best profession in the world! This is because the work we do for our students is vital, and we want to do all that we can for them. But what's equally important is the need for you to take time for yourself, and to make time for your loved ones.

Because we want to do the best by our students, this can result in our time being swallowed up with planning, marking and feedback. As a result, you can end up squeezing time with your nearest and dearest into rushed weekends, half-hearted, half-term breaks when you are exhausted, or full-blown catch ups during your longer breaks—once you have made time to recuperate from the term you have just experienced.

My advice is to arrange your time each week so that you have an evening off for yourself. It may sound counterintuitive, however spending time with your family, friends and loved ones will enable you to be a more productive teacher, with more energy to do the right things for your students.

The bottom line is that you and your loved ones matter.

So build-in and safeguard the time that you spend with them: it will serve you well.

Bukky Yusuf is secondary school teacher, a leader and a consultant.

What They Didn't Teach Me About
Having a Sunshine Box

Hannah Wilson

The highs of teaching can be very high, but similarly the lows can be very low. In one day, you can move from your best lesson to your worst lesson, from your best class to your worst class. A child can make you cry with joy one minute and a parent can make you cry from shouting at you the next.

I suggest creating a 'sunshine box' (physical or virtual or both!), and have it somewhere you can reach in your classroom (at your desk perhaps), or save it as your first email folder. Each time you get positive feedback, a thank you, a card or a note put it in the sunshine box. When you hit those low points you can spend a few minutes reminding yourself of all of your successes and recalibrating your positive 'I can do this' mindset.

Hannah Wilson. Head of Secondary Teacher Training at University of Buckingham (former Executive Headteacher of two start up schools in Oxfordshire) and Co-founder of #WomenEd.

What They Didn't Teach Me About
the Importance of Empathy

Andrew Cowley

What essentially was missing from my PGCE was empathy; a core human value, abstract, but crucial to the wellbeing of ourselves and others. In reflecting on the years since undertaking a PGCE in the 1990s, I realised there was much I hadn't covered at the time; only through further reading and study did I expand my pedagogical knowledge. But expanding your pedagogical knowledge isn't enough. My time in various roles in our education system taught me that there is much more for you—especially NQTs—to learn.

For example, there was never any mention of looking after yourself or of work-life balance. There also wasn't a mention of the impact of not doing as we should, bar one of the course tutors ripping into a group who ambled into a lecture half an hour late, reminding them they wouldn't do this once appointed to a role.

This realisation led to my being part of founding Healthy Toolkit, with the specific goal being to address a perceived gap in the wellbeing sector. There was a lot out there about self-care, motivational quotes and making connections with nature—all valuable information—but is this really going to help the new teacher, enthused in September, but on their knees in December, burdened with the Nativity, end of term assessments, displays, difficult parents and a nagging virus?

In my estimation, the gap was two-fold. Firstly, there was nothing around about leading wellbeing; with all due respect to people in that type of role, organising a night out, team bonding games and sticking a bit of fruit on the staffroom table isn't wellbeing, it is tokenism.

Secondly, there was little out there about being part of a team and the impact of the individual on the culture of the school.

Everything we do, say and think has an influence and bearing on the young people we teach. What I was never told was that our deeds, words and beliefs also have an influence, positive or negative, upon our colleagues. We have all seen someone upset in the staffroom because of the sharp words of others. Maybe we have witnessed a teacher in tears because an idea has been unfairly criticised. Perhaps we know of someone who has been bullied, marginalised or socially excluded in the workplace.

My twenty-six years of experience has taught me a great deal, and one significant thing I return to is the importance of empathy. I would urge all courses to cover it, and if yours doesn't, then develop your own values to promote it. In embarking on your teaching careers, I wish you luck. This is a wonderful and rewarding profession. Please look after yourselves and each other.

Andrew Cowley is the Deputy Head of a primary school in South-East London, a co-founder of Healthy Toolkit and the author of The Wellbeing Toolkit.

What They Didn't Teach Me About
Investing in Myself

Katie Matthews

The number one factor of importance for teacher wellbeing has to be self-care and the prevention of burn out. I'm sure we've all heard the phrase 'you can't pour from an empty cup', but it was only upon entering the field of Education that I fully appreciated the truth of this phrase. Education is a calling; a burning desire to educate, support, develop, mentor and empower others through knowledge, opportunities and collaboration. We invest so much of ourselves into others and their learning journeys that sometimes we forget about ourselves, or at the very least we start to find ourselves slipping down the priority list. We find ourselves buried under mountains of paperwork, marking, IEPs, deadlines, reports, the list goes on... it is easy to see why we as educators are so drained by the end of each day! Investing so much in others is the job, but it is critical that we also invest in ourselves! You must afford yourself the time to relax and restore your own energy supplies before another day, week, month, year, of investing that energy into the development of your students.

The second piece of advice I would like to impart is to be mindful of every interaction you have. This can be tricky to do, especially when you're exhausted, stressed or not feeling totally on form. Sometimes you feel so drained that the last thing you want to do is slap on a smile and jovially indulge in fractions or algebra. However, as we know, children's brains are like sponges: they absorb everything going on around them, both spoken and unspoken. I have become so conscious of the power of language and the weight of my words on my students; before

I speak, reply or question, I try to take a couple of seconds to think properly about what I am going to say and *how* I am going to say it. I'm sure we've all been in the position of hearing somebody say something and cringing about the way it was said; perhaps the tone didn't quite match what was being said or their expression or body language didn't quite parallel the message they were trying to get across? My mum used to say to me (when I was being a moody teenager!), 'the problem is not what you've said, it's how you've said it'. I now find myself turning into my mother and repeating these phrases! As educators, we have a responsibility to our students; to empower, to educate, to support, to build confidence, to guide, to mentor, to challenge and to inspire them. We need to understand the true impact our words can have and how one throw away comment could inform a student's decisions, opinions of themselves or even their future!

Finally, I would say to never stop learning. Always be open to new ideas, methods, techniques and strategies, and never lose your passion for learning and self-development! Challenge yourself daily, set yourself targets and keep moving forward. Practise makes progress!

Katie Matthews is a multi-award-winning entrepreneur. She features in the Northern Ireland 40 under 40 list and won the FSB NI Young Entrepreneur accolade in 2018.

Chapter 12

What They Didn't Teach Me About Employment

One of the most exciting parts about training to be a teacher is that at the end of the course you will be applying for your first teaching post. Choosing where you would like to work is a big decision, and in this chapter, authors share their advice about finding the job that feels right for you.

What They Didn't Teach Me About
the Teacher Training Experience

Beth Ireland

May 2017: My teaching journey started when I received an email from Liverpool Hope University while I was out in the sun enjoying a Nando's. I remember being really excited when I saw it was an offer. I had no idea this was the start of a huge journey that was probably one of the most challenging years of my life.

September 2017: My first lecture room was full of people eagerly anticipating our PGCE student journey. I remember the first thing the head of the course said was, 'on my PGCE I put on loads of weight and cancelled my wedding'—I was worried. Luckily, I persevered. The rest of the session was a blur of trying to find new friends, meeting my new tutor groups and generally trying to figure out what was going on.

October 2017: First, we had to go on an early-years' placement. I did a childcare diploma in college, so I'm not exactly a stranger to nurseries, but spending five days in that childcare setting fully made me realise that KS1/KS2 is for me. I ended up retreating to the baby room and cuddling four-month-old babies all week. Every time the nursery manager mentioned the toddler room, a look of total fear must have passed on my face because she never asked again for the week. It was there I realised that staff in nurseries are underpaid and overworked—like most professions—but the care and love they had for the children really made an impression.

I remember the day I got my next placement clearly. I was sitting, choosing what to have on my jacket potato (an important decision) and we all got an email. The whole canteen froze and looked at their new placements; a huge sigh of relief came over me as I realised my placement was only a 15-minute drive from my house. Note: this is probably PGCE's worst kept secret but do not say on the form that you can drive. My friend did, and she was placed over an hour and a half away for her placement.

My first placement: My first placement was in Y6. I was placed with another student named Anna, who—even now—is my absolute rock. Everyone needs that one person in school that you can go to after a bad day, or who will help you when you have nerves before a lesson observation. This placement was the best experience ever. This school was exactly the type of school I knew I belonged in. I remember crying in that first placement because I had 'so much to do'. At this point, I was teaching two lessons a week, and the class teacher gave us PPA all the time as she knew we wouldn't get a lot in our next placement (she was right). It felt so strange having to re-learn dividing fractions and teaching the children about historical figures, some of whom I hadn't even heard of, but when my tutor came and commented on how well I was doing, it made everything worthwhile.

My second placement: This time I went from Y6 to Y1, and I had a very different experience. I went from dividing fractions to number bonds to 10. This placement was hard—and without a doubt taught me the most. There were two class teachers, one SENCO and the other the deputy head, but I started teaching as soon as I walked in the door as they were always put on other jobs. The school was lovely, but I essentially trained myself on that placement—no one checked my English planning for a whole term! You need to be prepared to step up straight away. The best advice I can give is to prepare for the unexpected; placements are hard, and you will be thrown in at the deep end. I remember getting some constructive criticism and I thought my whole career was ending. Criticism isn't to put you down, but rather to help you develop. It is really important to distinguish the difference so you can improve.

Job hunting: The lecturers told us to choose the school we would feel most comfortable in, but, in our PGCE-panicked brains, everyone felt the need to apply for almost everything. The walk-around is crucial as this is where you see if the school really is for you.

When you do decide to send out applications, and assuming that you are applying to multiple positions, double-check the application and make sure you don't put the wrong school name in—I've definitely done that before, and that's one interview you won't be getting! Another thing is to not be disheartened. I applied for around seven jobs and I got interviews for five of them. In the first four interviews, I crashed and burned, despite having worked in retail beforehand and feeling pretty confident in my interview abilities. However, I was far from being prepared to be interviewed by three governors and two headteachers all in one room, or being interviewed by a school council, or having to spend full days in school being watched every second. However, I don't regret any of my interviews, because they provided me with the valuable feedback I used in my last interview.

The moment where I finally got my job is one beyond words. The complete relief and excitement I felt was immeasurable. I went for a KS2 job and they offered me a job is working in a reception/Y1 class—and I love it. I've always liked a challenge, but taking on two curriculums means there's a new challenge every day. I spend every day being so grateful for my wonderful class, and although there are really, really hard days where I find myself crying at the printer because it's sleeping and you desperately need it to print, I wouldn't have it any other way.

Enjoy every second of your PGCE: it's an amazing profession to be in.

Beth is a recently qualified teacher working as a Nursery teacher in Liverpool.

What They Didn't Teach Me About
Becoming a Teacher at the End of the Course

Ros Wilson

It was during the last few weeks of my wonderful experience in higher education when Martial Rose (Senior Education Lecturer and International Expert on The York Mystery Plays) gazed at me in some bewilderment after I appeared on his doorstep in a mildly inebriated state one evening to thank him for all he had done for me.

'Have you got a job sorted?' he enquired in mild bemusement. 'Where are you going to teach?'

My jaw must have dropped… the idea of getting a job had never occurred to me. And—to be fair—I had been totally oblivious to the fact that all those around me in my year were busily writing applications and attending interviews. It was Martial Rose who scanned the columns of the TES, made a phone call and ordered me to present myself for interview in one week's time at Normanton Secondary Modern School.

Fortunately, as soon as I settled in my art room with no tutors breathing down my neck and absolutely no classroom visits—let alone observations—in the whole five years I was there, I discovered that there were ways of teaching that were diametrically opposite to the way I was taught. They involved teacher/pupil interactions that were always positive and often fun, and thus I realised I had had a very fortunate accidental bumble into a wonderful profession.

Of course, there were many things the college never prepared me for—how could they when I didn't even know why I was there? But we all know it takes five years in the classroom to make a true teacher…

and so I did, eventually, learn the essentials of the trade; how to write on a blackboard, how to balance a full mug of instant coffee on a mountain of unmarked exercise books as you hurtle down a maze of corridors and—possibly the most important—how to only feel the need to use the loo at 10:25 am, 12:40 or 3:45 pm!

Ros Wilson. Education consultant and creator of Big Writing/Power Writing.

What They Didn't Teach Me About
Getting a Job

Theodore Griffiths

Getting appointed to a teaching job can sometimes be tricky. There are two aspects of securing that perfect job:

- Your application
- Your interview

A. The Application

The aim of any application is simple: it is to get shortlisted. More specifically, it is to get you shortlisted as the favoured candidate.

Five Mistakes That You Could Make in Your Application

1. Not finding the job vacancy
2. Not applying for the right job
3. Not following instructions
4. Not understanding what it's all about
5. Not making it easy for the school

So let's look at these five mistakes not to make.

1. Not Finding the Job Vacancy

You don't find the vacancy because you don't look in the right place. Look at the website of your local authority. They often advertise teaching posts, and a number of local authorities use Pools, especially for NQTs in primary. This is a centralised system for recruiting to induction posts, a bit like UCAS. The Guardian newspaper advertises jobs one day a week, but the main place to look is the TES. Using either their app or their main website, set up job alerts. Schools are also increasingly advertising positions using e-Teach.

2. Not Applying for the Right Job

Don't limit your chances by applying for only one sort of school. There are a whole range out there—community schools, foundation schools, voluntary-aided schools, faith schools, academies, free schools and independent schools—that may well be worth considering. But you need to consider two points about each school: *Is this the sort of school that I want?* (Find out about it first!), and *Am I the teacher that they want?* Simply put, apply for the jobs that you want and that you are qualified for. Don't apply for a job as second in department if you are still in ITT, and don't boost your application by misrepresenting yourself. You should also be specific about the positions you apply for. Avoid applying for multiple jobs through what I would call *scatter-gun applications*, where you send off 20 applications in one weekend, all with exactly the same letter of application or statement, hoping that one will reach the target; select the job that is right for you and apply for that.

3. Not Following Instructions

When it comes to applying for a teaching job, it can feel like there is no end to the advice and instructions you get offered; in fact, you are even getting instructions from me!

Obviously, some instructions are better than others, so cautiously maintain an open mind about what you hear—advice from experienced appointers (like me) and people such as a Head of department or Key Stage Leader who regularly participates in appointment of teachers to schools—can be very helpful. Beyond that though, you risk taking advice that is either biased or not fully informed by the relevant experience you need. Advice from a University Tutor should always be accepted courteously, but perhaps you should remember that they probably have little or no relevant experience here.

And advice from the internet, or from most, but not all, books on job applications, is of little value as this advice usually has an American bias and almost always is angled towards applying for jobs in industry or commerce.

Having said this, what I really mean about following instructions pertains to the school offering the specific position you seek. They tell you both implicitly and explicitly what they want you to do. So you should do it.

They ask for a letter or statement from you, so it should be written by you, not copied from someone else. They expect two sides of A4 paper using a normal font; don't make it too long or too short or in a miniscule font to cram more in. They ask for your education and employment history, so don't leave gaps in the chronology. They ask you to fill in a form, so neither leave a section empty nor write *See letter*. And pay attention to the people they require references from, for example, you are always required to give your current Head. Just follow the instructions.

4. Not Understanding What It's All About

Remember that saying by President Kennedy? *Ask not what your country can do for you—ask what you can do for your country.* This perfectly encapsulates something many applicants get wrong: It is not all about you. Don't focus on yourself with sentences such as '*This post would provide the support I need for my NQT induction year/allow me to develop my career/give me the opportunity to...*' It is about the pupils, and what you can do for them, and what you can offer the school.

Your letter or statement should briefly explain your philosophy of education and your experience and skills, but putting it all in the context of your contribution to the school. It should be custom tailored to that specific school, noting what that school's requirements and needs are, not the same bland thing sent to every single school.

In addition to your letter, write an Executive Summary; an at-a-glance way of showing the school that you match their person specification. Between these targeted parts of your application, you will demonstrate that you are a very appropriate candidate who should be shortlisted.

5. Not Making It Easy for the School

There comes a moment in the tide of applications when one is tempted, sorely tempted, to throw an application in the bin in exasperation.

Because the candidate has made it too difficult to assess their qualities, or—even worse—has made it difficult to invite them to interview.

These are the candidates whose application is not very legible (tiny print, or—horrors—handwritten badly), where they don't give full contact details for themselves or their referees, where their letter or statement is uncertain or vague, jumps about with no clear structure, and/or doesn't seem to relate to my school. That's where an Executive Summary comes in handy, of course. It feels extraordinarily surprising to have to say this, but focus on grammar and spelling, proofread to be sure, and understand the common courtesies required for a professional communication: I still shudder as I remember an e-mail enclosing an application that began 'Hi Theo!'.

Make your application clear, structured, neat, pleasant to the eye and to the mental ear that is reading it.

B. The Interview

The aim of the interview is to get the job; however, you also don't want to lose it subsequently because you misrepresented your skills, abilities and experience.

Five Mistakes That You Could Make in Your Interview

1. The wrong first impression
2. The wrong self-presentation
3. The wrong sort of talking
4. The wrong sort of preparation
5. The wrong questions at the end

1. The Wrong First Impression

Knowing that people often make split-second judgments at first sight, plan for this not to happen negatively to you. Don't arrive late and flustered is the first point, because it can all go downhill from there. Be super polite and friendly to Reception—and anyone else you meet in the school. Give an air of confidence as you walk into the interview room, but don't be pushy. Watch your body language; no sprawling legs, no flirtingly pushing back your hair, and no slouching or hunching forward nervously. Make the first impression one that makes the interview panel glad that they selected you.

2. The Wrong Self-Presentation

This can be a delicate issue to talk to you about. You may well feel that you have a right to express your true self in the way that you dress or wear your make-up, and you may feel that your qualifications are what matters and it's not up to the committee to assess you on your appearance. Fair enough, but a school is going to expect you to conform to their written—or even unwritten—rules on clothes and appearance, and to conform to the conventions for interviews. This means basically one level higher in neatness and formality from the everyday wear you'll see in the teachers round school.

Check the neatness in particular; make sure that you have the right shirt with no missing buttons, the skirt with no hem unsewn. To ITT candidates, used to casualwear at most times and disco outfits at the weekend, I would say *You are trying to get appointed, not dated*, so you may even need a set of clothes for interview that you rarely, if ever, wear at any other time.

The final point about self-presentation is even more delicate. Take care to avoid all horrid habits; for example, not changing your socks or not showering before getting dressed. Smelly candidates are unwelcome, as are those who chew gum, pick their noses or have other horrid habits. Yes, people *do* do this; generally because they are nervous.

3. The Wrong Sort of Talking

The wrong sort of talking is talking too fast, too slow, too much, too little, too soon or too negatively. We see this often in interviews, again because people are nervous. You would be surprised by how many candidates talk themselves out of the job, sometimes speaking so fast we can hardly understand a word. These candidates also often speak too much, going on and on and on, usually not very relevantly or intelligently either. You can almost see them saying to themselves, '*Quick! What can I say next, I must say something!*', so they just say the first thing that comes into their heads—and then the next, and the next.

If you don't keep to the point, you won't get a chance to show how you are the candidate that we need; at some point during your endless talking we shall just switch off and put our energy not into listening, but into trying to make you stop. Almost as bad is the candidate who has to be drawn out, because they answer in as few words as possible. It's like drawing teeth to get information out of them. Then there's the candidate who talks too soon, jumping in halfway through the question, and often therefore not answering correctly because they didn't hear it all. And no brownie points for interrupting the Chair of Governors either.

But the easiest way to talk yourself out of a job is to talk negatively. Just don't. Say nothing negative at all about your training, your mentor, your placement school, your current post or your Headteacher. Nothing. Similarly, avoid the word *unfortunately*. Once you've started a sentence with that you are showing that you know you haven't got the skill or experience that they are seeking.

4. The Wrong Sort of Preparation

There are two sorts of preparation: wise and unwise. Obviously, you want to be the candidate using clever, effective and wise preparation. Let's look at the unwise, even daft, techniques.

One bad idea is relying on books or websites with titles such as *Effective Answers to Difficult Interview Questions* or *All the Answers for Interviews for Teachers*—i.e., answers written by someone else for a different job that will have been seen and copied by countless other candidates. Guess what? The interview panel can recognise when you have done this.

Connected to the idea of using someone else's pre-packaged ideas is simply learning answers off by heart. We aren't impressed when we can tell that you've a long list of answers that you can drag out and repeat, parrot-like.

The interviewer(s) want to hear your ideas, particularly thoughts based on the likely areas that that particular school will wish to explore with you. Identify these areas, both the general ones (including achievement, safeguarding, etc.) and the ones specific to that school, and then draw up mind maps for them.

Then, practise responding to questions by visualising the relevant mind map and answering based on that—do it while sitting in front of a mirror to see your impact.

5. The Wrong Questions At the End

At the end of the interview, there is usually an opportunity to ask questions. I'll let you into a secret here. Usually, we hope that there won't be any, because we are at least as tired as you. We will generally be delighted if you say *No, thank you, your documentation and the walk round the school with the colleague gave me all the information that I need.* There may, however, be a very important question that hasn't been answered, and on it may depend whether or not you could reasonably accept the job, if offered. This is the only sort of question that is appropriate. Usually only one.

Sometimes candidates are advised to ask a list of questions to show that you are interested in and committed to this school, but that should already be clear from your thoughtful answers to our questions.

Resist the urge to ask a question to impress us with your up-to-date knowledge of all things educational, and especially resist the urge to ask questions that may highlight any shortcomings the school has, or has had in the recent past, such as questions about the Inspection Report.

And my final piece of advice is this: the interview has only ended when you are off school premises and out of sight. Maintain your professional decorum the entire time.

Theodore Griffiths, otherwise known as Theo Griff, started teaching 1966. Her professional career includes college, school and university leadership, and developing and teaching BEd and PGCE courses. For over a decade, Theo was the job seeking expert on a popular online advice forum for teachers. She has two downloadable books on Amazon about applications and interviews for teaching posts. Theo is currently teaching is as a volunteer in an Estepona state primary school in Andalusia, Spain.

What They Didn't Teach Me About
Finding a School You Can Thrive In

Claire Mitchell

'In less than 12 months' time, you'll be in front of your very own class'. That bombshell was how I remember my PGCE starting. January soon arrived, and one-by-one our cohort started to secure NQT positions. I applied for anything and everything, but at least had the good sense to seek interview feedback when I got that far. It was not overly reassuring as you can see:

- 1st interview: too inexperienced.
- 2nd interview: too casual ('The Governors felt you were too informal for the occasion and laughed too much; we are an outstanding school...').
- 3rd interview: not Catholic enough.

Adverts dried up over the summer term, and then the big holiday arrived. While my colleagues laminated display items and collected cushions for their book-corners, I considered a change in direction—maybe teaching wasn't for me after all?

Late in the summer holidays I saw an advert for an October start. The interview was great fun. The school was home. I loved everything about it from the minute I walked in. It 'felt right'. I got the job.

What this ended up teaching me is that whether you end up being one of the lucky students who quickly get cherry-picked for a great placement, or the end of the school year comes without your having found a position, try to be discerning in your quest for securing a job. I look back now and see that none of those first 3 jobs would have been right for me; the fourth was the right fit. I only realised the type of school that I really needed when it came along.

So my advice to you is to use the unique wealth of opportunities your PGCE year brings to work out what you need to thrive, and then find a school that can offer this. Try new things, network with new people; work out the beginnings of your philosophy which will grow and change as your career develops, but ultimately seek to find a place where it can be nurtured.

As a headteacher now, I feel disappointed when people apply for jobs without having visited our school. How do they know if it's right for them? How do they know if they will get the opportunities and support they need? Our school is special and wonderful, but—like anywhere—it's not for everyone. In the same way you shouldn't buy a house without a clear wishlist and several viewings, by working out what you want and visiting prospective schools, you'll eventually find the one that fits. Plus, you'll have much more to talk about in your application and interview. Schools vary massively in ethos, what they offer and how they do things. You'll get a good feeling when you find one that's right for you. If you're not quite right for the first, second, or even tenth job you apply for, don't lose heart. Your time will come.

Don't—like I did—consider leaving this wonderful profession before you've danced with it. You were called to teaching for a reason, and by embarking on this journey, you have already come so far. Trust that you will find your place to shine. Your PGCE is the beginning of something much bigger; trust yourself and my hope is that you will look back fondly at all of this and smile at how fate, your hard work and a few good decisions got you where you needed to be in the end.

Claire Mitchell completed her PGCE at the University of Leicester after a last minute interview in 2004. She started her NQT year late in 2005 at Latimer Primary School and has been there ever since. She has job-shared her Headteacher role with incredible women. Claire had her first baby halfway through her NPQH in 2011 and had her second baby in 2016. She is proud to champion part-time working and lead the fabulous Latimer team.

What They Didn't Teach Me About
Asking Questions at Interview

James Hollinsley

So you are looking around potential schools for your first year as a teacher. You learnt all your phonics sounds, behaviour strategies and how to create medium-term plans. But did your training provider really get you ready to ask the pertinent questions at interview or did you arrive and then learn you made a huge mistake? The wellbeing of staff is paramount to an effective school. As such, this is one of the main aspects you need into focus on before you even say 'Yes' to a post. Here are some things you may want to keep in mind, or even ask, before signing that contract.

Does the mission of the school match the values in your heart?
This may seem like a silly question. After all, so many schools seem alike on a quick tour when deciding on which school is best for you. Listen to the headteacher talk about their mission—what are they trying to achieve and what is the school all about? Does it make you excited listening to the mission and does it fit in with what drives you? The reason I ask this is because teaching can be tough. When you are digging deep for energy on those long days, it will be your passion for what you want to achieve for your class and the collective that will get you through.

How effective are the wellbeing ethos and systems in the school?
Ask leaders what they have done over the last two years to increase wellbeing of all staff. Listen for answers revolving around reducing workload; look for things such as reducing marking, simplifying assessment and reporting to parents. If their answer is yoga sessions on a

Wednesday (which can be all well and good) but they aren't acknowledging and being proactive in workload reduction, this may not be the school for you. On the flip side, you will want to know how extensive the wellbeing package is at the establishment. Workload reduction is the number one factor in increasing teachers' wellbeing but the 'experience' of being at the school is nearly just as vital. A cohesive team that is positive, due to a collective vision from the SLT, is paramount to a school not only being a place of work but a place of 'being'.

Does the school have a wellbeing committee for staff?
Are there plenty of opportunities to take part in activities outside of school? This is very important for teachers coming from afar or overseas who may need a wider social network. It is also a positive attribute to a school in bonding staff together through different opportunities. If they don't have a wellbeing committee to review activities and workload, do they plan on having one?

How does the SLT focus on the quality of learning?
Is it through arduous observations and high stakes according to performance in the classroom or is it through ongoing discussions and shorter, positive visits to explore learning?

Ask plenty about the marking policy.
This is crucial, as it has a significant impact on a teacher's workload. Get a copy and see what is expected. Is the policy clear in its intent and does it outline a reasonable expectation whilst still developing pupils?

Think about your expenditures.
So many teachers spend a substantial amount of their own money on developing their classrooms and for additional resources. A school should be keeping this in mind and provide as much scope as possible to reduce teachers' expenditure. Ask what the school supplies within each class—some schools provide teachers with an individual allowance for the start of the academic year or send a wishlist round to reduce such spending.

If there is staff movement, try to learn why.

It is perfectly natural for people to move schools. However, it is helpful to ask how many have left in the last two years and the main reasons why. If there is a huge movement of staff, can the SLT give a clear picture as to why this happened? Mass exodus does not necessarily mean that alarm bells should be ringing, but be mindful of the working environment you are walking into.

Ultimately, teaching is the best thing to do in the world. If you get the setting and wellbeing right, you will be waking up each morning with a spring in your step and a desire to get in and make that difference.

I wish you every success in your teaching career and hope that in 20 years you are as happy as I am—it really is the best!

James Hollinsley is the head of Longwood Primary Academy. The school was recently awarded TES Employer of the Year and also winner of the biennial Place2Be School Community award. James is the founder of AllSupportEd—an online organisation focusing on the mental health of school staff. He is a LLE in Essex, a qualified SENCO and former school inspector.

What They Didn't Teach Me About
Job Applications

Poonam Mattharu

I work with many NQTs to find them a position, either during their training or once qualified. I am always keen to hear people's journeys when qualifying to becoming a teacher, and I am always thinking about how I can help them find their dream job or what tips I can offer when applying for positions.

A few questions I ask teachers include:

- Why teaching?
- How did they find each individual placement?
- How do they cope with the overload?
- What obstacles did they face?

Many enjoy it, whereas others tend to decide teaching isn't for them; perhaps they find it too challenging or they prefer to do a support role within a school instead. So, after conversations with teaching professionals and through my expertise in recruiting, I have listed some practical advice regarding how to tackle obstacles during your studies/placements and how to apply for jobs.

During your training

- Accept **constructive criticism.** Don't walk into your first placement and expect to be outstanding—of course, obviously it's great if you are!
- **Reflect** on what you did well and what you didn't. How will you change it for next time?

- Watch and learn from others. Take notes, look at what you can incorporate into your lessons and then add your own **individual style**.
- **Utilise** the people around you. Your mentor, family and friends who are in teaching and your work colleagues on your placements are all valuable resources; don't be afraid to ask them questions, even if you think the answer is obvious.
- **Share experiences** and ideas with other students.
- Give yourself some time away from studying. **Take time out** to socialise or just reboot yourself. Overloading yourself is never good!
- **Enjoy** what you are doing! You have worked so hard to get to where you are; you will have good days and bad days, but start each day with a positive. Remember, you are changing a child's life by contributing to their learning and development.

  It's so inspiring what you are doing; give yourself credit!

Tips when applying for jobs

When to apply

Schools tend to recruit 2–3 terms ahead for a September start, which you can access online or on the individual school website if you have a specific school in mind. For example, jobs starting September will generally be online from the previous January.

Some students qualify in January, so start looking at vacancies a term ahead; again, you can even register with an agency to find you a position or supply work. Experience in different schools is a good way for you to expose yourself and learn about other schools.

Application process

- Take time to research a school, visit schools, ask questions, and carefully read the job description; this way you can pick up points to add into your personal statement to make it individual and relevant to each job/school you apply to.
- Take your time when filling out your application form, and double-check for spelling, grammar and punctuation.

- Get someone to read your application and personal statement prior to applying.
- If you haven't found a position by April, don't worry; there may still be jobs being advertised right up until the beginning of term. Agencies often have vacancies which are not advertised online.

Interview preparation

- Prepare yourself by researching the school: form entry, ethos, values, Ofsted rating and your knowledge about the curriculum—then think about why you want to work there.
- Make it specific for each individual school.
- Don't over complicate your lesson plan—keep it simple and have a clear objective.
- Include lots of interactive elements within the lesson—ask pupils questions and build a rapport with the children.
- Have all of your resources prepared: pens, paper, worksheets, etc.
- Dress smartly and give yourself plenty of time to arrive.
- You may need your DBS and proof of ID, so be sure to take this with you to show at reception.
- Try to stay calm and relaxed during your observation and interview; show them your confidence and passion for teaching.

Accept the job that feels right for you!

When I speak with Newly Qualified Teachers, I find that most of the time they are worried that they wouldn't find a position as soon as they qualify, and so they tend to accept the first job they applied to just to have a position. I understand their need for security and to complete their induction; however, once they start they would find out that the school was not supportive enough and often end up leaving after a term or two. My advice is to really research the school, and, when completing your Induction at the interview stage or when you visit the school prior to applying, don't be afraid to ask questions about how the school can support you and what the process is.

You need to fulfil your own expectations as well as the school's expectations.

Find a school that feels right for you. There are always options, and that's why you are given a period to complete your induction.

Good luck and credit to you for aspiring to become a teacher!

Poonam Matharu, CertRP, is a School Governor and the Director of Arden Education, a recruitment specialist agency placing teaching professionals into primary schools across the West Midlands on a temporary and permanent basis.

What They Didn't Teach Me About Writing Work-Related Letters

Theodore Griffiths

Throughout your professional life as a teacher, you will be required to write formal letters. Some of these will be a pleasure to write, as you write to accept a new job, or even to resign from a toxic one. Some, however, are less simple to draft. I am giving some suggestions for how to set about writing an effective and courteous letter in some of the difficult situations that you may face as a teacher, despite nobody telling you about these on your PGCE.

I will add that these difficult situations most probably will not arise for you, as most people have a rewarding and fulfilling career in teaching. But here these letters are, as a backup, just in case.

1. Letter of application
2. Letter accepting a job offer
3. Letter resigning a teaching post
4. Letter requesting a part-time post after maternity leave
5. Letter from part-timer asked to attend Inset on non-working day
6. Letter from part-timer asked to attend Parents' Evening on non-working day
7. Letter declining to carry out tasks during sick leave for work-related stress
8. Letter requesting school not to contact during sick leave for work-related stress
9. Letter declining to attend a meeting during sick leave for work-related stress

1. Letter of Application

This is the one letter that I am not going to draft for you, as it is very important that you write your own. But I will give some general tips.

The letter or statement must be professional in its appearance with no grammatical or spelling errors, so that it impresses at first glance and is also professional in its content. It should be well-structured and address the points made in the documentation sent by the school. Where possible, back up your statements with data, and check and re-check that you are sending it to the right person at the right school. It is not unusual to receive an application mentioning a different school.

Overall, the emphasis will be not so much looking back at what you have done, but, as much as possible, looking forward to what you will do for their pupils and for that specific school overall.

2. Letter Accepting a Job Offer

The aim of the letter is not only to accept the offer, it is to set out clearly what you believe to be the conditions of the offer. So you should specify that it is full-time or part-time (and the %), and whether it is permanent or fixed-term, if that was what the job was advertised at, even if it's not stated in their letter, so that there is no misunderstanding later on. Include the salary offered, adding *pro-rata,* of course, if part-time. If the job offered in their letter is more specific than just *Teacher*, copy this in your reply: *Teacher of KS1* or *Teacher of MFL.* Check that your contract, when you get it (which may not be until half term after you joined), also has the full details. Address your acceptance to whomever sent the offer letter, normally the Headteacher, unless the post is Headteacher or Deputy, when it is likely to be the Chair of Governors.

21 May 2019

Dear Ms Greene,
Thank you for your letter of 20 May 2019.

*I confirm that I accept the full-time permanent post of teacher of Mathematics in Treetops Academy, with effect from 1 September 2019, at a starting salary of £xxx (*write it in*).*

I shall shortly provide you with the documents that you have requested. I look forward to joining your team of staff and contributing to the further success of the school.

Yours sincerely,
Alan Browne

Sometimes a school makes you an offer on the phone, but doesn't send you the written offer quickly enough. In that case, you could write to accept the verbal offer, which has contractual force, but is not easy to prove.

7 June 2019

Dear Ms Greene,

Part-time (0.75) permanent post of Teacher of English

I am writing to confirm my acceptance of the offer made to me on the telephone by Ms. Oliver, Head of English, on the evening of Thursday 23 May 2019.

She offered and I accepted during that conversation the part-time (0.75) permanent post of Teacher of English in Treetops Academy, beginning on 1 September 2019, at a starting salary of £XXX, pro-rata.

I would be pleased to receive a written copy of this offer for my records, plus details of any other paperwork that I should provide for you prior to the beginning of my employment.

I look forward to joining your school and contributing to its continuing success.

Yours sincerely,
Alan Browne

3. Letter Resigning a Teaching Post

Make sure that you know the deadline dates for handing in your resignation.

Whether you are sad or delighted at leaving a school, whether you have been well or badly treated, you write exactly the same resignation letter. You neither try to score points nor get things off your chest. The letter is written to the person who wrote your offer letter, or their successor in that role.

22 May 2019

Dear Ms Greene,

I wish to confirm that I am resigning my post of Teacher of Mathematics in Treetops Academy with effect from 1 September 2019. My last date of employment will therefore be 31 August 2019, and my last date of attendance will be (put in date of last day of term, unless you are in the leadership team or otherwise required to attend during the holidays, such as a Head of Department on Results Days*).*

I would like to thank you and the rest of the teachers in Treetops Academy for the support that you have all provided for me throughout my time here. I have much enjoyed working as a part of this team of teachers, and appreciate the opportunities that I have had for personal and professional development. I shall ensure that my remaining time working with the students in Treetops Academy will be as successful as earlier.

Yours sincerely,
Alan Browne

4. Letter Requesting a Part-Time Post, e.g., When Returning from Maternity Leave

You can request part-time working at any time, but after maternity leave is popular. You should be aware that the change is permanent; you cannot require the school to reinstate you as a full-time teacher, although they might agree to do so if it suits you both. This letter is a draft for making a statutory (formal) request.

The onus is on you, by the way, to suggest what problems may arise and how they could be solved. In teaching, these are normally communication issues.

22 May 2019

Dear Ms Greene,

I would like to apply to work a pattern that is different to my normal working pattern, under my right provided in law.
I would like this new pattern of working to begin on 1 September 2019.

I comply with the requirements for this request since:
** I have been employed continuously in the school for the last 26 weeks; and*
** I have not made a statutory request to work flexibly under this right during the past 12 months.*
The proposed new working pattern that I am applying for is part-time 60%, three days a week.
This will affect you as an employer in that ....
This impact on you as an employer can be lessened or removed by ....
I understand that according to the legislation, my request will be considered and decided upon within three months of the receipt of the request. I also understand that employers must have a sound business reason for rejecting any request.

Yours sincerely,
Jane Browne

5. Letter from Part-Timer Asked to Attend Inset on Non-Working Day

Your school has asked you to come in for Inset on a day when you are not employed as a part-timer. You may be happy to attend this Inset, although it means working unpaid. Or you may be unable to do so because of another commitment, or prefer not to simply because unpaid overtime is unfair. Here is the type of letter to write.

22 May 2019

Dear Ms Greene,

*I see that on the School calendar there is an Inset session which is to be held on a (*insert day, e.g., Wednesday*).*
I am afraid that I shall be unable to attend this training session.

*EITHER, if you have another job Wednesdays or whenever, write something along these lines:
*As you are aware, my contracted days of work are (*Monday, Tuesday and Thursday*). I am contracted to another employer on (*Wednesdays*), and so am unable to attend.*

*OR, if you don't have another job on Wednesdays or whenever, write something along these lines:

*As you are aware, my contracted days of work are (*Monday, Tuesday and Thursday*). I have another commitment on (*Wednesday 4th September*) and most (*Wednesdays*), and so am unable to attend.*

I am sorry if this causes any inconvenience. If you feel that it is important that I receive this training, then if payment were to be given at the supply daily rate, this could enable me to make alternative arrangements for my commitment so that I could attend.

Yours sincerely,
Angela Browne

N.B. You do not have to justify in any way what that other commitment might be. *A personal commitment* is all you need reply if there is a query. It could be your turn to cook supper on Wednesdays—they don't need to know that.

6. Letter from Part-Timer Asked to Attend Parents' Evening on Non-Working Day

Your school expects you to attend a Parents' Evening on a day when you are not employed as a part-timer. You may be happy to attend, i.e., to work unpaid. Or you may be unable to do so because of another commitment, or prefer not to simply because unpaid overtime is unfair. Here is the type of letter to write.

22 May 2019

Dear Ms Greene,

*I have noted on the School calendar the date of the Parents' Evening for Year (*8*), which is to be held on a (*insert day, e.g., Thursday*).*

I am afraid that I shall be unable to attend.

*EITHER, if you have another job on Thursdays or whenever, write something along these lines:

*As you are aware, my contracted days of work are (*Monday-Wednesday*).*

*I am contracted to another employer on (*Thursdays*), and so am unable to attend.*

*OR, if you don't have another job on Thursdays or whenever, write something along these lines:

*As you are aware, my contracted days of work are (*Monday-Wednesday*). I have another commitment on (*Thursday 2 July*), and so am unable to attend.*

*I am sorry if this causes any inconvenience. If you feel that it is important that parents receive my feedback, and especially if some are specifically requesting it, I could perhaps telephone those parents on the afternoon of (*Wednesday 1 July*), if someone else were to relieve me of teaching my classes so that I was free to do so.*

Yours sincerely,
Brian Browne

N.B. You do not have to justify in any way what that other commitment might be. *A personal commitment* is all you need reply if there is a query. And you could also suggest being paid for this evening.

7. Letter Declining to Carry Out Tasks During Sick Leave for Work-Related Stress

When you are signed off by your doctor, it means signed off from all work; this includes marking, reports, lesson preparation and all curriculum planning. Now if you have a broken leg and are bored to tears, you might wish to do something—although the key is that you don't have to. However, colleagues signed off with anxiety or work-related stress should most certainly not do any work-related tasks. None at all.

22 May 2019

Dear Ms. Greene,

I have today received a letter/e-mail/phone call from you/my HoD/a colleague asking me to set work/mark coursework/write reports for my classes.
I am afraid that I must decline to do this.

*As you know, I am currently signed off from work with a Fit Note that expires on (*give date*).*
During this period, I must concentrate all my efforts on returning to health, and so am unable to carry out any of the duties normally associated with my post as a teacher in Treetops Academy.

*You will understand that in order to ensure that my health improves and I am therefore able to return to my duties on (*date Fit Note says*), I must follow the specific advice of my GP and neither undertake any work related to school, nor deal with queries.*

I would therefore be grateful if you would ensure that all my colleagues are aware that they should not contact me about any school matter at all. Thank you for this.

I am sorry that you and my colleagues will be inconvenienced by my absence, but I am hopeful that by following strictly the advice that I have been given by my medical practitioner, my health will improve sufficiently to enable me to resume my duties at the end of this predicted period of absence.
If, however, my health does not improve and I am not deemed fit for work as soon as I had hoped, then I shall inform you as soon as possible so that you can make any further arrangements to cover my classes and other duties.

Yours sincerely,
David Browne

8. Letter Requesting School Not to Contact During Sick Leave for Work-Related Stress

Colleagues signed off with anxiety or work-related stress should most certainly not do any work-related tasks and should not feel pressured by being contacted by colleagues with requests or queries. So as soon as you have a diagnosis from your Dr, let the school know not only that you will not be attending, but that you should not be contacted with requests to carry out any tasks. Write an e-mail like this, for example.

22 May 2019

Dear Ms Greene, cc Head of Department.

*I am being treated by my GP for a work-related condition. I am sending by post the Fit Note issued by my doctor. The current assessment is that I shall not be fit to return to work before (*insert date from Fit Note*).*

*You will understand that in order to ensure that I return to health and I am therefore able to return to my duties on (*date on Fit Note*), I must follow the clear advice of my GP and neither undertake any work at all related to school, nor deal with queries. This would include all normal tasks, including marking homework, examinations or other assessments, writing reports for parents or internal use, curriculum planning, etc.*

I would therefore be grateful if you would ensure that all my colleagues are fully aware that they should not contact me about any school matter at all. Thank you for this.
I am sorry that you and my colleagues will be inconvenienced by my absence, but I am hopeful that by following strictly the advice that I have been given by my medical practitioner, my health will improve sufficiently to enable me to resume my duties at the end of this predicted period of absence.
If, however, my health does not improve and I am not deemed fit for work as soon as I had hoped, I shall inform you as soon as possible to enable you to make any further arrangements to cover my classes and other duties.

Yours sincerely,
Barbara Browne

9. Letter Declining to Attend a Meeting During Sick Leave for Work-Related Stress

When you are on sick leave due to work-related stress, it can be upsetting to receive a letter or e-mail from school asking you to attend a meeting to discuss your absence. They may even suggest meeting at your house to make it less stressful for you, and even tell you that the union has been informed. If you don't feel up to the meeting, then you need to say so.
You should go to see your GP as soon as possible, so that you can tell her/him about the request being made, say how upsetting and stressful you find this, and if your GP agrees then get medical advice that you

shouldn't be involved. At that point, you should send a letter that might be based on this draft below. You must not, of course, send this letter if you haven't received this advice from your doctor.

22 May 2019

Dear Ms Greene,

Thank you for suggesting a meeting to discuss my ongoing absence from my duties at school. I appreciate the fact that you are trying to support me during this period of poor health, which is causing inconvenience to you and my colleagues.
However, the advice from my medical practitioner is that I should not attend any sort of meeting at present, either on school premises or elsewhere, as this would be prejudicial to my health and thus further delay my return to work, currently predicted to be (give date from last Fit Note).

You will understand that in order to ensure that I regain my health and I am therefore able to return to my duties as soon as possible, I must follow the clear advice of my GP and not meet up with anyone from school to discuss my health, my date of return to work, or any other matter. I have passed this advice from the GP to my Union representative.

I am sorry that you are being inconvenienced by my absence, but I am hopeful that by following strictly the advice that I have been given, my health will improve sufficiently to enable me to resume my duties at the end of the current predicted period of absence.

Yours sincerely,
Clive Browne

Theodore Griffiths, otherwise known as Theo Griff, started teaching 1966. Her professional career includes college, school and university leadership and developing and teaching BEd and PGCE courses. For over a decade, Theo was the job seeking expert on a popular online advice forum for teachers. She has two downloadable books on Amazon about applications and interviews for teaching posts. Theo is currently teaching as a volunteer in an Estepona state primary school in Andalusia, Spain.

What They Didn't Teach Me About
Being an NQT

Chanel Knight

Imagine. It is September, the training course (be it SCITT, PGCE, or Teach First) has been completed and now you hold the title NQT. You now know not to run away when the photocopier breaks, because you will be found; you know to watch what acrobatics you attempt in order to reach the books on the top shelf; you know you need to be a complete a one-man band when decorating your classroom because of Health and Safety; and you know any food left in the middle of the table in the staffroom is fair game!

However, the issue is not the photocopier, your flexibility or the food. It is that first group of students you have in that perfectly-kitted-out classroom, when you take a breath and think 'right, what do I do now?'

Over the coming months, you find your feet, and support systems are developed both in your professional and personal environments. You know what to do and are constantly working hard to improve everything about your teaching—even if you are, at times, a little too hard on yourself. As time passes, you also discover that there are three different types of people that you come across during your NQT year. The first are those who will see you as a normal teacher, nothing more, nothing less, just part of your department. Then, there are those who see that you do have potential—and in some ways see you as better than you think you are. Finally, you will encounter people who see you as still—despite the blood, sweat and tears during your training year—'just a trainee'.

Being seen as 'one of your department' is both perfect and terrifying. You can blend into the background and become a wallflower when you are lacking confidence in some areas, or you can show your strengths and point out that there are different ways to approach the multitude of content that you need to cover. We all put on our CV's that we are 'team players', ready to help anyone who needs it, no matter the experience. That's what being 'one of the department' is. You recognise the different people in your department and fit in where needed, becoming the resident comic, the maverick or the devil's advocate; you join the puzzle and plug the gaps because everyone has a different experience and way of teaching—which, of course, is not only okay, it is needed.

You don't have enough experience. You are new. You are 'only an NQT'; words which I have told myself many times. I do the job to the best of my ability because that is what the students deserve. So why are we so hard on ourselves? These are the moments in time which we need the second group of people. Those who build us up and see a potential that can make us question their sanity. 'Are you sure?' is often a question I have when colleagues say that the lesson was really 'interesting' when only walking past, or when they put you forward for opportunities which you wouldn't dream of going for in your first 'proper' year; coaching others, good practice sessions for the rest of the school, becoming the guinea pig for 'change'. These are the colleagues I think you need the most. They push you to challenge yourself, to aim high and be ambitious. They see 'something' in you that you don't see, they know more about you then you do.

'Just a trainee'; this is a phrase which is a personal bugbear. Anyone who works in education knows that it is a tough job and not everyone could do it. Those who have trained to be teachers understand the hard work that goes in during those first few years to meet teacher standards, discover the teacher you want to be and to find the routine that works for you. I am not disputing that each year you teach has different challenges. I am disputing the fact that trainees are assumed to be inept or unable to provide what our students need. My other gripe is that I am not actually a trainee. I am a newly qualified teacher who works hard for my students; who understands my areas of weakness; and who seeks out ways to help my department and to bring a few more 'positive vibes'.

I often contemplate back to when I completed my training year, and I remember thinking that my NQT year would be 'easier' or 'less stressful'. In actual fact, it was just as hard and just as much stress; however, in some ways I feel more rewarded. While I thought I wasn't ready to be a teacher during my SCITT training, my NQT year has taught me that even though you never feel fully 'ready', you put the game face on, and you become the teacher your class needs.

Chanel Carol Knight is an English teacher currently employed at a Multi-Academy Trust School in Birmingham. She completed a combined Bachelor of Arts in English and Drama at Manchester Metropolitan University before becoming a teacher through South Birmingham SCITT.

What They Didn't Teach Me About
Supply Teaching

Alice Cowell

Teacher training, no matter the route, focuses on becoming a class teacher, and all that that entails. This is very different to supply teaching. Obviously, there is a great overlap of skills and knowledge required for both roles, but no one seems to tell you that supply teaching can be a positive option once you have gained QTS; not just what to do if you do not get a class teacher job before September.

Doing supply is a great way to try different schools and year groups. You find out, as I did, that not all schools are the same. This includes how well they look after their supply teachers. Make sure you come prepared with lunch, water and good bladder control (you may not be shown where the staff toilets and staff room are and, if you are, you may not remember how to get there!); take many stickers, no matter the age of your class; arm yourself with a good range of behaviour-management techniques and activities/websites and games to fill time; be prepared to teach from a detailed lesson plan, a single sentence, nothing at all and everything in between.

Supply is a great way to develop certain skills, such as building quick rapport with children and colleagues and thinking on your feet. It also allows you to take self-care days when you need them, and to find out so much more about the sort of teacher you are and the sort of school you want to work in.

You can complete your NQT induction while doing supply. In England, this is only possible if you do long-term supply for at least the equivalent of one term. However, in Wales, each half day of supply counts towards your NQT induction. It should be noted that you cannot combine both English and Welsh NQT inductions.

You do not have to be with an agency or Local Authority supply register to do supply. You can approach schools directly.

Supply is not how I thought I would spend the second half of my first year of teaching; I must admit though, I love it more than I ever thought I would.

Alice Cowell, BSc (Hons), MSc, is a mature NQT, currently working as a supply teacher. She spent 12 years in the environmental sector, over half of that as a freelance environmental trainer and consultant. After four years as a Teaching Assistant, circumstances were finally right for Alice to make the final move into education and begin her PGCE.

What They Didn't Teach Me About Working as a Teacher Overseas

Jamie O'Dowd

What they don't teach you during your PGCE is that your teaching qualification, coupled with a couple of years' experience under your belt, is a passport to a world of travel and adventure. Picking the right school in the right country is key; for every teacher who will tell you they have landed their dream job somewhere around the globe, there are many others who will tell you they have landed in hell. Don't expect an extended holiday though. Working in an ambitious international school is tough work; parents pay good money and expect the best education for their kids. Having said that, provided you do your homework, moving abroad to teach could be the best move you ever make. Student behaviour is often much better than back home, and although the community can be quite transient, expats generally stick together and look out for each other. Moving your family abroad might seem daunting, but the lifestyle offered in warmer, sunnier climates often negates those early feelings of homesickness. Many ex-pats teaching abroad find a whole new world of opportunities open to them, whether it be a new hobby such as windsurfing, boating, trekking or simply being able to make health and fitness more of a priority—working overseas is life-changing in many ways.

Moving overseas isn't for everyone of course, but if you have ever leafed the International Jobs pages of the TES, you will already know that British Schools exist in every corner of the globe and British teachers are highly sought after for jobs in these schools. Of course, in the UK, British schools also need qualified teachers, so taking your teaching status and experience overseas is frowned upon in some circles, but don't let that put you off considering international teaching as an exciting and rewarding career choice.

Jamie O'Dowd. Assistant Headteacher of St Christopher's School, Bahrain.

What They Didn't Teach Me About

Being a Mature Student

Carmel Gibbons

I completed my second PGCE at the age of 56 (just!), and am now completing my NQT year in a challenging but rewarding school in Bradford. The reason I retrained was that I was coming to the end of a six-year project and felt a strong desire to belong to a team (my previous work involved short contracts in China), and to connect to a subject that I felt very passionate about (English). When I applied for the PGCE, I received a call from an advisor who helped me through the process, but in fact it was relatively straightforward. It is worth speaking to teachers, and also getting onto 'Get into teaching' websites, because there is a lot of information out there.

I ended up applying to a SCITT at the school that my daughters had attended. I was very nervous, but they couldn't have been more helpful. I enjoyed the SCITT route because it was quite gentle. We had a month in the classroom with lots of excellent lectures and a lovely cohort of trainee teachers before we were farmed out into schools. I was surprised that there were quite a few people not too far from my age who were also training, as well as younger (but very friendly) teachers straight out of university. I am still in touch with several of those people.

Our SCITT had excellent links with many schools in the area, and we all had placements. We also had subject leads for each subject; before we went out on placement, we spent a couple of days visiting the school where our subject lead was based—we had the chance to lead part of a lesson, which was a great confidence boost. It turned out that our subject lead was one of the best English teachers in the country (according to the results at the school), and we had sessions with her every Friday for six months. That part of the training couldn't have been better. Everyone on the course was very impressed with this part of the training.

I had two placement schools. The first placement was in a large Catholic school with a very big English department. I was teaching for six hours a week. Once I got over the fact that my mentor was half my age, I settled down really quickly—and it also helped that my host teachers were great! I loved the school, and it was brilliant to have the chance to meet so many teachers and watch their lessons. I strongly advise you to get into as many classrooms as you can at any stage of your teaching!

My second placement was at an Islamic all-girls school, where my subject lead was based. I spent the whole of Christmas worrying that I wasn't going to be good enough, but it was such a waste of time. I was welcomed with open arms. Training is lovely; you can ask as many questions as you need to, and your host teachers and mentors are so helpful. There is also the support from your SCITT in case there are any problems (such as personality clashes). The important thing is not to be afraid to ask for help. Humility goes a long way in education. I think I was scared because, being older, I thought people would expect me to know it all, but actually I couldn't have been more wrong. Teachers are delighted to be asked for their opinion and are often very humble themselves (and very funny too!).

I found my training year to be a very happy and fulfilling experience. It is the best thing I have done for ages. It prepared me for my NQT year, which has been more challenging in some ways; but then, I do put a lot of pressure on myself to get things right the first time. My advice would be to find your own style and to enjoy and get to know your students. There are some hilarious moments in the classroom. Every day is different. Don't ever feel you have to control the students. Controlling yourself is much more important. The students are responsible for their behaviour and you are modelling it for them. I am so proud of the students I am teaching this year. Their progress is amazing, and what a good feeling that creates!

Carmel Gibbons started her teaching career in Further Education. She made the transition to secondary school teaching because she feels passionate about making a difference to the lives of young people.

Chapter 13

Parting Words of Wisdom

Teach

Matthew Roberts

A fifty-minute, one-man show as advertised in the Edinburgh Fringe Festival 2019.

The lesson that changed his life.
A school in struggle and strife.
A government that uses a knife.

EPILOGUE

IF I stay—IF I go —
IF…
IF, I am 'class', then I am higher or lower.
IF, I am 'gay', then I am Muscle Mary—'do you know 'er?'.
IF, I am 'son', then I am my fathers' legacy.
IF, I am 'teach', I am more than my identity.
IF, I am 'teach-able', I am free.
IF— We—DARE TEACH.
Each other.
Each sister.
Each brother.
Each father.
Each mother.
Each friend.
Each lover.
Each 'other' —
Together.
In common unity.
Ignorance dies.
Lives are set free.
We become each other's amnesty.
I believe in you.
To be, to do, to process, manifest! What is in our DNA—Do you see?
Oh! What this life, this world, has in store for thee, and thee, and thee.
Draw your dragons.
Paint your colours.
SHINE YOUR LIGHT.
Each morning.
Each afternoon.

No matter how GREY the day
No matter how DARK the night.
DELIGHT—In—'not knowing'.
DELIGHT—In—'growing'.
DARING…
TEACH—To transform.
TEACH—To transcend.
TEACH the heart to heal and mend,
Our fractured times,
That are out of *joint.*
TEACH,
So they TEACH,
The next generation,
To TEACH it better, and better, and better, and better, and better—isn't that the *point?*
I need a cuppa tea!
Let's reflect,
over a brew,
'The brief chronicles of our times.'
Stir. Ideas.
(One lump or two?)
And experience things anew.
TEACH
inside or outside a classroom
TEACH
'them' to
REACH FURTHER THAN THEIR GRASP
…Is that too big an ask?
A brand new start.
To live the life imagined.
TEACH —
That transformational lesson.
(Like Mrs Raymer/ Thank you Mrs Raymer)
TEACH —
The warmth in your heart,

That lives on in me, and thee, and thee, and thee
AND—MAKES—LIVING…
…ART!
LET'S BEGIN!

Matthew Roberts is passionate about the transformative power of the arts. His work with the Shakespeare Schools Festival, Digital Theatre +, The South Bank Show and Sky Arts illuminate just some of his contribution to the arts on a local, national and international level.

What They Didn't Teach Me About
My First Day

Flo Awolaja

'From little acorns grow oak trees'—as a child I often wondered what that meant. You see as children; many things are said that we only ever understand when we reach adulthood; even then, we often struggle to make sense of them.

On my first day at school, I clutched my Dad's hand tightly. As a child it is so reassuring to have a parent walk you to school and guide you on your first day, secure in the knowledge that if you fell over in the playground and grazed your knee, coming home and telling your parents would put everything into perspective, soothe your woes and help you to move on. However, going to school as a teacher on your first day as an adult is quite different. Here is my story.

Little Acorns

Her day-to-day existence had recently merged into an all-day cloud. The monotony of shoving envelopes into the communal box was more than she could bear. She looked at her watch: in a few more hours, the shift would be over. She had to get back to complete her application. Why she'd ever decided to do it, Lord knows. She was impulsive like that—see something, do it. Now reality was dawning, the deadline loomed, she had to get it in.

Sitting by her makeshift desk, she took a last look at the application: spell check, name check, date check. She signed it, sealed it, put it in the envelope and sent it off.

A few days later, she heard the clang of the letterbox. Looking at the address on the envelope, she realised that it was from the school. Turning it over, she took the letter opener and slid it through the top. She quickly skimmed the contents, her eyes moving a second behind her brain: *Dear Ms, We are pleased to...* She'd gotten through. She swallowed hard. Would she ring to confirm her attendance? Now what?

The next few weeks were a blur. The day was upon her. She'd washed and lain her clothes out the night before, cleaned her shoes, dusted off her rucksack, bought a new set of pens, all in anticipation of her first day. 2:30 am, 3:30 am, 4:30 am… The alarm clock rang at 7:00 am but she hadn't got much sleep. A little queasy, she had butterflies; the smell of breakfast didn't help. How was she to hold down anything? Taking deep breaths, she tried as best she could to stem the rising panic. After a few minutes her breathing returned to normal levels. Throwing the covers back, she swung her legs off the bed, sat up and stared at the heap in the corner. She hadn't felt this surge of anticipation since she was a child. 'Come on!' she said to herself, psyching herself up: 'you've got this, you've only to walk through the doors'.

Stretching her arms, she stood up, shook the remaining sleep from her system before jumping in the shower. The cool flow of water evaporated her creeping thoughts. Reaching for the towel, she dried herself and set about getting ready. Keeping an ever-watchful eye on the clock, she noticed it was going quickly. No time to amble. The bus would be here soon; like all sensible folk, she'd taken the time to check the timetable. Her first day, she would not be late, it just wouldn't do. Taking a last look in the mirror, she checked herself once more, and all was well. Putting on her coat, grabbing her rucksack and keys, walking through the door, she was gone.

As she proceeded to the bus stop, she muttered to herself, getting weary looks from those approaching. 'This talking to myself must stop'; her nerves had gotten the better of her again. It would take some serious breathing to get them down.

Before long., the bus arrived, she squeezed on and found a seat. She wasn't in the mood for conversation and promptly stared ahead, focused. Even so, people tried to engage her, and she was grateful when she got to her stop. She quickly stood, excusing herself and with that she was off.

Crossing the tree-lined road, she entered the gates filled with the bustling throng of students, inhaling a last thought: 'This is your first day'.

Putting her best foot forward she strode to the reception;

'Hi, I'm the new teacher'.

Flo Awolaja is a mental health advocate and creative consultant. Flo has enjoyed a successful career as a graphic designer, allowing her to combine her passion for art and design with teaching. As a lecturer, Flo works to raise achievement in all learners, encouraging them, raising their self-esteem and aspiring confidence in them. Flo is currently working towards an MA in Education.

What They Didn't Teach Me About
Being a Super Hero

Corinne Latham

You've been accepted. You're on the course. Now it's time for hard work to begin. This is the start of an amazing journey; you are about become a teacher, but to some you will be a superhero. The young people you encounter will look to you to impart all that you know, not just about your subject, but also how to be an amazing adult. All young people need love. It's a very challenging world they are negotiating. They need you.

Be the Teacher by Corinne Latham

Be the teacher who is prepared.
Be the teacher who shares values.
Be the teacher who claps first.
Be the teacher who listens.
Be the teacher who laughs with the class rather than at them.
Be the teacher who is the cheers for the underdog.
Be the teacher who radiates positive energy.
Be the teacher who goes the extra mile.
Be the teacher who is known for knowing them.
Be the teacher who is generous in words and deeds.
Be the teacher who is relentless in their pursuit of excellence.
Be the teacher who inspired you to be a better version of yourself.
Be the teacher who loves their pupils unconditionally.
Be the teacher who is confident in the knowledge you can change the world by the lessons you impart.

Enjoy your training, embrace the opportunities and learn from your challenges. Over your career, you will create a legacy that will influence generations—and in my opinion, there is no better superpower than that.

Corinne Latham, B.Ed (Hons), MSc, PQH, MCCT. Corinne is a Primary School Principal in Belfast.

Parting Words of Advice Written by Teachers for Teachers

A collection of narratives

Making a difference: My teacher training programme did not teach me how important it would be to serve as my students' advocate when it came to discussing events that could determine their future, or—because it may not happen at home—how important it would be to celebrate all the little milestones that are achieved in the classroom. Every day in my classroom is a new opportunity to make a small difference in one student's life, and I've learned that these students have such an impact on my life. Every student I have had has shaped me into the teacher I am today, and I am forever grateful for that experience.—**Jessica Reed.**

Seek help from your colleagues: Although other teachers in your school may not know your exact subject area, they do know general things about teaching that could be helpful to you. For example, your colleagues could help you with classroom management techniques, how to read and understand policies, the characteristics of students and the culture of the school. In addition, there will be times when you have had a troublesome lesson and your colleagues are best placed to support you in these instances.—**Ben Zunica.**

Finding a job: I completed my PGCE from Goldsmiths College in the summer of 2012—the very month and year that London hosted the Olympic Games. I thought that the euphoria surrounding the games would match my teaching practice, especially going into teaching with the extensive management and technical skills I had from twenty plus years in the Civil Service. I remember feeling quite dismayed when, by the mid-point of the programme, fellow students were already securing NQT positions, and I had yet to even get interview invitations. Just after that point, I managed to secure some supply work, which boosted my confidence that I would secure an NQT position. It was just before the end of that school year that I had heard a school not far from where I live was recruiting; apparently, they were so impressed with one of my fellow students who had been offered a post that the Headteacher of the school wanted to see more students from Goldsmiths. Within less than two days of requesting an application, I was interviewed and offered a post at the school.—**Allen Tsui.**

Relationship building: Prioritise getting to know your students, and making time for fun activities. I forgot this at times during my PGCE and NQT year. As soon as you start screeching at a class, you've lost them; go back to basics and start again. Relationships can break down at any time, so it's important to invest and sustain them. I don't recall anyone telling me how attached I would get to some students. This is particularly the case with SEN and alternative provision; you invest so much time in relationship-building because you cannot make any progress without it. I'm still in contact with some ex-pupils—in fact, just this week an ex-pupil and family member called in to school to see me. Don't underestimate the impact we can have on young people and the impact young people can have on us.—**Helen Abbot.**

Be authentic: My best pieces of advice are: Remember that each child is someone's baby, so treat each child with empathy and care. Greet every child with a 'Good morning!' and a smile every day. Don't do anything differently for Ofsted; if what you're already doing is right for the children, it'll be right for Ofsted. Don't try putting on a show; the children will drop you in it! Be a good listener, with a friendly face. Appreciate your teaching assistants and ensure you communicate effectively with them. They are a Godsend and so are the office staff. Thank them regularly.—**Lisa Atkinson.**

Use reverse psychology: Ask yourself the following question: why do children display challenging behaviour? Not every case is the same of course, and there could be many issues that the child is dealing with that can lead to this, but most children will present as a challenge because they are desperate for attention, be it positive or negative.

Some children live in a world where they receive very little, if any, positive attention from their families. All they are used to is the negative attention they receive. Shouting at these children will have little, if any, impact, and the result will be a 'no win'. Why not reverse the process? Diffuse the challenge, continue the lesson, and then afterwards spend some time with that individual, discussing with them the result of their behaviour. I have found this tool to be one of the most effective ways of winning over those children that present the most challenge.—**Jamie Parkinson.**

You'll always be adapting: Experience has taught me that all the systems and structures in the world are only a toolkit. What you use or don't use is dictated by the needs of the children in front of you. Sometimes that may mean you work off gut instinct. It certainly means you constantly tweak and adapt your approach.—**Sue Parkes.**

Accept when you've been defeated: If a fly enters your classroom, it's lesson over. Admit defeat!—**Laura Bacon.**

Social dynamics: The classroom is actually a microcosm of social dynamics and its environment is one of the most important elements of good teaching. Students are not empty vessels to be filled or quiet and inquisitive beings willing to soak up your wisdom. It is important to consider the social environment; I classify it into three Fs: Facebook, Frenemies and Friends.

Facebook—Okay, any social media. The ability to connect people rapidly across time and space is one of the great change agents of the internet age. However, the relatively anonymous world of social media may lead to increases in negative activity. Young people are growing up in a totally different social landscape.

Frenemies—the social dynamics of the first three years of secondary school can be a whirlwind of groups, sub-groups, being in/out/whatever. Besties one day could be frenemies the next.

Friends—not the opposite of frenemies! These are students who will always get on with one another. They aren't likely to upset the peaceful social dynamics. Used wisely, friends can help stabilise your class, calling others to get into line and generally getting on with things.—**Dr Paul Ganderton.**

The welcome: After starting my career in an inner city school, I now know that the phrase 'they will find and push your buttons' is a complete understatement. My first lesson with a class of 15 Year 11 girls was welcomed with 'Who the **** are you and do you think you are teaching us now?' It was a warm welcome that continued for weeks. Through some hard work, determination and music from the band Rudimental, we built in a class anthem: 'Not Giving In'. It was played at the start of each lesson, and woe betide me if I forgot to play it. I had to quickly become an expert in fashion, prom dresses and boybands to relate every task to them to get their buy-in. It was a tough learning curve, but a great lesson in perseverance and challenge.—**Danny Bullock.**

The Most Common Feedback Given to Trainee Teachers

Chris Powell

Avoid 'dead time'…

In other words, try to make the transitions between the different tasks in your lessons as smooth as possible. Have the resource for the first task already on their desks at the start of the lesson. Hand out the resource for the second task whilst they're doing the first. Have the YouTube clip already set up in the right place, and ensure the speakers are working before the lesson. You get the idea. This is important because the engagement and flow of a lesson can be instantly flattened if the students find themselves sat with nothing to do whilst the teacher goes round the room handing out a worksheet or is frantically fumbling around on the computer trying to find the right slide with their back to the class.

Do some teaching…

Some teachers were brought up to believe that in a 60-minute lesson a teacher must not talk for more than ten minutes; essentially the idea is that chalk and talk is bad, while kids doing stuff is good. This has meant I've observed lessons whereby the teacher provides 60 minutes of different activities. Complete a worksheet, watch this video, answer these questions, do this card sort. At no point did the teacher actually stand at the front and *teach* anything. Don't be afraid to stand at the front and explain the concept your lesson is about. I bet your favourite teacher at school enthused you because of how they spoke and explained things—be like them!

Stay focussed on your lesson objectives…

It's very easy to find a really good activity and try to crowbar it in to a lesson, but if it has nothing to do with your lesson objective, it's a waste of valuable lesson time. Your lesson objective is what you want the students to have learnt by the time the bell rings. Therefore, everything you get the students to do during the lesson should be with the aim of getting them to meet that objective. Ask yourself *why* you are getting the students to do this; remembering this key point actually makes planning lessons much less scary!

Be enthusiastic!...

You should love the subject you teach. If you don't, then teaching is going to be a tough job. Sometimes I have seen lessons delivered by teachers who seem to find their subject the dullest thing on the planet, or who explain things in a monotone voice that does little to motivate the class. Be nerdy about your subject: embrace your inner boffin! The teaching standards emphasise promoting a love of learning and being a good role model. Show your students that you love learning—and, more importantly, that you love learning about **your** subject. Your enthusiasm might just rub off on your students and inspire the next generation of geographers, historians, mathematicians, biologists, etc.

And finally...

It truly is an honour to be allowed to observe another teacher's lesson. I am grateful for all the lessons I have observed over the years, and if any of the above is remotely helpful, then that'll be great.

Chris Powell is the Initial Teacher Training Lead for Parmiter's School and the Herts & Bucks TSA. Chris has been teaching for 13 years and is a Founding Fellow of the Chartered College of Teaching. Chris is also the Geography subject specialist for ITT at the University of Hertfordshire. @_Training2Teach.

What They Didn't Teach Me About
Getting Through Your First Year

James Hilton

Having been a headteacher of one of the largest primary schools in the UK and having twice been seconded to support NQTs across our local authority, it would be fair to say I have witnessed the highs and occasional lows that many teachers experience in their first year. Let me humbly offer my advice on dealing with some of the pressures of the first year.

1. Teaching can be one of the most rewarding jobs in the world, and yet we rarely know the long-term impact we have. I was approached by a theatre director in Birmingham a couple of years ago. Turns out he was a formal pupil of mine who fell in love with acting after I cast him in our leavers production years ago. When times get tough, remind yourself why you went into the job.
2. Most NQTs 'hit a wall' in terms of tiredness at some point. This is perfectly normal. To counter this, try and get your body clock set during the week, keeping regular going to bed and waking times.
3. Eat breakfast! You would be surprised how many teachers don't, but without it your metabolism has nothing to fire on, and you will struggle. Avoid sugary snacks during the day. Foods such as blueberries and bananas give a slow, steady, release of energy. Drink plenty of water.
4. Be realistic about what you can achieve each day. Many teachers over-schedule, and then their time is taken up with pastoral

issues, leaving them frustrated at the end of the day because they have not achieved all that they had hoped.

5. Teaching is one of those jobs where there will always be more that you can do. Do not burn yourself out; it is a marathon, not a sprint, and as one very wise director of education once told me, sometimes okay has to be enough.
6. You will feel swamped at times by your 'to do lists': that will never change. Try breaking your list for each day into 'Must', 'Should' and 'Could'. It only takes a couple of minutes, but it helps you prioritise.
7. Plan one evening when you will do something that is non-school related so that your brain gets a break.
8. In the staff room, choose your friends carefully. Without being rude to anyone, avoid the serial moaners (you will soon find out who they are). Align yourself with positive people, and don't get drawn in to rumour mongering and complaining about the leadership team. You may be surprised at what gets back!
9. Stay in contact with the people you trained with. It is worth investing the time; you may be far flung, but social media makes it easy. They can be a valuable source of support, but remember, you also have to give in order to receive.
10. It's okay to not feel okay. Don't beat yourself up about it. It's okay to have a bad day, week, or even month, but if you feel like you are struggling, talk to someone. You don't have a glass head, so they cannot see what you are thinking or feeling. Whilst people expect you be professional, they don't expect you know everything. People will want you to succeed, so don't be afraid to ask for help.

James Hilton is a former Headteacher and an international writer, author and speaker. He helps people to navigate the stresses and strains of the modern workplace in both the public and private sectors. He is the author of two books on leadership, resilience and stress management.

Parting Words of Wisdom from School Principal of the Year

Marie Lindsay, BSc (HONS), MSc (Dist), PGCE, PQH
St Mary's College, Derry, Northern Ireland

Don't Sweat the Small Stuff

When I started teaching, I remember worrying so much that I didn't know all the Science and Maths well enough to teach it. Don't worry about this: I realise now that I will never know everything, as there is new knowledge everyday. So don't worry about what you know or don't know—you know enough. The most important thing is to keep learning. Keep improving what you do. Be relentless about this! As you start leading learning in your classroom and your new school, remember that you too are learning and you will continue to learn as long as you teach. Learning is a bit like exercise—it is addictive! The good thing about this is that you don't have to know everything or get everything right—just keep learning and enjoy it!

Like the Children You Teach!

This sounds too obvious, but I have met a few teachers over the years who expect the students to be mini-adults. You will be a much better teacher if you care about your students, and if you try to help them to develop socially and emotionally as well as academically. Get to know them, be interested in them, be a good listener, be fair and consistent, kind and respectful; be especially kind to the challenging ones, the ones with attitude—they have their struggles and their own story. Your kindness might be the only kindness in their day. You can make them or break them. You are gifted with an unbelievable privilege; use it with great care and compassion, no matter how difficult or how challenging the situation. You have the chance to help, to heal and give them hope.

Help Those Who Are Struggling

Look around your new school. Look and listen to the staff, both teaching and support, and notice what they say and do. Decide who you think are enthusiastic, positive and happy people in their work, and stick with them. Their positivity and enthusiasm is infectious, so stay close. Same is true for the cynics and the moaners; while we all have off days, staff who are negative all the time will impact how you feel and drag you down, so avoid them as much as possible. If someone is struggling, just ask if you can help in any way. Try to avoid staff gossip, especially toxic talk about staff or students. We are all human, we all have family, and we all have our failings. Try not to judge or condemn—offer to listen and to understand instead.

Remember—You Are Good Enough

Take good care of yourself. It's important to put your family first always, eat well, exercise regularly, switch off from work, stay connected to friends and family and laugh often. Ask for help when you need it, build good people around you, be yourself—you are enough, in fact, you are more than enough. Enjoy transforming the lives of the children you teach. There is no greater honour!

Marie Lindsay is the Principal of St. Mary's College in Derry, Northern Ireland. She is a board member of School Employer Connections, the Walled City Music Partnership, the Shared Education Learning Forum (SELF) and a member of Derry City and Strabane District Council's Education and Skills working group. Marie was named Principal of the Year at the Foyle Blackboard Awards in 2016 and in 2018, she was inducted into the Business Excellence Hall of Fame.

Afterword
by Professor Barnaby Lenon CBE

Dean of Education, University of Buckingham

I did my PGCE at Cambridge in 1978. In those days, it was one term of teaching practice and two terms of study in the university (my special subjects were Plato's Philosophy and Victorian Education); this was my preparation for 35 years of teaching.

The thing which annoyed me most was that they did not teach me how to drive a minibus full of teenagers, something I had to do from day one in my first job. Very dangerous. Nor did they teach me how to control a difficult class... an unbelievable omission. But the PGCE year did give me time to improve my subject knowledge.

Looking back after many years of teaching, there are two things I would add. Well three, really. In my one term of teaching practice, I was living in someone's garage, which had been converted into a spare bedroom. It was one of the coldest winters in history; the garage had three outside walls and a flat roof, so I was forced to prepare my lessons in the pub every evening. But that was only a short-term problem.

What I really wish is that I had been taught more about the history and structurc of schools and qualifications in England. Why are so many schools run by the Church of England? What are Catholic schools? Grammar schools? These days, as things have becoming even more complicated, what exactly are free schools and Academies?

I also wish I'd been taught something about the importance and value of teaching. Now in my sixties, I have become fairly visible in the media; this has prompted a number of former pupils, some only a few years younger than me, to get in touch and tell me what impact I had on their lives. Who knew! Fortunately, no day, no lesson, was ever boring to me—even if I was teaching the same topic for the twentieth time. The pupils change, and it is that what makes all the difference.

At the end of a career, I look back and am so pleased that I stuck with my decision to be a teacher.

Professor Barnaby Lenon taught at Eton School for twelve years, was the Deputy Head of Highgate School, Head of Trinity School and the Head of Harrow for twelve years. He then helped to establish the London Academy of Excellence in East London, one of the most successful state sixth form Academies, where he is Chair of Governors. He is also the Chair of the Independent School's Council and has been a governor of sixteen state and independent schools. Professor Lenon is a director of the New Schools Network, which helps groups wishing to establish new schools under the government's free schools policy. He was a member of the board of Ofqal during the Gove reforms to GCSEs and A-Levels and is now on their Standards Advisory Committee. He has written six books and researches the characteristics of effective teachers in the UK and USA. Professor Lenon is the Dean of Education at the University of Buckingham in the UK.

About the Curator

Sarah Mullin, BA (HONS), PGCE, PG Cert, Ed PG, Dip Ed, MA, CTE, MTLA, FInstLM, CMgr, FCMI, FCCT, FRSA

Sarah Mullin is an experienced Deputy Headteacher who has been coaching and mentoring teachers for over fifteen years. Sarah studied English with Linguistics at Queen's University Belfast, and she is currently in the final phase of her Doctorate in Education. Sarah is a Chartered Teacher of English and a Chartered Manager; additionally, she is a Fellow of numerous organisations, including the Royal Society of Arts, the Chartered Management Institute, and she is a Founding Fellow of the Chartered College of Teaching.

Sarah Mullin has supported teachers and school leaders across the UK; she is also a DfE Women Leading in Education Coach. She has been shortlisted as a finalist in a number of award ceremonies, including 'Headteacher of the Year' and 'Teacher of the Year' by the West Midlands Education Awards, and she was shortlisted as a finalist from over 28,000 nominees by the ITV National Diversity Awards as a 'Positive Role Model (Gender)'. Sarah received the 'Contribution to Education Award of the Year' by the Birmingham Awards in 2019.

Sarah Mullin is passionate about breaking the barriers to learning, providing equal and equitable opportunities for all. As a skilled practitioner who is committed to driving social change, Sarah has helped thousands of children to maximise their learning potential, enabling them to achieve academic and pastoral success which has increased their future life choices. Out of all her accolades, Sarah credits becoming a mother to her three children as her proudest achievement in life.

Printed in Great Britain
by Amazon

35382711R00233